AF713044

Empowering Negotiators

Empowering Negotiators

Successfully Bargaining Salary Offers, Prenuptial Agreements, and Other Stressful Life Events Using the TABLE Method

Lynn A. Epstein
Professor Emerita of Law
Nova Southeastern University College of Law

Elena Maria Marty-Nelson
Associate Dean for Diversity, Inclusion, and
Public Impact & Professor of Law
Nova Southeastern University College of Law

Carolina Academic Press
Durham, North Carolina

Copyright © 2019
Carolina Academic Press, LLC
All Rights Reserved

See catalog.loc.gov for
Library of Congress Cataloging-in-Publication Data

ISBN: 978-1-61163-842-4
eISBN: 978-1-61163-991-9

Carolina Academic Press, LLC
700 Kent Street
Durham, North Carolina 27701
Telephone (919) 489-7486
Fax (919) 493-5668
www.cap-press.com

Printed in the United States of America

Contents

APPENDICES

Preface and Acknowledgments

Our goals for this book are described in Chapter 1, the Introduction. This preface is instead our opportunity to thank and acknowledge those who have contributed their wisdom, time, humor, and guidance to this project.

General Acknowledgements

We wish to acknowledge with appreciation the following authors and publishers, who have graciously granted us permission to reprint excerpts from their publication.

> Rutkin, Oldham, & Hogan, § 50:57. Sample Prenuptial Agreement 8A Conn. Prac., Family Law & Prac. § 50:57 (3d ed.) Westlaw, Reprinted by Permission of Thomson Reuters, all rights reserved.

We are both grateful for Samantha Gozlan, a third-year law student at Nova Southeastern University College of Law, who provided excellent research assistance with astonishing efficiency, judgment, and good cheer. We also thank Mariana Muci, Gabriel Fernandez Galiana, and Scherherazade Ferrand for their outstanding research assistance.

We are also grateful for the wonderful illustrations used throughout the book. All of the illustrations are by Christopher J. Carter, currently a law student at Ave Maria School of Law, a truly talented artist.

We both are also exceedingly grateful to David Weiss, Esq. for his thoughtful editorial suggestions, insights, and guidance. He generously shared his wisdom from his years of experience negotiating complex transactions with us and the book is truly enhanced by his efforts.

Our thanks also to our many students over the years not only in our negotiation courses, but also in courses as varied as evidence, professional responsibility, torts, federal securities regulations, income tax, property, international tax, wills, and trusts. Our students' insights, questions, and enthusiastic participation have greatly enhanced our teaching in this complex and fascinating world of negotiations.

Personal Acknowledgements

Lynn A. Epstein

To my husband, David, the best negotiator I know. Thank you for your guidance and optimism; my love and admiration always. To my son, Alex, thank you for being my millennial consultant. <3. To my father, sisters, and brother-in-law, thank you for your support and for providing me with years of practicing arms-open negotiations. To my mother, I am grateful to you for teaching me years ago that in a dispute you should "always let them save face." That advice has been invaluable, not only in negotiations but also in life. I miss you every day.

Elena Maria Marty-Nelson

I appreciate and thank my husband, David Nelson, an exceptionally skilled attorney and negotiator, whose brilliance and humor inspired me throughout this project. Thank you for being the best partner. I am also grateful to my sons, Scott and Matt, for their encouragement and wit. Finally, I thank my inspiring mother, Judy Marty, who continues to teach, lead, and negotiate with the best of them.

Empowering Negotiators

Chapter 1

Introduction

Parties engage in negotiations to resolve conflicts, reach compromises, and achieve objectives. Negotiations may involve couples, families, business associates, friends, or strangers. They could take place by text, phone, online, or in conference rooms, courtrooms, or living rooms. The skills associated with negotiations are considered essential for both personal fulfillment and professional success. For example, negotiations can affect a person's professional life including her salary, working arrangements, and business opportunities. Negotiations can also affect a person's personal life including her relationships with a future spouse, friends, or family. In addition, negotiations play a pivotal role in major life events such as buying or selling a home. Negotiations, on behalf of others, such as an attorney negotiating on behalf of her client, may encompass the range of personal and professional issues. For example, an attorney may negotiate the client's prenuptial agreement or the client's purchase of a business.

This book teaches the process of negotiating from planning to agreement through a unique method. Negotiators are empowered to negotiate even stressful events by learning and practicing the TABLE method. We chose TABLE as the acronym for the five negotiating stages for several reasons. First, the word table is routinely used in the context of negotiations. For example, parties often ask, "What is on the table?" They may ask, "How do we get the parties back to the table?" Also, commonly used negotiating phrases include "I am walking away from the table" or "I left something on the table." The common use of the word table in the negotiating context will make it easy to remember the acronym for the five-stage process. Another reason we chose TABLE as the acronym is that it is an actual word tied to the concept, unlike other commonly used negotiating acronyms. The use of a vivid real word, such as TABLE, may be especially useful for millennials, Generation Z, and their descendants who routinely use words in different contexts and who have the facility to write and speak in abbreviations and emojis. Finally, whether negotiating for yourself or on behalf of others, the TABLE method develops effective negotiation skills that will minimize conflicts, reduce stress, and streamline resolutions. The TABLE method provides guidance for both personal and professional negotiations.

The TABLE method of negotiating is a five-stage process:

Tactical Planning: Planning for the negotiation is a critical, but often overlooked, pre-negotiation stage. Chapter 2 explains the steps for planning the negotiation. Planning is facilitated through the use of a Tactical Planning Worksheet, which is included in the materials as Appendix A. The T serves as a reminder that without the T in tactical planning, one may be ABLE but not TABLE ready to negotiate.

Arranging the Negotiation: Traditional negotiations usually occurred in person in an office conference room setting. However, with the ubiquity of technology and our on-the-run lifestyles, negotiations may take place at any time and location. For example, parties may be thousands of miles apart and choose to negotiate by email, cell phone, Skype, or even by text messaging. The A in TABLE focuses on choosing from among the vast array of negotiation forums to begin or continue a negotiation session. Chapter 3 explores both the positive and negative aspects of the various settings that may be used for a negotiation.

Bargaining: Bargaining is the meat of any negotiation and appropriately the B is centered in TABLE as the main course. As negotiators would say, "this is what we came for." Chapter 4 breaks down the bargaining process and focuses on offers, counteroffers, and concessions. It also provides insight into certain tricks and tactics negotiators should be aware of and includes suggestions for appropriate responses.

Letting Go or Resolving: The bargaining phase ends in one of two ways: resolving the issues or reaching an impasse. Although at first blush these two opposite results hardly seem to warrant a chapter, the manner in which a negotiation concludes affects not only the current negotiation but also may impact the future relationship between the parties. The L in TABLE discusses when and how to determine if it is time to let go of either the particular negotiation session or, more drastically, the entire negotiation process, or to continue to try to resolve the matter. Chapter 5 also discusses if the parties reach a resolution, the steps they should take to ensure the final agreement accurately reflects the parties' understanding. The transition from a handshake at the end of a negotiation to a signed agreement is fraught with missteps. This chapter guides the reader through that process.

Ethics and Equity: Throughout a negotiation session, negotiators should expect honesty and fairness from their fellow negotiators. The E in table is a reminder that effective negotiators must embrace ethical behavior, and that bias and discrimination have no place at the table. Despite these aspirational goals, realistically, unethical behavior will occur in some negotiations. Chapter 6 focuses on recognizing this type of behavior and discusses some responses.

Once empowered with the TABLE method described in Chapters 2–6, Chapters 7–9 provide opportunities for practicing the method in various stressful life event settings, by introducing fundamental legal principles to use with numerous negotiating problems centered on stressful life events, including salary offers, non-compete agreements, and prenuptial agreements. Combining the TABLE method with legal principles is a unique feature of this book and provides a realistic approach to developing effective negotiating skills, as researching and recognizing the law is integral to negotiating many significant life events.

A word of caution is in order regarding the laws referenced in this book. This book is designed to teach negotiations skills. It is not intended as a primer in any specific area of the law nor intended to provide legal advice. Rather, general legal principles in certain areas of the law are introduced to emphasize the importance of examining and understanding the law when negotiating. Although this book describes general legal requirements for some states, the statutes and cases cited are subject to revision and local rules may somewhat vary the analysis.

Authors' Notes on the Exercises and Problems

Mastering a skill, such as negotiating, requires many hours of practice. Throughout the book, we have provided numerous exercises and problems for you to practice your negotiating skills before you arrive at an actual negotiation table. We distinguish between exercises and problems for specific reasons. In Chapters 2–6, we introduce and explain the TABLE method, and provide exercises to reinforce the various components of the method. These exercises should be completed after you have read the portion of the book to which the exercise is directed. Minimal preparation is needed for these exercises, and most of them can be completed in five to ten minutes.

Chapters 7–9 provide full-length negotiation problems centered on the specific life events addressed in each of the respective chapters. After you read the legal principles in each chapter, you are given the general information of the problem, which consists of the basic facts of the negotiation. All negotiating parties will know the general information. You should consider that the facts in the general information presented are accurate and true.

Following the general information, you are given the structure for developing confidential information. Confidential information means what it says. It is information that is known to one side only and is not meant to be shared initially with other parties to the negotiation. Typically, in order to preserve the confidentiality of that information, negotiation books will separate confidential information from the general information by placing the confidential information in the back of the chapter or leaving a blank page and separating the confidential information in that way. However, we know that some readers just cannot help themselves and will read confidential information that is intended only for the other side. Once they know that confidential information, the negotiation problem is tainted and loses its realism. While we would hope our readers would not succumb to temptation, especially after reading the Ethics section of this book, we did not want to offer that temptation. Therefore, the confidential information in our problems is given in a different format. We refer to the confidential information as bargaining positions. In essence, we permit you to create your own confidential information within the parameters of the problem. We pose questions to you in which your answers become your confidential information. For example, when you are asked to state your bargaining position as to the maximum amount you are willing to offer to settle the matter, if you decide your bottom line is $10,000, that amount is your confidential information and included on your Tactical Planning Worksheet. How do we know that you will not "change your mind" in the middle of the negotiation and come up with different bottom line than was reflected as confidential information in your worksheet? At the end of each negotiation session, you will be asked to exchange planning worksheets with the other side. This exchange not only allows you to see the planning process undertaken by the other side, but also is a check on the accuracy of your confidential information. Obviously, what was written as confidential before the negotiation must remain part of your confidential information (and worksheet). Furthermore, while you are permitted to reveal confidential information during the negotiation as needed, you may not change confidential information. By presenting the problems in this manner, we hope for a more realistic negotiation experience.

The problems in Chapters 7–9 are self-contained. We believe you will be able to practice several complete negotiations, using the TABLE method, by referencing the legal principles given at the beginning of each chapter. However, there are many ways to expand on these problems. For example, in a classroom, you may be asked to conduct more extensive research geared to a specific jurisdiction. Also, the facts of each problem can be modified. Further, in a classroom, confidential information could be dispersed in a more traditional format, such as by the instructor distributing copies of confidential information to each side. We are confident that either way, the problems in Chapters 7–9 provide many opportunities to practice negotiating skills.

Our purpose in writing this book is to provide a practical method to negotiate and resolve realistic, everyday life events. Practicing the TABLE method helps you to develop confidence in your negotiating skills. Life is filled with events in which we need effective negotiating skills. After reading this book, you will hopefully find yourself at the head of the table for all your negotiations.

Part I

The TABLE Method

Chapter 2

Tactical Planning

Just Winging It

Planning for a negotiation may be extensive or may be limited but having a negotiating plan is critical. Skilled negotiators should engage in tactical planning by first identifying the relationship and then proceeding with a five-step planning process to achieve their goals. The five-step process requires: (1) conducting research; (2) setting a highest realistic goal, and determining a minimum acceptable level; (3) formulating alternative options; (4) devising questions and responses to anticipated questions; and (5) preparing opening offers, concessions, and counteroffers. The time dedicated to each of the five steps will vary depending on the particular negotiation. Moreover, the actual number of steps is semantics. Lists with fewer steps generally combine several tactical steps into more general categories and lists with more steps elevate subgroups into full-blown steps. Moreover, as discussed in Chapter 4 on Bargaining, once the negotiations are underway, additional adjustments may be necessary. There is a constant, however. Preparation is key and completing a planning worksheet (see Tactical Planning Worksheet in Appendix A) prior to negotiating can lead to more successful negotiations. This planning process is the beginning of an adventure and an opportunity to develop your bargaining position.

Identifying the Relationship

Your initial step in preparing for an upcoming negotiation is to identify the relationships involved. This brief moment, which includes honest self-reflection, can help to provide necessary perspective. It is an invitation to consider the bigger picture in light of the relationships and personalities involved. This self-reflection moment is an important initial step in the planning process. It can often be completed quickly, but should not be overlooked. Identifying the relationship includes determining whether the upcoming negotiation is arms-length or arms-open, understanding the balance of power, and assessing personality styles.

Arms-Length, Arms-Open

Negotiations generally involve two distinctive relationships types. An arms-length negotiation presumes the parties are independent and unrelated and involve parties with no prior or continuing relationship. For example, a buyer negotiating a contract for the purchase of a house from a stranger may be willing to walk away from the table if the offer is not desirable. If the parties come to an agreement, the title to the house will transfer, and they are likely never to meet again.

By contrast, an arms-open negotiation involves dependent or related parties such as family members or business partners who know each other. An arms-open negotiation requires protecting that relationship as a goal. Since the parties have a prior relationship, each side must determine if they want to risk that relationship through negotiations. For example, assume a father rents a room in his house to his son for $300 a month. If the son stops paying the rent, the father must decide if he is going to demand the payment or have the son move out, negotiate alternative terms, or simply forgo asking for the rent. By demanding payment or negotiating alternative plans, the father runs the risk of ruining the relationship. However, if the father needs the income from the room and has given up the opportunity of leasing it to a third party, the father may negotiate, even if the process puts the relationship at risk.

Finally, there are situations where one type of relationship could transition from an arms-open to arms-length or vice versa. For example, family members who had an arms-open relationship may transition to an arms-length relationship when involved in an intra-family will contest. This type of negotiation is particularly difficult. The parties were initially connected, and therefore the parties may have emotional reservations about negotiating. Further, the family members may be unclear as to whether they want their relationships ultimately to end up with the parties together or separate. Conversely, a relationship may start as an arms-length relationship and transition into an arms-open relationship. For example, assume two neighbors who had not previously met, have a confrontation about one neighbor's loud music at night, which is disturbing the other's sleep. After several repeated incidents, the loud playing music neighbor takes the initiative and invites his sleep-deprived neighbor to his next party. The sleep-deprived neighbor attends the party, and the neighbors begin to discuss compromises so they can live in harmony. Subsequently, they become social friends, not just neighbors, and now have an arms-open relationship if, and when, they need to negotiate any future disputes that arise.

In order to determine if a particular negotiation is arms-open or arms-length, you should answer the following questions:

1. Do you have personal knowledge of the other side that is helpful in planning the negotiation?

   Yes ___ (arms-open) No ___ (arms-length)

2. Do you want a continuing relationship with the other side once the negotiation has concluded?

   Yes ___ (arms-open) No ___ (arms-length)

It is important to consider these questions carefully. For example, assume you are planning to negotiate a prenuptial agreement with your fiancé. In this case, both questions would hopefully result in a "yes" answer and the relationship would be clearly characterized as arms-open. In other words, presumably before contemplating marriage, you have acquired significant personal knowledge of your spouse-to-be and you also want the relationship to last "till death do you part." In identifying the relationship as arms-open, you are including your insights of your fiancé's negotiating style and interests in your planning, while, at the same time, being mindful that one of the goals of the negotiation is to preserve the relationship. Moreover, because this is an arms-open relationship, you may be willing to make more concessions, make fewer demands, and negotiate more openly than in a different type of negotiation.

By contrast, assume you were involved in a car accident with a stranger. Since you have no prior knowledge of the stranger and do not want the relationship to continue, your answer to both questions would be "no," and the relationship is properly characterized as arms-length. In identifying this relationship as arms-length, since you do not have insights into the other side's negotiating style or interests, you will need to focus carefully on your own negotiating style so that you are ready to respond to their unknown style. Moreover, because this is arms-length and you are not interested in continuing the relationship, you may plan to make fewer concessions and may even make higher demands than you would in an arms-open relationship.

Sometimes the answers to the two fundamental questions are not self-evident. Also, as mentioned previously, a relationship may transition from one type to the other. For example, assume you are casually acquainted with a competitor in your area of business and are now contemplating buying his business. Since he is only an acquaintance, you may not have sufficient knowledge about his negotiating style or interests to be helpful in planning the negotiation. Thus, your answer to the first question of personal knowledge would be "no." However, your answer to the second question of whether you want a continuing relationship might not be a simple "yes" or "no" and may actually be a "maybe." In this example, even though you have no personal knowledge about the business owner prior to the negotiations, you recognize that you might want the relationship to continue in some form, such as keeping the original owner working for the business for a couple of years as a consultant, after you acquire the business. In this case, this relationship is more properly identified as arms-length, which may transition to arms-open. In planning this type of negotiation, you have to be particularly flexible in your bargaining positions. You may plan on making more or fewer concessions depending on how the relationship develops during the negotiations.

Balance of Power

Parties rarely have equal power in a negotiation. Usually, one party has more to lose or more to gain than the other party. Sometimes one party holds all the power and has no incentive to negotiate. For example, assume a Hollywood producer is auditioning actors for a walk-on role in a new television series. The producer may have auditioned hundreds of actors, all eager to get the nod. When he finally selects the actor for the role, there may not be a need for a salary negotiation at all. The actor is so thrilled to have received the part that the producer may, in fact, be able to say, "this role pays $50, take it or leave it!" If the actor tries to negotiate a higher fee, there are a few hundred other actors waiting in line, ready to take the role. In this example, the producer has all the power. The actor in effect has no power. This power struggle is not just limited to Hollywood but may occur in everyday negotiations. For example, assume Ava is the hiring partner at a law firm. The job market is full of promising young attorneys with outstanding resumes for associate positions. Ava has narrowed her search to three candidates. Ava and her partners have set a very lucrative starting salary, aligned with starting salaries at similar firms. If the final candidates want to negotiate a higher salary, will Ava engage in that discussion? Probably not. The risk of losing one of these candidates may not justify paying a higher salary. If Ava can hire a great associate for the standard salary, she would likely forgo the negotiation. She holds all the cards.

In the above examples, one party may be like the character Oz from the classic movie, the Wizard of Oz. In that film, Oz's voice emanated from behind a curtain, and his demanding and stern voice made him appear as all-powerful. However, once the curtain was removed and Oz appeared in person, he appeared quite vulnerable. At this point, the film's protagonists, Dorothy and her crew, could "negotiate their demands." As in the Wizard of Oz, if a party cannot get behind the curtain in dealing with an all-powerful person, the all-powerful person will dictate, not negotiate, the terms of the agreement. However, if a party can get behind the curtain, they may acquire negotiating power. For example, remember the actor with no negotiating power. Now assume that actor's research had uncovered that the Hollywood producer wants a certain A-list actor to star in his feature film and that A-list actor will be unavailable. If the non-A list actor, or his agent armed with this knowledge, can convince the producer of his unique acting "similarities" to the A-list actor, he may gain some negotiating power. The producer still retains more power since, after all, there is no film without his decision. Now, however, there is an opportunity for a negotiation. Both parties have something to gain, as well as something to lose. The producer may lose his best substitute for the A-list actor, and the non-A-list actor may lose the opportunity to get his big break!

If the parties are willing to negotiate initially, the power may be more balanced. Keep in mind that if you are negotiating with someone who has more power than you, he is likely to negotiate less and demand more. Therefore, in planning the negotiation, you should make an initial determination as to your relative power, as this determination will allow you to plan the limitations and expectations of your negotiation strategy. Remember that determining this initial relative power encompasses many of the other tactical planning steps, including conducting research and formulating options, as discussed below. Furthermore, even if you start the negotiations with less bargaining power, you may be able to increase your power during the course of the negotiations as information is exchanged and concessions are made. Recall the previous example involving the hiring of a new associate for a law firm. Assume Ava offered the job to Brett for the standard salary. Brett attempts to negotiate a higher starting salary. Ava initially suggests she will not negotiate the salary and that the salary is fair because it is the going rate. In response to Ava's position, Brett informs her that he is more qualified for the job and deserves a higher salary than the standard set salary because he will be able to bring to the firm several corporate clients based on his connections. By providing this information to Ava, Brett has not only distinguished himself from other job applicants but has also moved towards equalizing the power in this negotiation.

Personality Styles

Once you have examined the initial balance of power, it is important to determine the personality styles of those involved in the negotiations. People tend to overestimate or underestimate their negotiating abilities, based on their successes and failures over the years in negotiating life events. Negotiation experience develops early in life. Examples include negotiating allowance money from parents; negotiating which restaurant to go to with friends; and negotiating with a spouse over who is going to walk the dog after work. Even if none of these negotiations involved formal negotiating sessions, people have developed a personality style as to how they negotiate. Nevertheless, they may not have thought much about their negotiating personality and more importantly, whether it can or should be improved. While they may have been told that they are a tough negotiator or a pushover, these terms are better described as competitive or cooperative. Professor Charles B. Craver, a renowned expert in negotiations, in discussing different negotiating styles, notes that "[m]ost negotiators tend to exhibit a relatively "cooperative" or relatively "competitive" style."[1] The chart on the following page describes some of the typical characteristics of these negotiating personality types.[2]

While some individuals are consistently competitive, and others are consistently cooperative, most negotiators develop characteristics of both styles. In fact, Professor Charles B. Craver maintains that "[m]ost successful negotiators are able to combine the most salient traits associated with the cooperative/problem solving and the competitive/adversarial styles."[3]

In planning a negotiation, you should first determine your own personality style as to whether you are more cooperative or competitive. Figuring out your own negotiating personality style may not be particularly difficult as long as you are willing

Competitive Negotiator	Cooperative Negotiator
Appears confidant, often to the point of boastful	Appears open and trusting
Appears experienced, often highlights the actual or perceived inexperience of the other side	Does not boast about their experience, or highlight other side's inexperience
Makes high, often unreasonable offers and demands	Makes reasonable, sometimes too conciliatory demands
Takes an aggressive posture, often with threats	Takes a collegial posture, rarely uses threats
Tries to maximize positions by working against the other side	Tries to maximize position by working with the other side

to assess your style honestly based on your prior negotiating history and you are willing to listen to outside assessments of your style.

The next step in personality analysis is slightly more difficult. In fact, it may be quite difficult to determine the personality style of the other side. In an arms-open negotiation, that task may be easier in that you are familiar with the other side and have some insights into her personality. In an arms-length negotiation, however, you may have no insights into the other side's personality at all. Research may help. For example, you may seek out other persons who have negotiated with the other side in other deals. Your research may uncover that your negotiating opponent has a reputation as a competitive negotiator. This research must be evaluated carefully to ensure it is reliable and that others' assessments as to what is competitive conform to your definition of competitive.

Recognizing personality styles of the negotiating parties is particularly important during bargaining, especially if the styles differ greatly. For example, if the negotiating opponent tends to be the competitive type, a cooperative negotiator may want to try to adjust his cooperative tendencies in order to stay in the game and not get bowled over by his opponent's extreme demands and competitive behaviors. Adjusting to differing negotiation styles is more fully discussed in Chapter 4 on Bargaining.

Step 1: Conducting Research

After the self-reflection moment, it is time to proceed with the five-step tactical planning process. First, tactical negotiation planning requires research. In their well-known negotiation book, the authors Roger Fisher and William Ury, suggest that effective negotiators should find objective criteria to support their negotiation goals and positions.[4] The term objective criteria is sometimes referred to as standards or simply sources of legitimacy. Another way to think about this is to recognize that research is necessary to determine if goals are realistic. The research involved in finding objective criteria often includes discerning the significant facts and determining the applicable law. There are often other sources of objective criteria. For example, when a homeowner is planning on selling her house, comparable sales in the neighborhood within a relevant period of time may serve as objective criteria. In a litigation example, assume Dylan is seeking $10,000 for injuries caused by a fall on a supermarket's floor that he claims was wet. Dylan will need to support his claim with relevant proof of his related expenses such as medical bills. In addition, Dylan or his attorney would need to research and determine the applicable law related to a supermarket's liability for wet floors. Once this objective criteria is determined, Dylan is prepared to make demands with confidence because he has the law and facts to back up his offers. Moreover, research also requires becoming familiar with the norms and standards of the industry involved. For example, the standard commission for real estate agents is generally 6%. By contrast, standard percentages for licensed talent agents for union actors is 10%.[5] Research is not complete without factoring in these norms.

It is also important to make sure your sources of objective criteria are truly objective, especially when researching online. With so many sources available online, it may be difficult to determine if the information you obtain from researching online is accurate or fake. In conducting research, follow some simple guidelines. First, investigate your sources. Look behind the information from the website and determine if it is a legitimate site; in essence research the cite. Is it a recognized source such as a newspaper or periodical? Is it a blog that does not have supporting information? Is the website created or sponsored by a group, individual or organization that is supporting a particular agenda? Second, do not be fooled or captured by the headlines. The headline may be a slanted or exaggerated description of the actual text of the piece. Moreover, the information may have popped up on the screen because your search terms were exactly what you wanted to find. While you might say of course "I searched for exactly what I wanted," there may be a drawback to only searching in this way. For example, if you are researching for the lowest price on a microwave, in addition to doing an internet search "What are the lowest prices on microwaves" you might also try "Compare prices on microwaves." The "lowest prices" search may give you advertisers who may be advertising a low price on a microwave as a marketing promotion for their other products. By contrast, a "compare prices" search may give you a price comparison site from independent sources that have recently researched and reviewed various models. Both search terms are useful but be aware of the sources of information. Third, check the date of the source. You may be surprised to find that what you think is current information, may actually be outdated. Always try and get the most current information to use as objective criteria.

Clearly, the more complex the transaction involved in the negotiations, the more research is needed. If, for example, the negotiations involve a possible merger of a company with a competitor, the research involved even in the planning stage would be extensive and multifaceted. In such complex negotiations, typically, the research planning requires the engagement of advisors to investigate legal, regulatory, and financial hurdles. These advisors would often be further deployed once negotiations were underway, for due diligence, valuation, and financial evaluation. Note that research, even in less complicated negotiations, may be adjusted during bargaining.

Exercise 2-1: Conducting Research

Exercise 2-1. Your local professional basketball team is playing this weekend and your college roommate is flying into town. You want to surprise her with tickets. Research at least three ticket selling services for the best price for courtside seats and describe the results of your research. If no courtside seats are available, research the next best level of seats available. If basketball season is over, research another professional sports team. If you are in an area without a professional sports team or if your team's overwhelming losing record makes tickets too easy to obtain, try this exercise with other ticketed events such as a music concert or theater performance.

Step 2: Setting a Highest Realistic Goal and Determining a Minimum Acceptable Level

The second step in tactical planning requires significant thought. Not only do you have to plan your highest realistic goal, but you also need to formulate your minimum acceptable level. Your highest realistic goal is the optimum outcome you hope to achieve in the negotiation.[6] Your minimum acceptable level is the lowest outcome you would accept. If you are negotiating on behalf of a third party, the minimum acceptable level it is the lowest outcome the third party would be willing to accept. Setting your highest and your minimum levels allows for a range of acceptable outcomes between those two markers. Depending on the particular negotiation, the range may be wide or quite narrow. In order to determine both your highest realistic goal and your minimum acceptable level, you need to conduct research to support them with objective criteria as discussed in Step 1 above.

Having a high realistic goal leads to significantly better outcomes in negotiations. Research has shown that negotiators who set their highest legitimate goals achieve objectively better outcomes than those who focus on a more moderate levels.[7] Moreover, social psychology studies have shown that individuals perform significantly better when they set harder goals rather than moderate or easy goals.[8]

There are, however, psychological hurdles to overcome when setting high goals. Certain personality types fear failure and thus are hesitant to set high goals unless they are confident in the outcome. In cases where this fear of failure concern is admitted or obvious, it may help to discuss the high goal setting objectives with someone the negotiator implicitly trusts, such as a friend or relative. Moreover, if the negotiator is adamant about setting a significantly lower than optimal realistic goal, it might be productive to switch negotiators. For example, assume a will contest involving the children of the deceased against the director of a nursing home. Suppose further that the will in question was executed by the parent in the last stages of dementia, was signed under suspicious circumstances, and left the parent's entire estate to the director of the nursing home who had only known the parent for two months. After researching the issue, the children determine that they have an excellent chance of successfully challenging the questionable will and inheriting their parent's entire estate under the laws of intestacy. Assume, however, that one of the children decides that the goal of the negotiation is to obtain 20% of the estate, because that child fears failure. The other children may, and perhaps should, talk to that one sibling and convince him to allow the other siblings to take the lead in the negotiations. If the sibling agrees to step aside, the remaining siblings could attempt to negotiate the settlement of the will contest themselves.

The highest goal also needs to be realistic. Poorly designed high goals that are unrealistic can backfire in spectacular ways, even in non-negotiating settings. For example, prior to January 1, 2017, Wells Fargo, one of the United States' largest banks, had in place a notoriously unrealistic sales goals incentive program for its retail bank employees. Under that sales goals incentive program, retail bank employees were urged to sell at least eight financial products per bank customer.[9] Those cross-selling sales goals were unsustainable and were so unrealistic that they were deemed to have encouraged cheating and the opening of fake accounts. In addition to reputational issues and losses of thousands of jobs, Wells Fargo's fake account practices, which was attributed in significant part to its unrealistic sales goals, cost the bank $185 million in fines, including a $100 million penalty from the Consumer Financial Protection Bureau, the largest such penalty the agency had issued. Wells Fargo's new compensation and incentive program for its retail bank employees now focuses primarily on customer service.

Setting realistic goals is critical not just for major banks, but also for everyday negotiations. Assume a couple, Lucas and Victoria, are contemplating a prenuptial agreement. Suppose Lucas sets the goal of keeping everything he brings into the marriage and, in the event of divorce, obtaining everything earned during the marriage by either of them and keeping any income earned from their marital property for himself. That goal is not realistic. Rather, such a one-sided goal perhaps suggests that Lucas is not truly ready for the current romantic relationship to progress into a legally binding relationship, because he is not setting a goal that indicates a willingness to negotiate.

Similarly, setting an unrealistically high sales price of a house that far exceeds comparable house sales, and does not factor in the poor condition of the house, can backfire on the prospective seller. An unrealistic sales price could lead to the house remaining on the market for a significant time period, which can make it appear less desirable to prospective buyers. Furthermore, having to keep lowering the price because it was set too high initially leaves the seller in a particularly weak bargaining position.

In addition to a realistic goal, the goal needs to be specific and take into account monetary and non-monetary concerns. Focusing on a specific, rather than a general goal, helps to focus the negotiation strategy. Keeping with the sale of the house example, assume a realistic goal is to sell the house at a price that is slightly above comparable sales in the neighborhood, because the house includes additional amenities. That goal may be realistic, but may not be sufficiently specific to be as helpful as possible. In truly setting the negotiation goal, it is important to think through additional questions. For example, how quickly must or should the house sell? For example, does the seller need to move within four months because of a pending job transfer? Alternatively, does the seller have time flexibility? Might the seller with an external deadline consider renting the house, if the house might not sell at her realistic price within her expected or needed time period? In addition, how much higher over comparable sales is the seller anticipating receiving?

Another transactional example where setting a specific goal is helpful is putting together a partnership agreement. Many clients might have the general goal of creating an equitable partnership agreement. That is a fine general goal, but again it is more helpful to have in mind a specific goal for the negotiations. For example, if one partner is expected to contribute more initially, or to be more actively involved in the ongoing partnership, the goal for an equitable partnership agreement needs to be examined carefully before entering into the negotiations and needs to include those issues as part of the goal. The more complex the transaction, the more likely that there will be numerous components to your goals.

Specific highest goal setting is also important in negotiating litigation issues. For example, a client's general goal may be to settle a dispute for a reasonable amount and to avoid a trial. That could be worthy and valuable information, but without specificity, it is not particularly helpful in settling the dispute. It is important to translate the client's idea of a reasonable amount for avoiding a trial to a specific monetary goal.

In addition to setting your realistic highest goal and a minimum acceptable level, it is important to attempt to predict the other side's likely goals and minimum acceptable levels. Consider particularly how important non-monetary factors or related issues might be for the other side. Moreover, as discussed further in Chapter 4 on Bargaining, there are instances where a negotiation could actually result in both sides ending up in a better position than their individual highest, specific, goals might have initially suggested. By anticipating the other side's goals in the planning phase, the negotiator is in a position to achieve a better combined synergistic goal in the negotiation. This high synergistic result requires both parties to be willing to think collaboratively and creatively to discover areas where their combined interests work to achieve a goal that singularly they could not achieve. Conversely, information may be obtained during the bargaining that requires you to reevaluate your minimum acceptable level. Both sides might wind up accepting an agreement below their anticipated minimum level once new information comes to light during the bargaining phase of the negotiation. Even in this unlikely event, the planning is crucial because it provides a framework for the negotiations.

Exercises 2-2 and 2-3: Setting Goals

Exercise 2-2. Assume your high school reunion will take place in 3 months. Since you will be seeing many of your old high school classmates whom you have not seen in many years, you want to "get in shape" for the event. How would you formulate your general goal of "getting in shape" to a specific, realistic goal? How would you achieve your "highest specific, realistic goal?" In formulating your specific goal, take into account the following:

(1) Monetary and non-monetary factors

(2) Your personality type

(3) Necessity of consulting with others to facilitate setting your goals.

(4) Additional information you may need to obtain before setting your goals

Exercise 2-3. Assume you have accepted a job in a different city and need to sell your current house. You have conducted research and determined comparable prices for houses in your current neighborhood range between $400,000 to $600,000. You have to move within two months to start your new job and you need to net a minimum of $300,000 from the sale of this house in order to be able to afford a comparable home in your new city. Your outstanding mortgage on your current house is $100,000. You expect closing costs to be about $20,000. The housing market has been somewhat sluggish with the last comparable home in your neighborhood taking four months to sell. If your house does not sell within two months, you will need to rent a house in the new city. Rental housing for the size you need for you and your family average between $4,000 and $5,000 a month. Currently, you have $40,000 in savings and your monthly expenses not including your mortgage on your current home are $5,000 a month. Based on these facts determine:

(1) What is your highest realistic goal and why?

(2) What is the minimum acceptable level you would accept for your house and why?

(3) What alternatives do you have if you fail to negotiate the sale of your house within the two-month period?

(4) What other information would be helpful in preparing your worksheet?

Step 3: Formulating Alternative Options If Negotiations Fail

The third tactical planning step is to consider options if the negotiations fail. If you do not come to an agreement, what happens next? What is your best alternative? Is maintaining the status quo acceptable? This concept of exploring alternatives to the negotiation is often referred to as determining BATNA (the Best Alternative to a

Negotiated Agreement).[10] Regardless of the nomenclature, the one with the power to leave the table often has the upper hand. Accordingly, it is important to formulate specific and viable alternatives to negotiations.

For example, when a buyer is negotiating to acquire a company, the buyer should consider whether his current company would be able to continue to thrive in his existing business if the acquisition negotiations fail. If the buyer's business could not continue without an acquisition, the buyer's alternatives are limited. The buyer's research should include an analysis of other potential available acquisition targets. All of this information is critical in planning the buyer's range of acceptable outcomes in the negotiation with the designated acquisition target company.

In a litigation context, if the parties do not settle, the alternative to a successful negotiation may be going to trial. The risk of going to trial with an uncertain outcome and its additional costs, and time, are all important factors to consider in planning the range of outcomes for the failed negotiations. As with the acquisition example above, the research in this litigation context should include a determination of the additional costs, both monetary and non-monetary, of going to trial.

In addition, this step of the planning requires attempting to forecast the other side's alternatives to a negotiated agreement. For example, looking at the acquisition example from the lens of the target company, it is important to try to forecast whether that company needs to be acquired for its continued existence. Is the target company attractive to other buyers such that the target could easily walk away from this negotiation? In the litigation context, if the other side's reputation would be harmed by the publicity of a trial, would the other side be less likely to walk away from the negotiation?

Exercise 2-4: Formulating Alternative Options

Exercise 2-4. You flew across the country for an important client meeting. Unfortunately, when you arrived at your destination, your luggage did not arrive with you. Your meeting is in a few hours. The airline believes that they will be able to locate your luggage and get it to your hotel shortly. Since your meeting is within a few hours, and the gym suit you wore on the plane is not appropriate for the meeting, you reluctantly decide to purchase a suit. You do not want to spend much, however, because you have perfectly good suits at home and you are on a budget. The hotel directs you to two stores. In the first location, you find a suit that is appropriate for the meeting, is priced at $400, but unfortunately does not fit you properly and needs slight alterations. The store can do "emergency" alterations for an additional fee of $50. They promise that it can be done at least an hour before your scheduled meeting. You decide to run to the other location to see if you can just buy a suit there. The second location is a vintage shop that has a perfectly fitting designer suit, priced at $600. You look great in this suit and you clearly prefer this one in terms of style. When you tried it on, however, you noticed that it has a slight, barely noticeable, tear on the left sleeve, which might be difficult even for a professional tailor to repair. The store clerk agrees immediately to give you a ten percent discount due to the damage. To get a larger discount you would need to speak with the manager. The manager is at lunch and will return in half an hour. Your meeting with the client is now due to start in three hours.

In deciding whether to purchase the vintage suit now with ten percent discount, what factors are relevant in weighing your alternatives of (a) waiting a half hour for the manager in the hopes of getting a lower price or (b) returning to the first store and purchasing the suit that needs alterations? After considering these factors, which choice would you make?

Step 4: Preparing Opening Offers, Concessions, and Counteroffers

After conducting research to uncover objective criteria and having determined your highest realistic goal, you should generally be ready to formulate your opening offer for your worksheet. In fact, in an arms-open negotiation your highest, realistic goal may be your opening offer. In an arms-length negotiation, however, your opening offer may be slightly more optimistic than your highest, realistic, goal. Professor G. Richard Shell defines an optimistic first offer as "the highest (or lowest) number for which there is a supporting standard or argument enabling you to make a presentable case."[11] He explains that this optimistic opening offer "need not be supported by your best argument, just a presentable one."[12] Notice, however, that an optimistic first offer is still one supported by objective criteria. It is not a random or an extreme number. Once the negotiations get started, however, as discussed further in Chapter 4 on Bargaining, you may not use your planned opening offer. If, for example, at the start of the negotiation session the other side appears extremely motivated to enter into an agreement, you may obtain an even better outcome than your specific, highest, realistic goal or even your proposed optimistic first offer by opening with a more aggressive opening offer. Moreover, sometimes the opening offer has already been made before any negotiation planning has taken place. For example, if a tenant breaks a lease that contains an early termination clause requiring the tenant to pay four months' rent, then the landlord may demand the four months' rent from the tenant and that constitutes the landlord's opening offer.

Even if you have prepared your opening offer, during the actual negotiation, the other side may make the first offer, so your prepared opening offer now becomes a counteroffer and may need to be adjusted in response to the other side's opening salvo. It is important to prepare an opening offer but to be aware of the necessity of maintaining flexibility during the actual negotiations. Of course, having an opening offer at-the-ready does not mean introducing that offer first. See Chapter 4 on Bargaining for strategies on making and responding to offers.

Step four of tactical planning also requires formulating concessions. Concessions are used by parties throughout negotiations to help reach a settlement range. Although making a concession implies you are "conceding" or giving up something, think of concessions more like an exchange or trade off with the other side. You make concessions not just to give up something but to trigger the reciprocity of getting something in return, which moves the parties toward settlement. Therefore, in planning, you should make a list of concessions you are willing to make, and prioritize them based on your goals and interests, and the projected goals and interests of the other side. What concessions are you willing to make? How likely is the other side to value each of your concessions? Concessions can be monetary or non-monetary. For example, you may be willing to agree to an earlier closing date than you initially wanted on the sale of your house in order to get your price. Skilled negotiators make a list of proposed concessions. The list should rank the concessions in order of importance. Concessions serve many purposes including keeping the negotiation going if they stall. Also, non-monetary concessions may serve to preserve a higher monetary result.

You will also need a strategy as to the timing of making concessions. Do you want to begin with a small concession to show goodwill or do you plan to save concessions for a time in the negotiation session when the process is stalled, and you need to move things along? In determining your concessions, you need to consider your relationship with the other side. If you are attempting to establish a long-term relationship, as in going into a business partnership, you may be more willing to use concessions to establish a good working relationship that shows your flexibility. Conversely, if you are trying to settle a matter subject to litigation, you may use concessions sparingly to maximize the best result for your client without giving too much away.

Your plan also needs to anticipate concessions the other side may make. What is the strategy for handling the other side's concessions? For example, in negotiating an employment agreement the employer might be willing to concede one day a week of telecommuting if the employee signs the employer's standard non-compete. This employer's concession on telecommuting might be the first one made, especially if the employer already offers some other employees that option or if the employer was planning to make that offer to all of her employees anyway. Keep in mind that even if this is the least important concession to the employer, the employer may have insight that this is a perk that the prospective employee values highly, so it is a valuable concession to make. Many companies are adept at offering concessions that appeal to prospective employees that are relatively easy to concede.

Concessions and counteroffers go hand in hand. As you plan your counteroffer, you should anticipate their concessions. For example, if you are attempting to buy a house and the seller offers the house for $400,000, you may plan to counter with an offer of $350,000, because the roof needs replacing which will cost $50,000. You should anticipate that the seller may disagree that the roof needs replacing but concede that the roof needs repairing. In this example, by anticipating that the seller may concede the need for repairing but not replacing the roof you are prepared to adjust your counteroffer.

One of the most difficult parts of the five-step tactical plan is anticipating the other side's concessions and counteroffers. If you do not have enough information to determine what concessions are valued by the other side, you should conduct research as part of your planning process. If you are new to an industry or profession, for example, researching the business norms and practices will be most beneficial in anticipating the other side's concessions. Research can involve anything from talking to those in the industry or reading articles, manuals, or treatises about an industry. For example, a negotiation with federal regulators may not follow the standard concession dance. Assume Bob, an officer of a public company, is being investigated by the federal Securities and Exchange Commission (SEC) for a securities law violation. In trying to negotiate with the SEC, Bob might think that if he agrees to a larger civil money penalty, the SEC might agree not to impose a long-term ban on Bob serving in the future as an officer or director of a public company. Such an assumption might not be appropriate, however. In this industry, sometimes regulators expect large money penalties to be tied to longer time sanctions. In other words, if Bob offers to increase the amount of his penalty in the hopes of reducing any time sanction, his higher monetary penalty offer could backfire as the SEC will now want to increase the time sanction to match the higher monetary penalty. This example simply shows that before preparing offers or concessions it behooves the negotiator to truly research, not just the law and the facts, but also the norms of the industry or practices of the opposing side.

In planning your offers and concessions, in addition to preparing the planning worksheet, it is sometimes helpful to role-play the negotiation with a colleague or friend prior to entering the actual negotiations. By actually "acting out" the negotiation, you have the opportunity to see how your planning plays to the other side, and gives you practice in responding to offers and concessions on the spot. Role-playing can be invaluable in bringing the planning worksheet to life. You receive immediate feedback as to the strengths and weaknesses of your plan. It is the difference between simply reading a script and a live rehearsal. While your plan may play well on paper, your performance may be lacking. By rehearsing offers and concessions, you have the opportunity to observe the process before the actual negotiation.

Exercise 2-5: Preparing Opening Offers, Concessions, and Counteroffers

Exercise 2-5. You have rented an apartment in a twenty unit building in downtown Atlanta for the past year. You pay $1,000 per month for a one-bedroom apartment. Your lease is up for renewal in two months and you indicated to the landlord that you would like to renew the lease for an additional year. Thus, your landlord sent you a renewal lease contract for your review. According to the lease, your rent will be increased by $200 per month. You happen to know that there are currently five apartments that are not leased, and two other apartments with leases expiring at the same time as your lease. You have talked to the two tenants whose leases expire on the same date as your lease. One tenant has told you he does not plan to renew his lease. The other tenant, who lives a few doors down from you and is very friendly with the landlord, told you he is unsure of his plans to renew and you should "work your own deal," and he does not want to discuss it further. You do not know the status of the remaining apartments.

You have also looked at two comparable apartment buildings in your neighborhood. One of those apartment buildings has a one bedroom available for $1,000 a month. However, that apartment is 100 square feet smaller than your apartment and located right next to the elevator and trash disposal. The other apartment building is fully occupied with the next one bedroom apartment available in four months for $1,100 per month.

You really prefer to remain in your apartment as you do not want to go through the hassle of moving. You also love the location of your apartment on the top floor of the building and enjoy the gym and swimming pool amenities. However, you do think your apartment should be painted and the refrigerator replaced. You also would like the landlord to improve the security in the building by installing security cameras at the entrances and hallways. While you can afford to pay the extra $200 per month, based on the information you know, you decide you are going to try to negotiate a lower renewal rent. If your landlord ultimately does not budge on the rent, however, you will stay in the apartment and pay the rent increase.

(1) What would be your opening offer? (Note: this is really a counteroffer since the lease renewal has set the opening offer at $1,200). You may include both monetary and non-monetary offers.

(2) What concessions are you willing to make? Make a list from the least important to the most important concession.

(3) What concessions do you anticipate the landlord is willing to make?

(4) What do you think the landlord is willing to accept?

Step 5: Devising Questions and Preparing Responses to Anticipated Questions

Skilled negotiators know the benefit of having prepared questions. Preparing questions to ask the other side is often omitted from negotiation planning but should be included. The process of preparing questions crystalizes for the planner information that he might be missing about the other side's case. For example, in a sale of a house, the seller might want to prepare a question asking the buyer how soon the buyer needs to move in. If the buyer needs immediate access to the house, because, for example, they have recently sold their prior house and are temporarily living with in-laws, that information could be useful either as a bargaining chip for the seller or as an agreed upon term facilitating the rest of the negotiations. Also, questions, if asked properly, can be a way to show the other side that the negotiator is interested in seeking common ground by getting their input. Finally, questions break up the negotiation intensity of making and responding to demands, which often leads to an escalation of stress and anxiety. Questions do not need to go just to the substance of the negotiations but can also be used to establish rapport. For example, asking the other side how they coped with the ten inches of rain in the last three days can be an easy way to establish a rapport. However, asking a follow-up question of whether he believes the rain is due to climate change may be a way of destroying the rapport. Again, planning is key.

In preparing questions, focus not only on the subject matter of the question, but also on the type of question. The two main types of questions asked during negotiations are closed-ended questions and open-ended questions.[13] Closed-ended questions are questions that require a brief answer, usually just a yes or no. For example, a close-ended question would be, "Did you run the red light?" This question simply requires a yes or no answer. An open-ended question usually requires a detailed answer because the question as framed does not lend itself to a yes or no answer. The question often begins with who, what, when, where, why, or how. For example, instead of the leading question, "Did you run the red light?" you could ask an open-ended question such as, "How did the accident occur?" This open-ended question will likely elicit a detailed response and will allow the responder to tell his version of the story of the accident. Of course, it is probable that the story of the accident will be very favorable to the responder, but at least the question leads to a discussion and to an opportunity to gather information.

In planning for the negotiation, you should prepare both closed and open-ended questions. Open-ended questions tend to be non-threatening and are likely to further the discussion. Closed-ended questions can be helpful to turn to if during the negotiations the other side is not forthcoming in sharing information. In such cases, the planner can resort to a relatively easy closed-ended question to try to pinpoint the answer and continue the negotiating process. Asking closed-ended questions can become somewhat tedious, in that the repetition of a yes or no answer to a question can lull both the questioner and responder into a pattern that hinders establishing a rapport between the parties. The best method may be to intersperse closed and open-ended questions during the negotiation.

In addition to closed- and open-ended questions, other types of questions serve objectives beyond gathering information. For example, a leading question suggests the answer with an objective of getting the responder to adopt the questioner's position. For example, "you were texting on your phone right before the accident occurred, weren't you?" This question attempts to get a response desired by the questioner (most likely a plaintiff's attorney) that the responder (most likely the defendant) was texting before the accident.

Confrontational and complimentary questions are two additional types of questions with different objectives. A confrontational question is an assertive question whose objective is to confront the other side when they have taken a seemingly disingenuous or aggressive position. For example, assume the other side starts with an extremely low offer that is completely unrealistic. A confrontational question might be something to the effect of "are you really expecting me to believe that you cannot offer more than this paltry sum of money?" Another version might be "are you really telling me that your client has not authorized you to offer more than that sum to settle the case?" Parties should use confrontational questions sparingly, if at all, because these questions may completely derail the negotiation. However, if you know or suspect that the other party is an overly competitive type of negotiator who tends to take an aggressive stance during negotiations, it is prudent to plan some confrontational questions in case the need arises. Conversely, a complimentary question is one whose objective is to build up the other side. An example of this type of question would be, "since you have so much knowledge and experience in these matters, would you mind explaining to us your position in detail?" It is probably best not to use too many of these questions either, as the party may give the impression to the other side that he values the other's opinion more than his own which will weaken his bargaining position. Therefore, a party should have a few confrontational and complimentary questions "in the bag," but delay putting them on display in the negotiation unless necessary.

The planning worksheet should prepare for questions to be interspersed throughout the negotiation. Questions should be centered on subject areas or particular goals. As in the example above, a party may want to ask questions to find out more about how the accident occurred and may also want to gather information about the damages. Instead of just listing all the questions together, separate liability questions about the accident from damages questions. This approach to organizing questions will allow you to quickly refer to questions during the negotiation on the same topic.

Preparing your responses to anticipated questions from the other side is as important as preparing your questions. Negotiators should expect that if they are going to ask questions, they will be answering questions as well. In planning for the negotiation, you should recognize weaknesses in your positions, and decide your approach if asked questions by the other side concerning these areas. A particularly important area of concern for planning is how to respond to questions that seek to elicit confidential information that you wish to protect or have a duty to protect from disclosure. This dilemma often arises when a party is negotiating in a representative capacity on behalf of another person, such as an attorney negotiating on behalf of a client. In that situation, the representative must make sure to reveal only the information that the client has authorized them to reveal.[14] If the client has not authorized the client to reveal confidential information, the attorney should decide in advance how he will handle these types of questions. For example, if you are a lawyer representing a client in a car accident and you are asked if your client ran the red light, there are three possible answers: (1) yes; (2) I am not revealing that information; and (3) no. If you choose option one and answer "yes," but your client has not authorized you to reveal this information, you are likely revealing confidential information that is protected. You may subsequently be sued by your client for malpractice, or disciplined by a court, or your state's bar association, for this breach of fiduciary duty.[15] If you choose option two and answer, "I'm not revealing that information due to attorney-client privilege," the other side may interpret the reluctance to reveal the information as the same as a "yes" response and infer that your client ran the red light. If you choose the third option and answer no and your client had actually told you that he had not run the red light, then the "no" response is one you are most eager to give as it benefits your client. What if, however, your client had told you that he ran the red light? In that instance, a "no" answer would be a lie. Not only would the lie be unethical and should compromise your moral code, but it could also have significant legal consequences for both you and your client. For example, if the case eventually settles, and that other side's attorney relied on that "no" response in entering into a settlement, the settlement is subject to being set aside for material misrepresentation.[16] Additionally, as the attorney, you may be subject to a claim for fraud based on the lie.[17] See Chapter 6 on Ethics and Equity.

Not every question needs a direct answer. If a party does not want to respond to a question directly for whatever reason, he should plan some diversionary responses. Diversionary methods include answering the question with a question, changing the subject matter, being offended by the question and refusing to answer, or simply ignoring the question. In planning such diversionary non-responses, you should be aware that any of these methods you use will likely be mirrored by the other side in responding to your questions. This diversionary interplay can result in little or no exchange of information during questioning. Therefore, it is best to plan to reveal some useful information to the other side and encourage them to do the same and use diversionary methods sparingly.

Exercises 2-6, 2-7, 2-8, and 2-9: Devising Questions and Preparing Responses to Anticipated Questions

Exercise 2-6. Closed-Ended Questions (two-person exercise). Assume you and a friend are having coffee. Your friend is interested in pursuing a profession other than the one in which she is currently employed.

Pair up with a person who will play the role of your friend. Instead of asking your friend what other professions would interest her, ask only closed-ended questions (i.e., ask only questions in which the answer is yes or no). For example, you may ask, "Does your new profession require a college degree?" or "Does it require an advanced degree?" Your friend must limit her answers to a "yes" or "no" response only. By asking a series of closed-ended questions, see if you can discover your friend's desired profession. After completing your questioning, switch roles and repeat the exercise.

Exercise 2-7. Open-Ended Questions (two-person exercise). Assume your 15-year-old son took the family dog, "Mellow Mary" to the dog park. While at the park, your son tells you that Mellow bit another dog. Your son then begins texting on his phone because he believes he has given you all the necessary information and that the conversation is over. You, of course, are quite upset at the situation and are imagining all kinds of fallout from the event, from Mellow having psychological issues to receiving a call from the owner of the other dog or his lawyer.

Pair up with a person who will play the role of the 15-year-old son while you play the role of the parent. Using only open-ended questions, try to uncover details about the incident from your less than talkative son. Remember these questions are describing and explaining questions, not questions that elicit only a yes or no answer.

Exercise 2-8. Mixing Closed-Ended, Open-Ended, Complimentary and Confrontational Questions (two-person exercise). Assume you stopped by a garage sale on your way home from work. You immediately see a television for sale that attracts your attention. You have been contemplating buying a television to use in the spare room in your apartment. You notice a tag on the television with a price of $50.

Pair up with a person who will play the role of the seller while you play the role of the buyer. In order to gain as much information about the television as possible, ask the seller questions as to both the price and quality of the television.

Exercise 2-9. Mixing Closed-Ended, Open-Ended, Complimentary and Confrontational Questions. A seller has posted a television for sale on Craigslist. It is a Toshiba 20 inch "smart" television and is two years old. The asking price is $499. Make a list of questions you would like to ask the seller.

Chapter 3

Arranging the Negotiation

Sensing that an in-person negotiation may not work, Petra was ready to switch to negotiating by text.

After completing your tactical planning, it is time to determine the logistics of the negotiation. In other words, deciding the when, where, and how of the negotiation. This is an important component often overlooked by participants. One consideration for determining logistics is whether the negotiation is arms-length or arms-open. An arms-length negotiation often requires a more formalized setting than an arms-open negotiation. For example, if Zoe is interested in purchasing a house owned by her sister, Zelda, they may have a series of in-person casual, informal negotiations in a variety of settings before they come to the actual agreement and specified terms. By contrast, if Zoe is negotiating with a seller with whom she has no relationship, the negotiations will likely be more formalized and be prearranged, often through an agent or attorney. As part of the planning process, the parties should determine the timing and location for their initial negotiation. Furthermore, present day technologies allow the parties to negotiate in numerous formats other than in-person, including phone, email, texting, and video conferencing. A negotiation may entail one or a mixture of several formats. In deciding which format to use initially, it is important to recognize the pros and cons of each.

Various Platforms for Negotiations

In-Person

An in-person negotiation is the traditional method of negotiation. When parties contemplate conducting a negotiation, they most likely imagine scheduling a time and place to meet to attempt to resolve their conflict. In-person negotiations have some advantages. Parties who meet in-person have already gone to the trouble of arranging their schedules and exerting the effort of arriving at a meeting place. These steps indicate a certain commitment to the negotiation process. Presumably, parties would not waste their time to meet in person, if they were not seriously attempting to work out their conflicts, unless, of course, these parties are ordered to do so by a court or by an aggressive human resources department.

Beyond the believed seriousness of the negotiation process, in-person negotiations also offer other advantages. When parties get together in a conference like setting, they are afforded a sense of privacy that may be lacking when conducting an email or text negotiation. Given that sense of privacy, parties may be able to more freely exchange information that they may feel reluctant to do by email or text.

In-person negotiation also allows parties who do not have a prior relationship to get to know one another through informal conversation, initially through ice breaking and subsequent small talk that may take place throughout the negotiation. Perceptions as to a person's warmth are important in a negotiation. In fact, one study has shown that our perceptions of others' warmth and competence make up for 80% of our judgment of them.[1] Contrary to what many would believe, negotiators observe warmth before competence and in some negotiation contexts, actually value warmth over competence.[2] Warmth encompasses traits such as trustworthiness, sincerity, friendliness, and kindness. These traits are undoubtedly discovered more easily in-person than through email or text. Through ice breaking and small talk, the parties may be able to establish a rapport and assess each other's warmth quotient. See Ice Breaking in Chapter 4 on Bargaining. While a certain amount of competitiveness is an important negotiating trait, overly competitive negotiators are generally perceived by other negotiators as suspicious. The ability to assess these traits is a positive aspect of having an in-person negotiation.

In-person negotiations also allow the parties the opportunity to complete the negotiation more efficiently. Since the parties have made the effort to get together in person, there may be a tendency to stay in the room until a deal is reached, especially if there is a positive rapport and the parties have found common ground. While there are many stories of the person who storms out of the room while shouting, "you're wasting my time," those stories are usually what makes good television drama. As noted, except for a few cases in which the parties are required to meet to negotiate, parties who voluntarily agree to meet may have a greater incentive to come to an agreement.

Phone Negotiations

Another traditional method of negotiating is by phone. Phone negotiations can be used to conduct the entire negotiation in certain cases, especially when you want to make a quick deal. Phone negotiations can also be valuable when used in conjunction with in-person or other formats of negotiations. Phone negotiations can be used early in the process of the negotiation for introductions and to gather some initial information from the other side. Phone calls later in the process are often valuable to follow up on a prior session or to settle issues that remained open from a prior session. For example, if a prior negotiating session was halted because there was a need for further research or investigation on certain issues, a follow up by phone would be appropriate once that research or investigation has been conducted.

Phone negotiation have both advantages and disadvantages. Negotiating by phone allows the parties to have real time negotiations much like in-person negotiations, but without the delay and expense of travel. While phone negotiations do not permit the parties to observe non-verbal clues of expression and body language, they do provide for interpretation of tone and inflection. Due to its somewhat informal nature, phone negotiations allow parties flexibility. For example, you could end a negotiation session that is heading in the wrong direction more easily than when negotiating in-person by saying "unfortunately, I need to jump off this call now." Conversely, it is just as easy for you to start a negotiation session by phone because a call can be made at any time or any place. In addition, phone negotiations allow for others to participate in the negotiations through the use of speaker phones or multiparty calling. Of course, all persons participating in the phone negotiations should be identified to maintain confidentiality and avoid deception.

There are some risks associated with phone negotiations. Unlike an in-person or video session, since you are not in "view" during a phone negotiating session, you might be tempted to multi-task during the conversation. This multi-tasking distraction may result in a less than optimal performance. In addition, negotiating by cell phone while you are commuting or are otherwise on the go may make it difficult to memorialize the terms of an agreement until a later time. At that time, you may not accurately remember the agreed upon terms. Another concern is that with the ease and informality of phone negotiations, you may be tempted to answer a call and start engaging in negotiations before you are properly prepared. This impulse to answer the call is generally a mistake. You should be sure to check caller ID before answering. If not prepared to negotiate, you should perhaps not answer the call.

Email Negotiations

Negotiation by email has many advantages not found in face-to-face or phone negotiations.[3] Due to its asynchronous nature, parties may send and respond to emails at any time and any place. Thus, email erases time and distance impediments that may act as stumbling blocks to in-person negotiations. Whether it is first thing in the morning or very late in the evening, a party can make an offer, accept an offer, or just keep the conversation going. No worries about cancelled flights, late arrivals, or any other actual or created obstacles to not show up. Although it is not unheard of for an email negotiator to complain that their server was "not working," or that they did not receive a prior email, such excuses should not lead to the significant delay that a cancelled in-person negotiation may entail.

Consistent with the ability to negotiate at the parties' convenience, email negotiation often proves cost effective. Costs associated with travel for face-to-face negotiations are avoided. If the negotiation involves multiple parties, an email meeting avoids perhaps several in-person meetings if all parties cannot attend at the same time. Furthermore, if the negotiation involves represented parties, clients can be included on email communications as they occur, thus avoiding time spent by attorneys updating clients as to what occurred in the negotiations. All of these benefits should result in reduced costs to clients.

Email negotiation also allows the parties to take a break from the discussions if emotions are running high, or if they have reached an impasse. Furthermore, the theatrics associated with in-person negotiations are mostly eliminated by email. For example, a negotiator who erupts in anger in an in-person negotiation is stymied from this behavior in an email negotiation. Even the negotiator who resorts to all capital letters wording in an email, trying to express anger, is unlikely to produce more than indifference or even a laugh from the other party. In addition, a party's failure to respond at all to an email can be interpreted in different ways. Are they done negotiating? Are they angry? Are they conferring with others to formulate a counteroffer? Did they decide to take an impromptu vacation or take ill? While ambiguity may afford the party taking a break time to collect their thoughts, the party not receiving a response may become frustrated or angry such that it derails the negotiating process. Thus, you want to ensure that your email responses are not misinterpreted. See Chapter 4 on Bargaining for more ideas on responding to others.

Email also provides a verifiable way to prove what occurred since it is memorialized in writing. This written communication, as opposed to the verbal communication in face-to-face negotiations, may have both a positive and negative effect on the process. A party may be more reluctant to "put in it in writing," since there will be a record of what occurred that cannot be easily erased. By contrast, in a face-to-face negotiation, there can be considerable disagreement as to what was said, or simply a denial that something was said.

Email negotiations, however, do not provide the opportunity to observe non-verbal clues from the other side. Some studies laud the ability to read non-verbal clues during an in-person negotiation.[4] For example, facial expressions such as lip biting may indicate anxiety. Body language such as crossed arms might indicate that the person feels defensive. Constant fidgeting may suggest impatience. However, other studies show that these non-verbal clues are greatly overvalued and may in fact be misleading.[5] Therefore, while in-person negotiations allow the opportunity to observe non-verbal conduct, the resulting benefit is mixed as a negotiating strategy. Without visual or vocal clues, email negotiators are left to convey their proposal solely with words. For some who enjoy the game of negotiation, this option may prove too mundane. However, other negotiators are bolstered by the clear meaning of words and prefer avoiding the distraction of deciphering non-verbal clues and emotional outbursts.

Because of the asynchronous nature, the effect of negotiating by email may be more thoughtful exchanges. While there is no suggestion in this book to ever "wing it" for any type of negotiation, those involved in face-to-face negotiations may be derailed from their plan by an aggressive party whose tactics throws them off. In an email negotiation, one is afforded the opportunity to take time to plan when responding, which may provide for more reflective and thoughtful responses than in-person negotiations. Further, the more strategic planning you apply in drafting your email responses, the more likely the negotiation will be successful.

Video Conferencing

Video conferencing is, in effect, a combination of in-person, phone, and email negotiations. It affords many of the advantages of email, phone, and in-person negotiations with some disadvantages. Many of the benefits of an in-person negotiation translate to a video conferencing negotiation. Due to its synchronous nature, video conferencing provides face-to-face contact similar to an in-person negotiation. Thus, the parties may have the ability to read verbal and visual clues. Video conferencing also occurs in real time, unlike an email negotiation. This real-time effect allows the parties to take the time to ice break and establish a more comfortable rapport. It further allows the parties the ability to wrap up the negotiation and make decisions more efficiently since, similar to meeting face to face in a conference room, they are meeting in the virtual conference room.

In addition to having some of the benefits of face-to-face negotiations, video conferencing also has many of the benefits of email negotiations. Like email negotiations, video conferencing saves time and money in that the parties do not have to physically meet, thus eliminating travel time and related expenses. Furthermore, although video conferencing does not have the benefit of memorializing exchanges in writing as in email negotiations, video conferencing can be recorded with ease and thus the conversations can be memorialized to some degree. Even if the parties do not wish to record the video conference, just the fact that a party is "on camera" may prompt a more thoughtful exchange of information, and a decreased likelihood of spontaneous outbursts.

Despite the many advantages of video conferencing, there are some downsides to using this method for negotiating. First, although a video conference allows the parties to "see" each other, it is less personal than an in-person meeting. Unlike an in-person meeting, negotiating by video conferencing requires the parties to stay on screen and in the picture, thus offering a somewhat stilted image of that person. With this fixed picture, the parties are not able to move around the room or display anything more than their image from the neck up. Therefore, it is possible to misread visual or verbal clues on the screen given the fixed image. Moreover, as with phone negotiations, with a fixed screen, the parties may be unaware of others in the room who are not visible on the screen. Second, there may be technical difficulties with video conferencing that may greatly interfere with the negotiating process. Remote connections are often shaky, networks are subject to intermittent failures, and the hardware or software may have compatibility issues that interfere with the connection. Third, since the parties are meeting in real time, they must be aware of time zone changes. While one party may want to video conference at 10:00 AM that time may translate to 2:00 AM for the other party. Differing time zones may eliminate some of the advantages of not meeting in-person.

Studies have shown that video conferencing and other virtual negotiations favor the less powerful party.[6] Research found that the party with less power did better in virtual forms of negotiation than in face-to-face negotiations.[7] The research suggests that when people negotiate remotely, power hierarchies have less impact on the outcome. Virtual negotiation particularly tends to level the playing field. Therefore, in situations such as an employee negotiating a raise from his boss, negotiating virtually may help to balance the power. That is, of course, if the employee can get the boss to respond on screen.

With many advantages but also disadvantages, it may be difficult to decide if negotiating by video conferencing is the best method for a negotiation. The type of dispute, the parties' locations, time restraints, and costs, are factors that may determine if this method is appropriate. As with other methods, video conferencing should be considered as a viable negotiation platform, even if only to supplement other negotiation platforms.

Text Messaging

Text messaging can also serve as a significant platform for negotiations. It has both advantages and disadvantages as compared to other platforms. One benefit of text messaging is that it is a quick and easy way for the parties to communicate, especially when used as part of the overall negotiation process. Text is often used to initiate or continue the negotiation in another forum, such as by email, phone, video conferencing, or in-person. Another benefit of texting in the negotiation setting is that it is generally viewed as more informal than email, which can be beneficial particularly in certain arms-open negotiations where the parties are amicable when starting the negotiations. Also, unlike an email where the other party might have blind copied another person into the conversation, and thus made it difficult to know who is "in the room," the members of a group text are generally visible, with a click or two, to all parties. There is no hiding in the text room. Texting can also be used as an advantageous alternative to a phone call. Although texting is not truly real time as a phone call, the ability to provide multiple rapid-fire responses with text can mimic the real time effect of a phone call. Unlike a phone call, however, since a text is not actually in real time, a party may be able to avoid direct responses more readily than by phone.

There are certain disadvantages to negotiating by text. Text messages are generally short and often lack content or details. The lack of explanation can lead to text being misinterpreted. Also, text messages are typically sent immediately after they are composed without the drafter first reviewing or editing. By contrast, email systems provide easier methods for saving drafts and editing and thus encourage the drafter to review before hitting send. Also, those who send text messages may try to clarify or amplify their texts by including emoticons (emojis). However, the use of such emojis can have the opposite effect and actually lead to more confusion. Emojis are not uniformly interpreted. For example, on a text, emoji tears may be intended by one party as signifying laughter and happiness but interpreted by the recipient as frustration. While this may not be a problem with texts among friends, in the negotiation context it could derail negotiations or even lead to a law suit. For example, in one case a prospective tenant, in discussions by text with a landlord, sent the landlord a series of emojis that included a smiley face, a comet, a champagne bottle, dancing bunnies, and a chipmunk.[8] Partially because of the emojis, the landlord believed an agreement had been made and took down the listing. When the potential tenant backed out of renting the apartment, the landlord sued. The judge agreed with the landlord that the prospective tenant had negotiated in bad faith and awarded rent to the landlord. Accordingly, use of emojis during negotiations should be used sparingly and with caution.

While some traditional negotiators would not generally use texting for negotiations, text messaging is often the preferred method of communication for millennials, and members of Generation Z, and must be considered as an available negotiation format. In fact, text messaging has become part of the negotiating process even in high stakes negotiations involving law enforcement agencies. For example, in 2011, police negotiator Andres Wells was pursuing a suspect in a gas station robbery who was threatening suicide.[9] The suspect began ignoring Officer Wells' telephone calls. Instead, the suspect sent the officer a text message. This was the first time Mr. Wells had ever encountered a suspect using a text message as a form of communication. The suspect, in a text, demanded the officer contact his girlfriend. Then, in a subsequent text, the suspect demanded water. Recognizing that he would be unable to successfully resolve the crisis solely through text messaging, Mr. Wells' strategy was to get the suspect to stop texting and pick up the phone. Eventually the officer was successful, as the suspect agreed to accept phone calls from the officer and the matter was resolved. Officer Wells was forced to use text messaging as a way to communicate in these high stakes situation. Because of negotiations such as these, law enforcement agencies are training their officers to address the challenges of crisis negotiations through text. In a situation such as crisis negotiating with a suspect, determining the suspect's mental state is crucial, and thus verbal clues are very important. In order to decipher these verbal clues, officers are now trained to encourage suspects to switch from text messaging to in-person or telephone methods of communication. Most negotiations do not rise to the level of a crisis. Nevertheless, negotiating by text messaging may be an integral part of the process.

Exercise 3-1: Text Message

Exercise 3-1. You are trying to sell your car and negotiating by text message with a potential buyer. You have never met the buyer, and the negotiation has been conducted solely by text messaging. You are moving and need to sell your car within the next five days. You have had several text exchanges with the buyer with multiple offers and counteroffers. You intend to text your final offer to the buyer and believe the price will be acceptable to him. However, you also want the buyer's payment to you to be in full and an all cash deal. Finally, you want to arrange the delivery of the car to the buyer within five days.

A. Translate what you believe buyer was texting. Do you believe you have a deal with the buyer?

B. Prepare the following responses to the buyer:

(1) Respond to buyer using only emojis to convey your message

You text this message to the buyer:

> My last offer is for $5,000
> with full payment and
> delivery within five days.

Buyer replies with the following text:

> 5👍Full😟Days

(2) Respond to buyer using only words to convey your message.

(3) Respond to buyer using both emojis and words to convey your message.

C. Compare the responses. What are the advantages and disadvantages of responding using emojis in this negotiation? What are the advantages and disadvantages of responding using words without emojis?

Choosing the Initial Platform for Negotiating

Which initial form of communication the parties decide to use in their negotiations is based on many variables including the relationship of the parties. For example, in an arms-open negotiation, such as negotiating a prenuptial agreement, it would be unusual to think that the engaged couple would start the negotiations in any other platform than in-person. In an arms-length negotiation, however, such as the purchase of a house from a stranger, the initial format for the negotiation may not be significant and would likely be determined by personal preference or practical issues such as time and costs.

Furthermore, similar to the crisis negotiator scenario above, the parties may begin a negotiation using one platform for the negotiation and move to another platform during the process. For example, a person negotiating a car purchase may meet with the car dealer in person, but if the deal is not completed on the lot, they may continue the discussion by email or phone and finalize it by a text message, confirming the agreed upon purchase price.

Exercises 3-2, 3-3, and 3-4: Choosing the Initial Platform for Negotiating

Exercise 3-2. You and your fiancé have decided to have a destination wedding in the Bahamas. You saw an advertisement in Wedding Weekly for a hotel in Nassau that specializes in destination weddings. The ad quotes a price of $30,000 for a four hour "all in" wedding, which includes a decorated room for the ceremony and reception, a DJ, a cocktail reception, a five-course meal, and a wedding cake. The hotel will even include a person to perform the ceremony. This offer is for a wedding party of up to 50 guests. The advertisement lists an email address to contact the hotel manager for further information.

Draft a one-page email to the hotel manager. Introduce yourself and ask a few questions in order to gather more information about the package. Also, lay the groundwork to negotiate for either a price reduction or more services. You plan to have only 30 invited guests. This is an introductory email only. Do not attempt to conduct the entire negotiation by email.

Exercise 3-3. (two-person exercise) Assume the same facts as in Exercise 3-2. However, for this exercise, assume that the hotel has an affiliate hotel near you and there is a representative, Mr. Representative, available to discuss your destination wedding. You made an appointment with Mr. Representative to meet in person to discuss the wedding.

Pair up with a person who will play the role of Mr. Representative. Introduce yourself and begin the groundwork to negotiate a lower price. Do not attempt to conduct the entire negotiation. You will have 10 minutes to complete this exercise.

After conducting both Exercise 3-2 and 3-3, answer the following questions.

(1) How did the email introduction differ from the in-person introduction?

(2) Which method did you find was preferable in this situation? Why?

(3) Would you successfully be able to conduct the entire negotiation using either email or in person?

(4) Would a combination of email and in-person negotiation achieve the optimum result? Why or why not?

Exercise 3-4. Assume you interviewed for a marketing position at a start-up company located in California. You live in Tennessee. Your interview was in person in their California offices. You left after the interview and two days after you arrived home to Tennessee, you received a text message offering you a position for a salary of $70,000 per year with significant benefits. While the salary is more than you are making currently in your present job, your research suggests that the salary offered is slightly lower for comparable jobs in California given the high cost of living. They have given you a one-week deadline to accept the offer. You have decided that you want to ask for a higher salary. Since you cannot do an in-person negotiation for practical reasons, you will need to use one of the other platforms to negotiate a higher salary. Answer the following questions for each possible platform.

(1) Assume you choose to negotiate by email. How would you draft an introductory email regarding the salary?

(2) Assume you choose to negotiate by text. How would you draft your text message? Would your text be different than your email and why?

(3) Assume you choose to negotiate by either phone or video conferencing. Draft an outline of the initial conversation you would use to introduce a negotiation concerning the salary under either phone or video conferencing. How would video conferencing be different than phone?

(4) Which platform do you think would work best for this exercise? Do you anticipate switching platforms at any point during the negotiations and why?

Chapter 4

Bargaining

I know you're really enjoying this ice-breaking, but it's time to negotiate.

Ice-breaking

Once the parties have chosen their initial negotiation platform, it is time to meet and begin the process of negotiating. No matter which platform the parties choose to initiate the negotiations, the start of the negotiation is often the most awkward part. The parties should think of the start of the negotiation as the beginning of a first date. Most people on that first date want to make a good first impression. Similarly, the beginning of the first negotiating session should strive for that good first impression objective.

Many inexperienced negotiators will just start the negotiations with their opening offer. Such an abrupt opening may not be optimal. Or, there are some negotiation pretenders who show up with no real intent to negotiate, but rather show up and make an unrealistic demand, appear miffed when it is rejected, and storm out of the room in a dramatic fashion. Why do they show up? Perhaps they were ordered to do so by a court or were under some type of outside pressure to make an appearance. Perhaps they did not read this negotiating book and believe this dramatic posturing is most effective. Such posturing is unlikely to succeed. This posturing signals to the other side that there is no genuine interest in negotiating an agreement. Parties who intend to negotiate in good faith would not start a negotiation in such a volatile manner. Rather, like a first date, the parties should spend some time getting to know each other and finding common ground before launching into demands. Parties that approach a negotiation in an overly aggressive manner, believing that establishing a rapport and seeking cooperation shows weakness, are often surprised by how quickly the negotiation dissolves. It is important from the outset for parties to show they are willing to collaborate to reach a successful outcome.

No matter which platform you are using for the initial negotiating session, if you have never met the other side, you should take a moment to introduce yourself. If you are meeting in-person for the first time, you should formally introduce yourself even if you have previously called, texted, or emailed the other person. A formal introduction may also save you the potential embarrassment of starting a negotiation with the wrong person or mispronouncing their name.

After the introductions, it is advisable to take a few minutes for ice-breaking. Ice-breaking is best accomplished by finding common ground with the other side. That common ground may be as insignificant as the weather. However, to avoid the mundane, if you are negotiating with a person you have never met you should do some homework to obtain basic information about them. Your biographical research may uncover common ground. Perhaps you attended the same college as the other party or grew up in neighboring cities. You may have a common interest in certain sports. A brief discussion on any of these topics helps to put the parties at ease.

After the introductions and ice-breaking, it is helpful for you to make a statement showing your willingness to make a deal. For example, "I'm happy we could meet today, and I hope we can work this out." You may think this shows weakness, but it does not, and is usually quite effective. A willingness to settle should be the reason you are meeting. Of course, this does not mean that if ten minutes into the negotiation the other side is making unreasonable demands and refusing to make counteroffers, that you should continue your amicable posture. At that point, you should make firm demands that are clear and supported by objective criteria. If there is no reciprocal willingness to negotiate in good faith, it may be time to end the session.

At this beginning stage of the bargaining phase of the negotiation, it is a good idea to present your proposed agenda to the other side. If your negotiation session has a time limit that you did not communicate when the negotiation was scheduled, inform the other side at this time. For example, "I have a hearing in an hour, so we will only have about 45 minutes to discuss this now." If you are limiting this negotiation to one issue in a case, for example medical expenses and not liability, state that at the outset. In other words, try to outline for the other side the scope of what you believe can be accomplished in this session. Also, be open to meeting again, if things are not resolved in this session. If the negotiation goes badly, you may not be eager to schedule the next session. In the beginning, however, it is a good idea to let the other side know that you expect an open line of communication that would continue beyond this session, if necessary.

After ice-breaking, it is time to start negotiating. Since you have a negotiation plan, you should feel confident to proceed. Recall, however, that this plan is just a guideline, as you may be off your game plan very quickly, if, for example, the introductions did not go as amicably as hoped, or if the other side institutes their game plan before you. However, no matter how the negotiation begins, negotiations typically include offers, counteroffers, and concessions.

Offers, Counteroffers, and Concessions

There is considerable debate on who should make the first offer in a negotiation.[1] As noted in Chapter 2 on Tactical Planning, sometimes a first offer has already been made prior to the negotiation. For example, if you are negotiating for the purchase of a home, the first offer may be the seller's listed sale price for the home. In that case, your first offer is really a counteroffer. In addition, the other side may make the first offer before you have a chance to take the lead. You will likely have to adjust your planned opening offer, if the other side makes the first offer. However, in many negotiations, the first offer has not been made. In these cases, you have to determine whether you should make that first offer or wait for the other side to make it.

Some experts believe making the first offer gives you the upper hand in the negotiation in that you have set a starting point. By making the first offer, you have "dropped the anchor," which often results in what is referred to as anchoring bias. Anchoring bias, which applies in numerous contexts not just negotiations, is a cognitive bias and describes a "common tendency to give too much weight to the first number put forth in a discussion and then inadequately adjust from that starting point, or anchor."[2] If the parties eventually settle closer to the initial offer than to the other side's counter offer, it may be the result of an anchoring bias. Negotiation research on anchoring bias "has shown that negotiators may be able to gain an edge by making the first offer and anchoring the discussion in their favor."[3]

A study on anchoring bias involving a sale of a house demonstrates the powerful effect of making the first offer. Professors Greg Northcraft and Margaret Neale conducted an experiment in which they provided real estate agents different randomly chosen list prices for a house that was for sale.[4] The random prices for the house in the experiment ranged from $119,900 to $149,900. The real estate agents were also given information about the house such as comparable prices and other data. In addition, the agents all took a tour of the house. After the agents were each given their individual randomly designated "list price," they were then asked to set their own list price for the house. The result of the experiment was that agents who were given a higher random list price set their own list price higher than those who were given lower list prices. Even though all the real estate agents were given the same additional information about the house and all took a tour, they were likely influenced by the initial randomly designated "list price" they were given, suggesting an anchoring bias.

Interestingly, all the agents rejected the idea of an anchoring bias and justified their estimates on unique features of the properties they were assigned.

Anchoring bias may be especially effective in situations where there is an unequal balance of power or when one party has more knowledge about the subject matter than the other and attempts to drop the anchor by making the first offer. For example, in a salary negotiation, typically the employer has more power and knows more about the salary range of their company than the potential employee. In this situation, the employer almost always drops the first anchor and makes a salary offer. How should the potential employee respond to the employer's attempt to anchor? The potential employee needs to be armed with objective criteria to uproot that anchor and perhaps pull the salary into a range more desirable to the potential employee.

A first offer does not always, however, result in anchoring bias. Generally, in a situation where there is a long-standing relationship between the parties, anchoring bias may lose its effect.[5] If, for example, a car manufacturer has been shipping cars to a car dealer for many years, the parties' negotiating pricing may be somewhat routine. Each side has nearly equal power and the same access to knowledge, such as profit margins and because of this awareness, each side will resist being anchored.

Furthermore, making the first offer may, in fact, be a disadvantage in certain negotiations. You may decide to let the other side make the first offer in the following situations. First, despite the risk of the other side attempting to drop an anchor as discussed above, it may make sense to hear the other side's offer when he possesses more knowledge about the matter at hand than you do, and you are unable to obtain that information through any further research. Second, it may make sense to allow the other side to make the first offer when your highest, specific, realistic offer is so novel and innovative that it is difficult to estimate its value. For example, Thomas Edison went to Western Union with a new invention to improve the telegraph machine. He had initially planned to ask for $2,000, but when Western Union asked his price, he decided to let them make the first offer. Western Union offered $40,000, which he accepted and used the funds to build a laboratory where he would later develop a better known invention—the light bulb.[6] A third instance in which it may make sense to have the other side make the first offer is where it is customary practice in a business or industry.

Notwithstanding certain situations where you should not or cannot make the first offer, in instances where you have significant information, you should plan to make the first offer. Making the first offer signals to the other side the value you have placed on the negotiation. An overly aggressive first offer may suggest a long battle ahead. Conversely, too low an opening offer may indicate to the other side a too eager willingness to settle, which may suggest weakness in your case. Since your planned offer is supported with objective criteria, you should feel comfortable in taking the lead and making the offer.

Communicating Objective Criteria behind Offers and Counteroffers

Experienced negotiators recognize the value of communicating objective criteria in support of their offers and counteroffers.[7] For example, you should not say, "I am willing to offer you $10,000 to settle this case." Instead, say, "I am willing to offer $10,000 because that amount represents half of your property damage and based on well-established law, you are 50% at fault." If the other side doubts your criteria, it helps to offer proof. Be prepared to offer to show the other side the case law, comparables, or other objective criteria and be ready to do a quick internet search, if there arises a question about such criteria. Similarly, if the other side makes an offer and does not support it with objective criteria you should ask her to support that offer with her objective criteria. If she has no basis, or if she tries to bluff a justification, you should refer to your planning worksheet to prove that her offer is not realistic and to justify your rejection of that offer. For example, assume you want to purchase a boat, which is listed for sale for $40,000. You meet to negotiate with the seller. After initial ice-breaking, you offer to buy the boat for $20,000 and you provide the seller with objective criteria supporting your offer. Assume the seller rejects your offer and reiterates that the list price is $40,000 but provides no objective criteria supporting that price. Instead of raising your offer, you should ask for the seller for her justification for the list price. The seller should provide some objective criteria as to why $40,000 is a realistic price. If she is unwilling or unable to provide objective criteria as to why the $40,000 is justifiable, you should reiterate your criteria for the $20,000 offer. For example, if your criteria included a range of comparable sales you could explain that the seller's offer is clearly outside the range. This discussion should cause the buyer to reconsider her initial list price.

Sound negotiations have a healthy exchange of offers and counteroffers supported by objective criteria. Obtaining a counteroffer from the other side typically propels the parties towards a resolution. Even if the counteroffer is not particularly attractive, it serves several purposes. First, it demonstrates a willingness of both parties to participate actively in the negotiation. Second, the counteroffer when coupled with the offer, serves to bracket the negotiation.[8] In other words, the offer and counteroffer reveals the upper and lower settlement limit of the negotiation. Bracketing indicates the actual range that the negotiating parties are in and should protect against future extreme offers outside the range.

Once the negotiation is bracketed, it is important to check your planning worksheet and compare that bracketed range to your minimal acceptable level. If the negotiation bracket includes your minimal level, you know that you are now in a range to settle, although you should continue to work towards moving the needle closer to your highest specific goal. If the bracket does not meet your minimal acceptable level, then you know that there is a lot of work ahead in this negotiation. For example, assume when preparing your planning worksheet, you determined that your highest specific goal was $50,000 and your minimal acceptable settlement was $20,000. In negotiations, you offered $50,000 to the other side, and she responded with a counter offer of $10,000. The negotiation is now bracketed, with the potential range of settlement between $50,000 and $10,000. However, since your minimal acceptable settlement is $20,000, even though the negotiation is bracketed, you are not in a range in which you planned to settle. Regardless, bracketing is beneficial, as you and the other side have now set the parameters of this negotiation with a settlement range between $10,000 and $50,000. Once the negotiation is bracketed, there should continue to be a healthy exchange of offers and counteroffers supported by objective criteria.

There may be instances, however, where the other side rejects your offer, does not make a counteroffer and thus no bracket is established. If no counteroffer is forthcoming, ask for one. If the other side is attempting to get you to revise your first offer before making a counteroffer, hold firm. If you adjust your initial offer, you have just made a counteroffer to your own offer. In essence, the other side has managed to get you to negotiate with yourself to obtain a better deal without putting an offer on the table. Stick with your negotiating plan and communicate that you will not make any further offers until you receive a counteroffer. Also, make sure that you check your plan so you do not accept below your bottom line and be aware of what your alternatives are to settlement. While it would be highly unusual to accept the first offer or counteroffer, bracketing will give you the ability to see how much work is ahead before you make a deal.

Along with offers and counteroffers, concessions are an integral part of the negotiations. Generally, once an initial offer and counteroffer have been made, the parties typically begin making concessions.[9] In other words, concessions should be interwoven throughout the negotiation. The timing of making concessions is a critical factor in a negotiation. Further, making smaller concessions at appropriate times is usually more productive than making one large concession. Also, making rapid concessions is often associated with a weak position, while holding off on making concessions is associated with a reluctance to engage in any meaningful bargaining. Getting the other side to make the first concession is advantageous in accessing her flexibility. If you have taken the lead and made the first offer in the negotiation, the other side's counteroffer may in fact include a concession. However, if no concessions appear forthcoming, it may be necessary for you to start the concession exchange.

Since you have prepared the Tactical Planning Worksheet, you have prepared concessions you are willing to make and the order in which you plan to make those concessions. You would usually begin with the concession that you have determined on your worksheet is of least importance to you, but is something valued by the other side. Furthermore, with thorough research, you are likely aware of the value the other side has placed on this concession. For example, assume Sally's dog allegedly bit her neighbor Cory in front of his house, causing a minor bite wound to his leg. Cory has sued Sally for monetary damages, including medical bills and emotional distress. However, the dog bite required minimal medical intervention, with no stiches or scarring. Since Sally's dog had all of his shots, there are no known diseases transmitted from the dog to Cory. Yet Sally may know from speaking with others in the neighborhood prior to the negotiation that Cory has strongly suggested that Sally's dog be removed from the neighborhood, even hinting to other neighbors of a drastic remedy that her dog should be euthanized. During the negotiation, after first offers and counteroffers were rejected, Sally may now decide to make a concession that she will not walk her dog on Cory's street in the future. This small concession is of minimal importance to Sally but based on information Sally has learned from the neighbors, is of great importance to Cory. Sally's concession may prove to move the needle on the big issues in this case, the amount of damages, and hopefully delay or avoid discussion of a more drastic remedy such as removing the dog from the neighborhood or euthanizing the dog.

Concessions are rarely made in isolation and are usually tied to offers. Therefore, the ultimate success of a concession may likely depend on the seriousness of the first offer. If the other side perceives the first offer to be frivolous, the concession will also appear lacking in sincerity and depth. For example, in the dog bite case discussed above, assume Cory presented medical bills of $800 to Sally in support of his damages claim. If Sally's first offer is $25 and she states to Cory, "that's all you deserve," Cory will likely not value Sally's subsequent concession of not walking the dog on Cory's street. Further, just as offers must be supported by objective criteria, so should concessions. When offering a concession, explain how the concession benefits the other side and that you are truly given up something of value.

While offering a concession should lead to a reciprocal concession and counteroffer, negotiations rarely run so smoothly. Generally, negotiation protocols suggest that when one party concedes certain issues the other party is expected to make similar compromises. Experienced negotiators know, however, that some parties do not follow negotiating protocols, at least not on every occasion. It is possible that a concession will be rejected with no reciprocity in the hopes that an outright refusal to cooperate may spur additional concessions and offers. It is important that you never get to the point where you are the only one on the room making concessions. In that situation you are increasing the attractiveness of your offer while the other side simply sits back and waits until the terms become acceptable. Similar to bargaining against yourself by making repeating unreciprocated offers, if you see that you are in the situation where the other side is simply rejecting whatever concessions you put on the table, it is time to put the brakes on making subsequent concessions. Instead, you should ask the other side for their next offer or concession. If none is forthcoming, it may be time to end the negotiation session.

Some negotiators like to avoid the possibility of unreciprocated concessions by making a contingent concession.[10] In other words, I will make this concession if you make that concession. In this way, your concession is contingent on a reciprocal concession. By using reciprocal concession strategy, you have clearly communicated to the other side that you not only expect him to make a reciprocal concession, but that there is a specific concession you want him to make. A contingent concession does have some drawbacks, however. By tying your concession to the potential concession from the other party, you have narrowed the possible concessions the other side may have made in response to your concession. In fact, the other side may have made a more beneficial concession in response to your concession than the one you proposed that he offer. Recall Sally's biting dog. If Sally simply makes a concession that she will not walk her dog on Cory's street and waits for Cory's response, she has left open all possible concessions Cory may make. However, if Sally says, "I will not walk my dog on your street if you agree to not pursue quarantining or euthanizing my dog," she has effectively made a reciprocal bargain of those issues only. If Cory says, "I was never going to pursue that course of action and give me my $800," her contingent concession has weakened her bargaining power. If she had simply said, "I will not walk my dog on your street," Cory may have lowered his damage request in response. However, if the continued welfare of the dog was in fact priceless to Sally, then she was wise to use the contingent concession even though she may wind up paying more in his damages. Given the uncertainty of contingent concessions, it is of the utmost importance that you conduct research prior to the negotiation, so that you are in the best position to place a value on the concessions you are making and accepting from the other side.

Remember during the bargaining phase of the negotiation to refer to the concession order you outlined in your Tactical Planning Worksheet. Also, remember to check off the concessions as you offer them and write down the concessions you have been offered during the negotiation. Some of the offered concessions will hopefully match the anticipated concessions you tried to predict in your planning worksheet. Keeping track of the concessions will ensure you make those concessions in order and will give you a quick picture of the number of concessions you have made in relation to the concessions made by the other side.

Exercises 4-1 and 4-2: Offers, Counteroffers, and Concessions

Exercise 4-1. Assume you started a resume writing business. You place an ad online about your resume writing business, provide your contact information, and state that pricing is dependent upon the client's specific resume requirements. Khloe, a potential client, emails you and explains her resume needs with some basic information about herself. Khloe also states she needs the completed resume in three days. She then asks for a price. You respond that based on the information she has provided, your price to prepare her resume in three days would be $100. Khloe responds that she does not want to pay more than $50. You counter with $75 but tell her that at that price you will not have her resume ready for a week since you cannot postpone working on other client's resumes to finish her resume in three days. Assume that Khloe states that your terms are unacceptable and asks you for a better price, but she does not counter. Assume that your business is doing fairly well but it is important for you to obtain as many clients as possible at a fairly consistent rate. You have never charged less than $60 to prepare a resume and your standard preparation time is one week. How should your respond to her?

Exercise 4-2. You are a salesperson for a large electronics store. The store is currently trying to sell a well-known manufacturer's latest mobile phone. The manufacturer mandates that the phone must be sold for its retail price of $799. However, the manufacturer will allow the store through its salespersons to offer perks, or concessions, to buyers that are not tied to the price. These perks include free service contracts, free service activation, a generous trade-in policy of no less than 75% of its value in the next two years, and a 50% discount on a case and headphones for the phone. What would be your strategy in selling this phone? How would you order these concessions to a potential buyer? Why?

Questions

Questions used during the bargaining process can be very effective for many purposes. They are valuable for general information gathering and for clarifying or justifying positions taken in the negotiation. They are also helpful for establishing a positive rapport or for altering the tone of the negotiation when needed, such as tempering an angry exchange.

As discussed in Chapter 2 on Tactical Planning, a thorough planning worksheet will include your proposed questions. However, it is not possible to plan all questions you may ask. Moreover, it is not effective simply to run through all of your prepared questions in the order you planned in your worksheet. Questions are best interspersed throughout the bargaining process. Good negotiators will constantly adjust questions during the negotiation depending on the answers they receive. Once an answer is given, a follow-up question may be necessary.

Listening is a critical part of the questioning process.[11] When and how to ask questions requires you to listen to what is being said by the other side and to pay close attention to the tone and manner in which it is being said. For example, assume you represent a client involved in a car accident. The other side claims that your client failed to yield the right of way at an intersection and hit his client's car, causing injuries. In your worksheet, you planned to ask a question early in the negotiation in order to gather information as to how his client perceived the accident occurred. However, before you can ask that question, the other side begins the negotiation by saying, "Let me tell you how this accident happened. Your client sped through the intersection and was totally negligent in hitting my client's car. End of story." In this scenario, if you were not really listening but reviewing your planning worksheet as he was making this testy statement, and you now ask, "Can you tell me how your client said the accident occurred?" it will be obvious that you were not listening at all to what was just said. Unless the other party thinks you were making a not too funny joke, your question will probably infuriate him and may put a damper on the negotiation. However, hopefully, you were paying attention to the question, and you abandoned your scripted question and asked follow up questions to get more details about their version of the accident. By asking follow up questions, you will be able to gather additional information, since it is highly unlikely that the other side presented a complete detailed version of the accident. It is more likely the other side presented a version very favorable to his client's position and thus left out key information that you would like to know.

Skilled negotiators use both open-ended and closed-ended questions as appropriate. Since you should have a prepared list of closed and open-ended questions in your Tactical Planning Worksheet, during bargaining you should strategically decide the best approach to interspersing these types of questions in order to receive optimal answers from the other side. Failing to use a strategic mix of questions could result in receiving unsatisfactory answers or no answers at all. For example, while you may have started with open-ended, non-threatening questions, if the other side's answers are not forthcoming, you may need to reframe your questions as more direct, close-ended, or narrow questions. These types of questions may be successful in that they may only require a yes or no answer. Of course, there is a likelihood that the other side may refuse to answer some or all of your questions. If you receive an answer such as "I am not going to answer that," or the more forceful, "Are you kidding me?" you should try to encourage the party to answer. You should explain that an answer would be helpful in moving towards a resolution of the case. For example, if you ask the other side "Was your client on the phone at the time of the accident," you may get the response, "I'm not going to answer," or "I don't know," or "You can ask my client in a deposition." If you receive any of those unhelpful answers, you may explain to the other side that providing an accurate answer will help determine how to apportion liability and that delaying this answer will only serve to delay a resolution. This type of encouragement may prompt a helpful response. However, it is human nature that people (and those who represent them) are reluctant to answer questions that may hurt their case, even though the answer will eventually be revealed. In the situation where the other side will not answer because his client has instructed him not to answer, especially if the information is protected by the attorney-client privilege, you may in fact have reached a dead end. In that instance, it is better to change course and move to a different issue or topic, which will lead to more effective bargaining.

As discussed in Chapter 2 on Tactical Planning, questions serve purposes beyond simply information gathering. Questions may also be used for purposes such as establishing a positive rapport with the other side. For example, during ice-breaking, you may want to ask a non-threatening question such as, "How was the drive to our office today?" Unless the other side was stuck in a two-hour traffic jam, this type of non-threatening question allows the parties to establish a rapport before getting down to the nuts and bolts of the negotiation. However, even the best non-threatening question may go astray. If you sense that the other party is simply not a person who enjoys any small talk, you may abandon the small talk questions and move forward with your agenda.

Questions may also help to clarify matters arising or justify positions taken by a party during the negotiation. For example, if the other party has offered a settlement proposal that is 1% of sales revenue calculated from the first date on the shelf to the expiration date, you should ask questions for clarification. For example, is the percentage based on gross or net revenues? Also, when is "on the shelf" determined? Do not assume that the terms will be explained more thoroughly when the terms are included in the contract. If you cannot explain the deal to others as it was explained to you, you do not have a clear understanding of it. Do not be concerned that you may appear less knowledgeable by asking questions. In fact, asking questions may highlight that there are missing links in the other side's proposal that can now be corrected.

Furthermore, questions are effective in situations where a party makes an offer without providing objective criteria. In those situations, you should ask, "What is your basis for the offer?" This question will help to uncover the other side's objective criteria, if there is any.

Questions can also be usefully employed when negotiations become contentious. They allow the parties to step back. For example, if you make an offer perceived as unrealistic or perhaps insulting, the other side may respond angrily, "That offer is absurd." In order to diffuse this anger and hopefully put the negotiation back on track, you should calmly ask, "What about the offer raises concerns for you?" Hopefully, a question like this would prompt the other side to offer a reasoned response and move the parties towards a productive negotiation session.

Just as you prepared questions to ask in your Tactical Planning Worksheet, your worksheet should reflect questions you expect to be asked and how you plan to respond. Since you have likely anticipated many of the questions posed by the other side, you should be ready with answers. The way in which you answer questions may be mirrored by the other side in the way she answers your questions. Similarly, if you planned to use some diversionary techniques to avoid answering questions, you can expect those diversionary tactics to be used by the other side. For example, in the car accident case discussed above, if you asked the question, "Was your client on her cell phone at the time of the accident?" you may receive this mirrored question as a response: "Was your client on his cell phone at the time of the accident?" This question to a question response is fine as long as you have a satisfactory answer. But if you do not want to answer that question, you should not ask it.

Finally, do not be discouraged if many of the questions you prepared go unanswered or unasked. There will be other opportunities to obtain information. You do not want questioning to consume the negotiation process. Use questions strategically and purposefully, but do not lose your focus on bargaining by asking an excessive number of questions.

Bargaining Tactics

Ideally, negotiators will deal fairly and honestly with each other and not resort to game playing or devious tactics. Unfortunately, negotiations do not take place in La La Land. Moreover, many negotiators employ these tricks. Thus, you should be aware of some of the most common tricks and tactics and how to respond effectively to them. Tactics involving lying and bias are covered in a full chapter, Chapter 6 on Ethics and Equity.

While there are a myriad of negotiation tricks and tactics, some of the most widely used tactics are described below.[12] Coupled with descriptions of the tactics are some suggested responses.

Extreme opening offer/demand: A negotiator may make an extreme offer or demand. This tactic may be used by a competitive, aggressive, negotiator who believes that the shock value of an excessive offer or demand will serve to send a message that he is no pushover and, in fact, may be the bullying kind. An extreme offer may also be used by a negotiator who is not adequately prepared and decides to just shoot from the hip with an extreme offer. Not surprisingly, extreme offers or demands are usually not accompanied by objective criteria.

Response: If you receive an extreme offer or demand, your first response should be to ask for the basis of the demand, i.e., the objective criteria, in a non-threatening manner. It is likely that the other side does not have an objective basis for the demand but more likely he will provide an emotional basis, such as "your client needs to pay for what he has done." If this is the case, you may explain why his criteria are lacking. You may further wish to make your own reasoned offer, highlighting the objective criteria you have employed. If the other side will not budge from his extreme position, this negotiation may be over before it had a chance to get started.

Take it or Leave it: A negotiator may set forth an offer followed by the statement, "take it or leave it." This ultimatum may have been preceded by an extreme offer or preceded by an offer worth further consideration but not necessarily acceptable on the spot. In either case, the negotiator employing the ultimatum of "take it or leave it" is attempting to circumvent any further discussion about the offer.

Response: While you might be tempted to respond with a hearty "I'll leave it," such a response would likely lead to an escalation of an already tense situation. Instead of responding by directly addressing their ultimatum, it is better to ignore the "take it or leave it" ultimatum and keep the focus on the offer or demand. You should ask the other party to explain the objective criteria for the offer and continue with further questioning if necessary regarding the basis of the offer. Also, be sure not to fall into the trap of bargaining against yourself and continuing to make offers that are not reciprocated.

Threats: There are many different types of threats a party may resort to in a negotiation. Assuming a threat is not illegal or criminal, such as extortion or blackmailing, a threat used in a negotiation is generally a desperate attempt to force a settlement when a party believes that things are not going well. One type of threat is a scare tactic that interjects a peripheral issue into the discussion in order to intimidate the other side. In these cases, the party using the scare tactic generally does not have the ability to follow through with the threat. For example, assume the other side says, "If you don't accept our offer to purchase your company, we will smear your reputation in the industry." Another type of threat is when the party may or may not have the intention of following through with the threat. For example, the party says, "If you don't settle, we are going to file suit tomorrow." The threat may be simply grandstanding, if the party has no intention of ever filing suit. The party may, however, believe he has a better chance of success in court than you do, and will actually file suit if you do not agree to his negotiating terms. Other types of threats may be grounded in fact and have to be given consideration. Sometimes, a party is using a hardline threat to set forth a viable alternative not previously discussed. For example, if the other side says, "If you do not accept our offer to purchase your company, we will continue our talks with one of your competitors, and if we purchase their business, you will likely not find a buyer in the near future, since we know we are one of few buyers available to purchase this type of business." This type of threat may prove to be an accurate assessment and must be considered more seriously than empty threats.

Response: When a party issues a threat during a negotiation, before you respond, you must first diagnose and try to understand the motivation behind the threat. Was the threat made out of frustration or was it made to introduce a viable alternative? If negotiations have become heated and the other side is simply venting frustration, you should try to express your concern and move the discussion back to the realistic proposals on the table. However, if the threat is actually an alternative that the other side is in a position to employ, you should ask questions to uncover additional information and determine the strength of that alternative. If you are unsure of the viability of the threat and a party persists in using the threat, it may become necessary to call them on the threat and if necessary, respond with a threat. For example, back to the example, "If you do not settle we will file suit tomorrow," you may feel confident to call them on it if you feel they are bluffing. You might point out that a lawsuit would be costly and the time it would take to get the case resolved would cause a disruption to their business. If the party is unmoved by this reasoning, it might be best to offer a counter threat such as, "If we do go to trial, legal precedent is in our favor and I believe a jury will be much more sympathetic to our position than to your position." Of course, you need to be prepared to back up these statements or else you are simply issuing an empty threat as well. In situations where you are unsure of the legitimacy and strength of the threat, the best approach in confronting the threat may be for you to use a mix of aggressive questioning and accommodating questioning.

Limited/Lack of authority: You may get to a point in the negotiation where you believe you are close to coming to an agreement, when suddenly the other side says, "This all sounds good, but I have to go back to my client, boss, husband, preacher, or mother before I can make this deal." If disingenuous, this is a classic stall tactic and an attempt to delay a resolution of the matter. If negotiations are going well, it may be baffling as to why a party would want to delay, but the "blame someone else" tactic is likely an attempt to get you to sweeten your offer by interjecting uncertainty of authority.

Conversely, there are cases in which a settlement requires approval by another person, such as where an attorney needs client approval, but the negotiating party refuses to try to obtain that approval. The party may respond to your offer by saying, "This offer is so insulting that I am not going to take this offer back to my client." In this instance, the party is using the ultimate insult tactic, i.e., your offer is so unworthy it is not even worth repeating to the client. The refusal to obtain the authority may be a stalling tactic.

Response: You should never be in a position where the other side can surprise you with a claim of a lack of authority. Before you begin negotiations, you should confirm that the party you are negotiating with has the full and complete authority to enter into a settlement. If the party does not have such authority, you should establish a procedure before negotiations begin for obtaining such authority. However, if you have not had a pre-negotiation discussion concerning authority, and you are surprised by this lack of authority during the negotiation, you should now establish the procedure for getting this authority by asking, "When will you get a response from your client?" If you receive a vague or unconvincing answer on authority, you can infer that the other side probably has no procedure set up to convey settlement proposals to his client and this authority issue is probably a bluff. In that case, you may want to set the parameters by setting forth a time frame for a response such as "how about calling me later today with your client's response." However, if you are in the position where the attorney will not even take the offer to his client, you should remind him that attorneys have an ethical duty to convey all offers to clients, and his client may later be surprised upon learning the attorney rejected your offer without notifying him. Then you can tell the attorney you expect a response once that offer is conveyed to the client.

Time Pressure: Many times, there are real time constraints in a negotiation. For example, if you are negotiating a matter in litigation with the other side and the trial is set to begin the next day, time is an important factor both parties must confront as the negotiation proceeds. Or, if the parties are negotiating a prenuptial agreement and the wedding is in a month, the pressure is on to come to an agreement, ditch the prenup, or the heart wrenching decision to cancel the wedding. However, you should be aware of a party who imposes a time constraint when no such constraint exists. For example, if a party says, "This is our offer and you have 24 hours to accept it," and does not give any reason for the 24 hour limitation, it is likely this is a fake deadline imposed by the other side to try to prompt you to quickly accept the offer for fear it may expire. Sometimes time constraints may be subtler. A party who states during a negotiation that he suddenly must leave in 20 minutes, or a party negotiating by email who writes that he will be unavailable by email for a week as he is signing off to his email is attempting to assert time pressure on you to quickly come to a resolution.

Response: You should be able to prevent a party from asserting an artificial time constraint during the negotiation by setting up a time schedule when planning the negotiation. If you are planning to meet in person, discuss the length of time you are available for the negotiation and inquire about time constraints for the other side. If you are negotiating in other formats, this may be more difficult.

Since email and text are not in real time, setting a time frame is difficult. You should, however, try to set an endpoint during such exchanges. For example, if you sent the last email or text and have not heard a response for 24 hours, you might send another text or email trying to prompt a response. If you still receive no response, it is time for you to back off from the exchange as the other side may purposely be trying to ignore you in the hopes that his silence will cause you to make a better offer.

Anger, sadness, and related personality traits: Negotiations tend to be emotional and not all negotiators are adept at keeping a poker face during bargaining.[13] Further, there are instances when showing emotion is not a tactic but is genuine. Showing emotion may humanize a party, and bring the parties closer to a resolution. For example, assume that grandma passes away, and two sisters are negotiating over who will get possession of her silverware. Sister 1 becomes teary eyed after telling Sister 2 that she would like grandma's silverware to eventually pass down to her daughter, who is a chef. Sister 2 is moved by her emotion, and Sister 1's emotional statement may in fact help to resolve the dispute. However, in the same scenario, if Sister 1 produces tears that appeared feigned, and says grandma said to her before she passed away, "Sister 1, I want you to have the silverware after I go," Sister 2 may believe the tears and the story are fake, and this emotional statement may actually escalate the matter.

Anger is also a common emotion expressed during negotiations. In most instances, anger complicates bargaining and is not helpful in resolving the conflict. A party may become angry simply because he has lost control during the negotiation or the anger is a tactic to intimidate the other side and force a solution. Furthermore, whether the anger is real or fake, when a party expresses anger, the other side often responds with anger. Anger is often expressed in personal attacks, which have no legitimate purpose in effective bargaining.

Response: In most negotiations, it is best to try to maintain composure when confronted with an emotional outburst from the other side. By keeping your emotions steady, you have the opportunity to consider the other side's emotional display in context. It may be that the party's expression of emotion is genuine and will bring you closer to a resolution. In arms-open negotiations, where the parties have a personal relationship, emotions may be easily triggered as negotiations become tense. However, if the emotion is a recognizable tactic, and does not serve to facilitate the negotiation but in fact makes the negotiation more tense, you should try to stay calm and get the negotiations back on track. This calmness is especially effective when responding to anger. Do not allow yourself to be bullied or intimidated. Unfortunately, in some circumstances, your composed demeanor in the face of anger may serve to make the other side angrier. If that is the case, you should take a break until the other side can approach the negotiation without anger. Furthermore, avoid the temptation to respond to anger with anger. If you start a yelling exchange, you will lose your focus and it will be difficult to get the negotiation back on track.

The above tactics are only a select few of the myriad of possible gamesmanship employed by negotiators. If you are involved in an arms-length negotiation, you should be on guard to potential tactics and be prepared with responses. If you are involved in an arms-open negotiation, however, because of your familiarity with your counterpart you are probably well aware of what, if any, tactics they may attempt and are already prepared with responses, and you can move right on to Chapter 5 on Letting Go or Resolving.

Chapter 5

Letting Go or Resolving

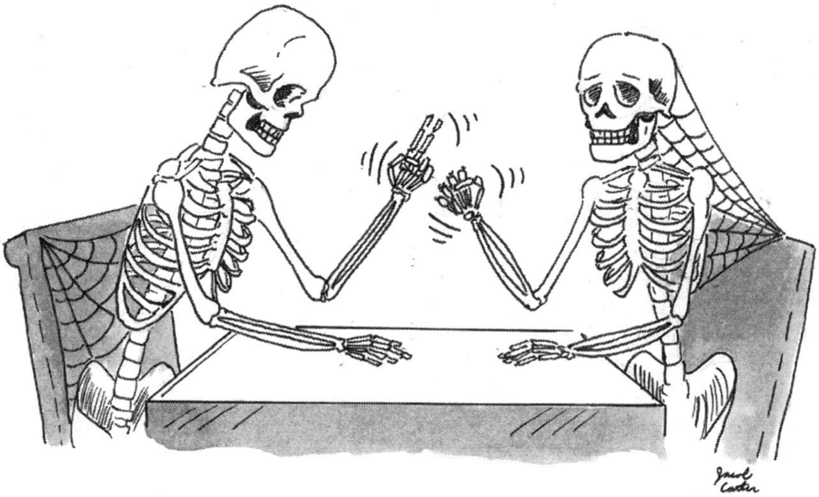

"We're so close, we can't give up now!"

Letting Go or Resolving

If you bargain effectively and efficiently, you will hopefully reach an agreement during bargaining and will not need to confront the letting go or resolving dilemma. However, there is a point in many negotiations where you begin to doubt whether there will be a resolution. This doubt may occur whether you have been involved in a series of negotiations on the matter or it is only the first negotiation. If the offers and concessions have slowed to a crawl and frustration is becoming apparent, it is time to either kick the negotiation up a notch or call it, either for the day, or for good. However, there are many factors to address before deciding if you should stay or go. These factors are considered below.

Time Constraints

Prior to or at the beginning of the negotiation, as discussed in Chapter 4 on Bargaining, you likely set the agenda, which hopefully included any time constraints on the upcoming negotiation session. There may be rigid time constraints that are out of the parties' control, such as pending trial dates, shipping deadlines, or expiration of contracts. If any of these are in play, then both sides know the clock is running and there may be a greater desire to keep the negotiation going, especially if alternatives are not attractive. There may also be more flexible time constraints set by a party, such as needing to adjourn for another appointment or catching a flight. These are flexible time constraints because they are self-imposed by the parties, and although the party may believe these future obligations are not movable, there is no third party deadline imposed as in a trial date. There may also be time constraints that are not pre-planned but arise abruptly during the negotiation. These abrupt time constraints may be real emergencies that arise or may be manufactured predicaments by a party who just wants to leave the negotiation. For example, a party's phone may suddenly ring followed by an announcement that she must leave. Was this a real or manufactured excuse? If the negotiation was stalled or emotions were running high, it may well be a subtle way of ending it.

If the negotiation is headed towards a time constraint that you are aware of, it is appropriate to take a moment to assess your progress and determine whether it is desirable to continue with the pending deadline looming ahead. In order to make that assessment, you should examine your current bargaining position and determine how close you are to resolving this negotiation and your alternatives if you do not settle.

Assess Your Progress

Determining if you are close to resolving the matter will help you decide your approach to the remainder of the negotiation. At this stage of the negotiation, you may be making real progress, some progress, or no progress at all.

Assume the negotiation session has been going well, with mutual offers and concessions, when it slows to a crawl and suddenly you are at an impasse. In order to get back on track, you should try to return to questioning, especially non-threatening questions.[1] Try to determine, through questioning, why the offers and concessions have stopped. It may be that the other side has reached his bottom line, or that he has reacted negatively to information you have given to him and does not want to continue. By asking questions, you may be able to uncover the reasons for the disruption.

It also may be that your negotiating counterpart is reluctant to make a deal for emotional reasons, not business reasons. For example, assume that Nate has owned and worked at his family deli for 40 years. He took over the business from his father, who had started the business. Nate is in poor health and he needs more liquid assets. His family members have not been significantly involved in the business and do not want to take over and run the deli. You want to purchase his deli and after several rounds of negotiations, you and Nate are very close to making a deal when suddenly Nate says, "That's it. I don't think we are going to make a deal." He then begins to gather his belongings and starts to leave.

It is apparent that Nate is having an emotional reaction to selling his business and trouble letting go. At this point, you should try to show compassion and discuss with him the difficulty of leaving his business. You should also try to brainstorm some creative solutions to keep Nate peripherally involved in the business. Perhaps Nate can be a consultant, or you might agree to consider hiring some of his family as future employees. However, these solutions must also be compatible with your goals. You should also ask Nate to examine his alternatives if he does not sell the deli to you. It is likely his best alternative is not as good as your offer. After exploring these options, you may now have convinced Nate to go through with the sale.

Sometimes, you may notice the mood in the room shifts for no reason that is apparent to you. In this case, you should examine the reasons for the shift in mood. If you had been having a professional and courteous exchange, you are much more likely to get the negotiation back on track.[2] However, if the mood and tone has been strained or negative, you, or the other side, may have reached the breaking point and the negotiation is collapsing under the strain. It is important to examine if there was a mood changing event that occurred during the negotiation, and attempt to get back on track. In this case, a short recess may be able to get the sides to break the ominous mood and return to productivity.

If your negotiation never progressed past the ice-breaking and initial offers stages, and now you are faced with a time constraint, it may be that this was never going to be a successful negotiation and it is time to quit. You are not really deadlocked because this negotiation was DOA. Any attempt to resuscitate it at this point may lead to a hurried bargaining phase with the potential for you to make too many concessions in the hopes of making a quick deal. If you believe there is still a possibility of working a deal, and are not confined by a rigid time constraint, you may want to suggest ending the negotiation session for the day, and reconvening at another time. However, do not make this suggestion unless you think the next negotiation will be different from this one. Moreover, if you have gained any information from this session, you may legitimately need to do additional research and investigation before the next session. Even if that is not the case, you should not meet again if there are no plans to take the negotiation in a more successful direction. Therefore, you will need to review your Tactical Planning Worksheet and determine if there is a different strategy you may need to implement the next time. Of course, it takes the other side to act reasonably also. If you were negotiating in good faith, but the other side was simply unreasonable, refusing to make offers, counteroffers, or concessions, there is no amount of strategy or revising of your worksheet that will help. In that instance, it is better to agree to meet again only if the other side truly wants to attempt to reach a resolution and will put more effort into bargaining.

In many negotiations, the bargaining is not all smooth or all rocky. You may be at a point where there have been some offers and concessions on both sides, but the brackets are wide and not close to your settlement range, and progress has halted. If you have proposed the last offer on the table, and no counteroffer is forthcoming from the other side, as previously discussed, make sure you do not make another offer and bargain against yourself in an attempt to move the negotiation forward. You should also maintain your composure and not be frustrated by the lack of progress, even if the other side vents his frustration. Asking open-ended questions, such as "What can we do to move the negotiation forward?" may get the other side to talk and lead to further progress. But be prepared for a response such as, "offer us more money." If you are unable to move past this point, and other attempts to move the negotiation forward fail, it is appropriate to evaluate whether there is anything else to accomplish in this session. If there was real progress that has temporarily slowed, you may be more readily able to suggest a recess or schedule another session. If there is a time constraint, a break may be possible but scheduling another session may not. At this point, it is time to examine your alternatives.

Examining Your Alternative Options

Before pulling the plug on any negotiation, it is important to compare the offer on the negotiation table to your alternative options if you do not reach an agreement. The offer on the table may be within your range of an acceptable agreement, but not at the top of the range, or the offer may not be within your range of an acceptable settlement. In either situation, you must decide whether to push for more or accept their offer and consider your alternative. If you are within your range, you may breathe a little easier, because you are likely assured of a positive outcome. However, if you are not in range, you may be sweating a bit. Either way, you should determine if the status quo or alternative is better than the last offer. Since you have prepared a planning worksheet, you have pre-determined your best alternative. Further, you have also estimated what the other side's best alternative is as well. During the course of the negotiation, you may have gained information that you must now factor in and adjust the other side's alternative. Taking in all these factors, assess the most desirable outcome for the negotiation. It may well be that continuing the negotiation and seeking a better resolution is better than accepting your alternative. If this is the case, you should assess time constraints and decide the best approach to keep the negotiation process going.

Splitting the Difference to Reach Agreement

Sometimes parties are stuck in the process and no matter how much they debate and use objective criteria, neither party is willing to budge from their last offers. Splitting the difference is a well-known technique implemented by parties to try to reach an agreement by using simple math.[3] For example, let us assume Buyer and Seller are in the midst of negotiations over the sale of a house. Buyer's last offer was $275,000 and Seller's last offer was $285,000. Despite offering objective criteria and asking questions to obtain more information, Buyer and Seller refuse to budge from their last offers, but neither party wants to walk away (even if they pretend they do). Buyer may now suggest that they "split the difference" and agree to a selling price of $280,000, which is the midpoint between $275,000 and $285,000. This technique may prove successful in that it seems a fair way to raise/lower offers without an emotional component.

Splitting the difference should be used sparingly and with caution. First, you should never split the difference in the early stages of the negotiation or when your respective offers are far apart. Splitting the difference between $275,000 and $300,000 is significantly different than splitting the difference between $300,000 and $800,000. It is likely with this vast range that you have not acquired information from the other side or fully stated your position. Negotiations should not be reduced to simple mathematical equations when there are real differences in offers and desired outcomes. Your Tactical Planning Worksheet set forth your research and objective criteria for you to use in order to make offers, counteroffers, and concessions. Do not abandon your planning to do mathematical computations when your bargaining position is so far apart from the other side's bargaining position as reflected in the offers.

Second, splitting the difference may simply be a tactic used by the other side and does not promote equality at all, despite the use of non-judgmental math. For example, refer back to the sale of the house. Assume Seller had first offered the house at $300,000 and Buyer's first offer was $220,000. After small concessions and counteroffers by Seller, Seller's last offer was, as stated in the example above, $285,000 while buyer's last offer was $275,000. They now decide to split the difference and agree on $280,000. However, under this scenario, Buyer has increased his original offer by $60,000, while Seller decreased his offer by only $20,000. Unless Buyer's opening offer was not justified by objective criteria, Buyer did not succeed in obtaining an equitable result by splitting the difference. Therefore, it is important to keep track of offers, counteroffers and concessions during the negotiation so as not to fall into the trap of splitting a lopsided difference.

Third, splitting the difference may result in re-bracketing of your offer. Therefore, it may be wise for you to avoid being the one to suggest the split the difference option. Even with this warning, you may still be tempted to use this technique in the throes of a negotiation when a deal may be imminent. If you decide to suggest splitting the difference, be aware that a savvy negotiator may use this split the difference offer as a chance to re-bracket the negotiation and ultimately make a better deal. For example, assume you are an attorney representing a doctor, who is the defendant in a medical malpractice action. During the negotiation with the plaintiff's attorney, your last offer on the table was $100,000 and the plaintiff's attorney's last offer was $120,000. It is late in the day and you are ready for this negotiation to end, so you throw out a "let's just split the difference at $110,000." Instead of jumping at your offer, the Plaintiff's attorney replies, "So you're willing to go to $110,000?" As you mumble "yes," he says, "Ok, let me take that back to my client and get back to you." A few hours later, he contacts you and says," my client will not go to $110,000 but will agree to $115,000." You are likely to either agree to $115,000 or you may try to get his client to split the difference again and agree to $112,500. At this point, because you are still close to settling, you are most likely eager not to derail the deal. However, your splitting the difference technique became an offer which permitted the other side to counter one more time for a higher amount.[4]

Scheduling Another Negotiating Session

If in fact, you cannot reach an agreement during the negotiation session but have decided it will be beneficial to continue the negotiation at another time, and have convinced the other side to continue, it is important to make sure you schedule the next meeting before you adjourn for the day. It is not enough to leave simply with a casual, "I'll be in touch." It is much more effective to attempt to set the next meeting at the end of this session. In this way, not only do you have a commitment from the other side to continue, but you have shown your willingness to try and further work toward an agreement.

In setting the next meeting, determine the forum in which to continue.[5] While you may have met in person for this negotiation, you are certainly not bound by that forum for the next meeting. In fact, logistics may prove it to be difficult for the parties to meet again in person, so alternatives should be suggested. As discussed in Chapter 3 on Arranging, video-conferencing, email, and text are all viable formats for negotiation and may be an easy and cost effective way to keep the discussion going.

After determining the forum, you should also try to schedule the next negotiation session sooner rather than later. Obviously if you are bound by a rigid time constraint, that time limitation will influence the next meeting time. However, if there is no immediate time constraint, it is still preferable to not to allow too much time to pass before continuing the negotiation. If you delay the next meeting, the incentive to continue the negotiation may decrease. Also, unanticipated issues may arise in the interim recess, which may complicate or derail the progress you have made. Further, although "absence makes the heart grow fonder" in personal relationships, in negotiation, "out of sight, out of mind" may prove applicable. This saying may be especially true if you are negotiating the purchase of a business or a job offer. In these situations, there are "other fish in the sea" and delaying discussions may prove the "kiss of death" for the deal.

Draft 57: "If you agree to put a semi-colon instead of a period at the end of the second sentence in paragraph 32, I will agree to put a subheading before paragraph 64 as you requested."

Executing the Agreement

If you reached an agreement during the negotiation, congratulations! Even if less desirable than you expected, hopefully your agreement was within your acceptable settlement range and was better than your alternative. While you may think the hard work is over, there is still much to do in order to finalize your agreement, which is the conclusion of a successful negotiation.

If you were negotiating in person, it is likely that you and the other party came to a verbal agreement, shook hands and said, "I'll be in touch." At this time, it is unlikely that you will have the time or resources to reduce that verbal agreement to writing and draft an immediate settlement agreement and make it legally binding. However, as is often noted, a verbal agreement is not worth the paper it is written on. While oral contracts may be enforceable, it will be a difficult road to prove the terms in the absence of a writing.[6] Therefore, before you adjourn, convince the other side to take a few minutes and reduce the key terms to writing. Memorializing key terms in writing at this time will ensure that you are both in agreement, and if not, allows time to resolve matters in which there remains confusion. If there is no time to reduce terms to writing before adjourning, you should send an email confirming the terms to the other side as soon as possible after you leave. Hopefully the other side will acknowledge the representations made in your email, and you will now have written confirmation.

If you have been negotiating by email or text, you have the luxury of already having some terms of your agreement in writing. However, negotiating through email or text rarely translates to a completed agreement. Nevertheless, emails or texts may serve as a written basis from which you can springboard to a completed agreement.

If your negotiation was recorded, the recording will be useful in several ways. First, it will confirm the terms to which you have agreed. Next, it will clear up any confusion as to what was said during the negotiation. Finally, it will help to prevent a party adding terms not agreed upon. Any discrepancies between the parties can be cleared up by playing the recording.

The next and final step in the process is to prepare a formal agreement. Most often the parties will draft a contract, which when finalized, becomes the operating document that controls the parties from this point forward. If a party does not live up to the terms of the agreement, he may be considered "in breach" of the agreement.[7] If the parties are unable to work out their differences, the aggrieved party may need to file a lawsuit or attempt to resolve the dispute through arbitration or mediation.[8]

Whether or not you were able to write down key provisions at the end of the negotiation, you should discuss whether you or the other side will be preparing the final agreement. In some situations, it is standard for one party to prepare the final agreement. For example, in the purchase of a house, the seller, most often through their agent, prepares the sales agreement. This agreement is usually a series of forms containing boilerplate language in which the key provisions, such as sales price, are filled on the form. Similarly, the seller of a business usually prepares the agreement. However, if you are settling a matter subject to litigation, either party may prepare the settlement agreement, depending on the circumstances. Notwithstanding an industry standard, if there is no objection by the other side, it is wise for you to prepare the agreement so you have the control and the ability to get the document finished in a timely manner.

Once it is decided who will prepare the agreement, the parties should agree to a schedule for completion for the agreement. It is customary for the person who prepares the agreement to send it to the other side, who may make non-substantive corrections, additions, or deletions to the agreement before returning it to the preparer. This back and forth may continue until the agreement is acceptable to both sides. Therefore, it is important to try and set a time frame for completion. For example, you might say, "I will prepare the agreement and send it to you by Friday. If you have any changes, I hope we can work on them at the beginning of next week and have this signed by next Thursday." In this way, both parties will have a completion date to strive for. In general, the sooner you can finalize the agreement, the better. Further, there may be valid time constraints in place which will dictate completion of the agreement, such as a pending trial date. If so, you will obviously be bound by those limitations.

In drafting the agreement, do not add any terms not agreed upon in the hopes of playing a game of "gotcha." Conversely, if you receive a prepared settlement agreement, make sure no additional terms were added as well. Changes made by either side should be merely formal or stylistic, not substantively altering the terms of the settlement. The preparation of the settlement agreement is not an opportunity to continue the negotiation, but rather should memorialize their agreed upon terms.

While you hope the process of finalizing the agreement goes smoothly as described above, unfortunately there may be times where a party does add terms to the agreement, either intentionally or mistakenly or he may suggest that the changes are not substantive. If you do not have any written or recorded "proof" as to what was agreed upon, you may need to jump back to negotiation mode to work out the differences. If you do have to re-negotiate terms, you should first try to narrow the discussion to the new disputed terms and resist the temptation to bring up other terms not in dispute. For example, if a home buyer now disputes that he agreed to a ten day closing, instead insisting he agreed to a thirty day closing, the seller should attempt to resolve the closing date instead of moving to other issues. For example, in response to the closing date dispute, the seller should not say, "Well I've decided not to repair that broken window that I had agreed to do." However, if the parties are unable to come to agreement on the disputed terms, it may be necessary to open up other related issues in order to resolve and salvage the deal. For, example, in the home purchase example above, if the parties cannot resolve the closing time frame, and the buyer is insistent on thirty day closing, seller may now say, "well if it is going to be a thirty day closing, you will need to pay me $100 over the agreed selling price as I will incur an extra twenty days of expenses with the house." Note how the disputed closing time frame has prompted the seller to renegotiate the selling price by linking the extra closing time to more added costs. Even though the seller takes the risk by renegotiating terms, he has tied the closing date to the objective criteria of increased expenses.

Drafting the Agreement

The actual drafting of the agreement can be a lengthy and time consuming process. As noted above, if you are in an industry in which forms are standard, or even required by law, you have a great head start in putting together the agreement. Even if you do not have standard forms, good research should provide you with sample forms for whatever contract you are preparing. For example, if you are preparing a settlement agreement for a slip and fall case, you will be able to find many samples of settlement agreements, even tailored to personal injury cases. However, a form is just a starting point and can only provide a framework for your document.

In drafting your agreement, keep the language simple. If you are drafting the agreement, make sure you understand every word you are placing in the contract and avoid the temptation to use complex language and opt for plain language. For example, instead of writing, "the undersigned" simply use their name. This is especially important if you are an attorney drafting a contract on behalf of a client. Attorneys often believe that must use complex legal language to impress clients with their "legal talk." Although certain legal terminology may be crucial in some contracts, and if so, that language should be explained to the client. However, most documents are littered with legal speak that only adds confusion to the agreement. Further, since this is the clients' agreement, they need to thoroughly understand the language of the agreement. A client should not have to hire another lawyer to explain the agreement to him. Also, drafting a contract with simple language provides protection for the attorney as well. If the client thoroughly understands all the language used, that client cannot come back at a later date to the attorney and now say they were confused by the terminology.

If you did not draft the agreement, thoroughly check the contents of the agreement once you receive it. While it is paramount to make sure the substance of the agreement is what you have agreed upon, it is also important to check even seemingly minor details. For example, check dates, times, and spelling of names of parties. A checklist that is specific to the type of agreement you are preparing may help. An agreement settling a lawsuit will have a much different checklist than a lease agreement. If you are unsure if the agreement thoroughly represents the terms you have agreed upon, you should enlist the help of a third party to review the document. This person may be a trusted associate, or even a friend with knowledge of the matter. However, if you are not a lawyer or being represented by a lawyer, when in doubt it is best to use the services of a lawyer since you want to make sure the agreement conforms to the requirements of the law.

Once the agreement is acceptable to all parties, it should be properly executed. Many times, the applicable law will require that the agreement be notarized. After those formalities, the agreement should be binding on the parties.

Exercise 5-1: Executing the Agreement

Exercise 5-1. (30 minutes) Assume Winnie sued The H Hotel for injuries allegedly resulting from a slip and fall in the hotel's restaurant. Winnie alleged that she slipped on water that had accumulated on the floor after a waiter had spilled a glass of water while clearing a table. She claims the H Hotel was negligent in failing to clean up the spill in a timely manner. The parties' attorneys met to attempt to negotiate a settlement. After several hours of negotiations, the attorneys reached an agreement. Before leaving the negotiation session, they wrote down the following terms:

1) The H Hotel will pay Winnie total damages of $15,000 in one lump sum payment within ten days of the execution of this agreement.
2) The H Hotel will give Winnie a voucher for three free nights at the Hotel for selected dates, excluding major holidays.
3) The H Hotel and Winnie agree to a mutual release of all present and future claims.
4) The H Hotel and Winnie agree to keep the settlement confidential.
5) The H Hotel and Winnie agree that there is no admission of liability by either party.

Prepare a settlement agreement for The H Hotel and Winnie. Conduct research to find a form suitable for a personal injury settlement. Use the form as a guideline, and edit the form to tailor to the terms of their case. Do not simply fill in blanks. If you do not understand the language, do not put it in the agreement.

Chapter 6

Ethics and Equity

A thorough analysis of the negotiation process requires examining ethics and equity, the E of the TABLE method. One would hope that negotiators would act ethically and treat all parties equitably, and therefore there would be no need to discuss effective responses to lapses in such conduct in a negotiation. However, the often private setting of a negotiation seems to be conducive to these troubling types of behavior, in that many negotiators believe the absence of formal proceedings or witnesses in a negotiation embolden them to behave in such a manner. Therefore, every negotiator should anticipate and prepare to respond to both unethical behavior and inequitable treatment.

Ethics

Negotiators often fail to consider ethics when approaching or conducting negotiations. In fact, many negotiators are unsure as to what is considered unethical behavior. They would not be entirely wrong in their uncertainty. It is difficult even for experts to agree, and certain types of conduct may be considered ethical by some and unethical by others. This gray area is often attributed to age, life experience, and education levels, which can form our personal values. For example, bluffing may be considered lying and unacceptable by some, or a legitimate part of negotiation strategy and acceptable by others. Professionals, such as attorneys, are guided by codes of conduct, which may help to delineate ethical conduct, but other negotiators are simply left to make decisions based on their individual moral and ethical standards.

Some negotiators do not concern themselves with ethical challenges because they take the approach that since the negotiating process is unrestricted in terms of both forum and format, whatever they say or propose is not easily discovered or proved outside of the negotiation room. Therefore, their conduct will not be subject to scrutiny for its ethical component. However, the "I can do it because I will not get caught" approach is shortsighted and potentially weakens a negotiator's effectiveness, especially when his conduct undoubtedly crosses acceptable ethical boundaries.

Furthermore, notwithstanding the frequent ineffectiveness of lying, negotiators who engage in unethical behavior can be penalized in many ways. For example, as noted in Chapter 2, on Tactical Planning, material misrepresentations relied upon by one party in entering into an agreement may result in that agreement being set aside when those misrepresentations are discovered. In addition, many professions have their own ethical rules and codes that impose penalties on negotiators who engage in unethical behavior in a negotiation. Furthermore, negotiators who act unethically run the great risk of gaining a reputation as one who is not to be trusted, a label that diminishes their bargaining power in future negotiations.

Most unethical conduct in a negotiation is linked to the exchange or withholding of information, usually in the form of dishonest communication.[1] Lying, misrepresenting, and deception are terms used interchangeably under the general heading of untruthful information and is the most prevalent type of unethical conduct that occurs in negotiations. It can often be very difficult to discover and address during a negotiation.

Why Do Negotiators Lie?

Negotiators lie to improve their bargaining positions. They may feel backed into a corner, having run out of truthful approaches to making offers, counteroffers, and concessions, and are unhappy with the offer on the table. In order to move the negotiation forward, they tell a lie. Alternatively, negotiators may feel that the other side has deceived them during the course of the negotiation, and their reciprocal lies are simply a tit-for-tat strategy.

Frequently, parties lie in a negotiation for the simple reason that they believe that everybody lies, and in fact, the other side expects such behavior. Even more confusing is that certain types of lies have long been supported by various professional codes and negotiation experts, under the theory that certain types of lies are part of the negotiation game. For example, in the legal profession, a lawyer will not be disciplined for unethical conduct if he claims during a negotiation that he has no authority to offer a higher settlement amount when he does have that authority.[2] However, a negotiator who claims his client told him he did not run the red light when in fact the client told his attorney he did run that light would be subject to attorney discipline. Under the Model Rules of Professional Conduct, making false statements of material fact is unethical but the rules carve out an exception for certain statements made in negotiations. Under the Model Rules, "estimates of price or value placed on the subject of a transaction and a party's intentions as to an acceptable settlement of a claim" are not statements of material fact and hence not unethical, because these types of statements are made under "generally accepted conventions in negotiation."[3] However, the attorney's lie about his client not running the red light is a false statement of material fact and thus a violation of the attorney's ethics code. The Model Rules make it clear that not all statements made during negotiations will fall under the "generally accepted conventions" exception and escape penalties under the ethics rules.[4]

In line with the exception in the model rules for attorneys involved in negotiations, many negotiators believe lies concerning settlement amount authority and similar negotiation statements are so integral to the negotiation process that lying in these areas is not problematic or unethical. False demands and misstatements about authority seem to be expected in negotiations and often set bargaining ranges for the negotiation.[5]

Types of Lies

There are generally three types of lies used during negotiations: 1) statements that are affirmatively false; 2) statements considered half-true, such that the statement in and of itself is true, but the negotiator has omitted a material fact making the statement misleading (this type of lie is referred to as paltering);[6] and 3) lies of omission, which involves a negotiator who knows the truth, but intentionally conceals the truth, misleading the other party.[7]

While outright lies are your typical everyday untruth, paltering and lying by omission are more intricate and likely take some talent, and practice. The following example demonstrates the differences in the three types of lies.

Assume you have decided to rent a house for the weekend for a 4th of July party. You find the perfect house and are in the process of negotiating with the homeowner about the rental. You especially like the backyard area because it has an outdoor kitchen complete with a large grill. You ask the landlord if the grill is in working condition. If the grill is not in working condition and the landlord answers, "Yes" he has made an affirmative false statement. If, instead, the landlord answers, "Last July 4th, we had a huge party here and cooked up dozens of hamburgers and hotdogs on that grill." This statement is an example of paltering. Assuming he had that huge party last 4th of July and cooked on the grill, his statement is true. However, he omitted the material fact that the grill is not presently working, which makes his statement misleading. Finally, instead of an affirmative false statement or paltering, the homeowner answers, "What would the 4th of July be without a cookout!" and he then points to the grill. This statement is a lie by omission. He has not answered the question about the grill's condition affirmatively "yes" or "no," or made a truthful but misleading statement about the grill. Instead, he has made a comment about the 4th of July, and cookouts in general, while omitting the answer to the question as to whether the grill is in working condition.

Consequences of Lying

Negotiators may feel that if challenged about lying, they will simply lie again and deny they ever made a false statement and therefore there are no consequences to lying. This repeated denial may only compound the initial problem and now the negotiator is caught in a vicious cycle of lies. Furthermore, once a party lies and is "caught" in that lie, it may be difficult to believe any further representations made by that party during the negotiation. This distrust may even occur when negotiators tell those "acceptable" lies. For example, assume a negotiator falsely states that "My client has not given me authority to pay more than $10,000 to settle this case." However, after trading counteroffers and concessions with the other party, the negotiator now states, "I am prepared to offer you $15,000." The other party is immediately thinking (maybe even out loud!), what happened to his $10,000 authority? Once the other party heard the $15,000 offer, he will now realize the lie, and the consequences may be that any further bottom line given by that negotiator will quickly be discounted as not factually true. Therefore, even though the negotiator may be within his ethical bounds to state a false authority under generally accepted conventions of negotiation, the consequences may result in a less effective negotiating posture.

Even negotiators, who believe they have gotten away with the lie during the negotiation, find their lies often discovered in later proceedings in the same matter, through depositions, or through other investigative methods. Then, once cornered, they engage in further unethical conduct to try to remedy the situation. There is a reason why prosecutors often say the cover up is worse than the offense.

Furthermore, deceitful negotiators develop reputations as untrustworthy, which greatly diminishes their effectiveness in subsequent negotiations. Negotiators who develop reputations as known liars have great difficulty in future negotiations in proving they are making honest representations. The "once a liar always a liar" label may stick to that person and greatly diminish his effectiveness in negotiations. For example, Professor Leigh Thompson describes one study where negotiators were observed over a 10-week period.[8] After that time, they were classified as either liars, tough-but-fair, or cream puffs. Those negotiators who were classified as liars had much greater difficulty resolving disputes in subsequent negotiations. Due to their reputations, their negotiations involved aggressive exchanges as they were consistently challenged on statements and representations they made during the negotiation, resulting in fewer settlements than the tough-but-fair, and cream puff negotiators.

The consequences of lying go beyond ruining your reputation and potential ethics violations. Lying can rise to the level of fraud. A negotiator commits fraud when he makes a statement that he knows is a misrepresentation of a material fact upon which the other side reasonably relies to his detriment, causing damages.[9] For example, an obvious case of fraud would be a car salesperson who knows that an odometer on a car was reset from 20,000 miles to 5 miles but represents to a buyer in a negotiation that the used car is in fact new, since the odometer shows 5 miles. If the buyer purchases the car, he will have an action for fraud because the salesperson knowingly made a material misrepresentation about the mileage on the odometer. Further, the buyer has damages in that he has purchased a car of less value since it is a used car when he believed he was purchasing a new car.

Other cases of fraud in negotiation may not be as obvious. For example, courts have struggled in fraud cases that involve negotiators making representations that they have other offers when they do not. Professor G. Richard Shell in his article describing risks associated with lying in negotiations, references an Oklahoma case where a real estate agent was held liable for fraud when she told a prospective homebuyer that if the buyer did not purchase the home now, another buyer was going to purchase the house and pay the asking price later that day.[10] In that case, however, the other buyer did not exist, and the court held given all the facts and circumstances that this misrepresentation was material and fraudulent. Further, courts have also found that self-serving statements about the value of a person's business may rise to the level of fraud in a negotiation, if the statement is verifiably false.[11]

The lesson to be learned from these cases is that the best practices for negotiators is to avoid the temptation to lie during a negotiation. Although there is some leeway in professional codes as to what constitutes unethical behavior, you may find yourself before a court who will decide if your factual statements rise to the level of fraud. If it does, you may be subject to damages and the potential unraveling of the deal you have made. Furthermore, if you develop the reputation as someone who plays fast and loose with the truth, you may find it difficult to effectively bargain with the other side in a negotiation, as each and every representation you make would likely be subject to scrutiny.

Uncovering Lies during Negotiations

Even though you have read this book and have been convinced not to lie in a negotiation, the other side may not be as well-read and ethical as you are and will in fact decide to lie during negotiations. Many theories have developed on the ways in which to spot a liar, and just as many theories have dismissed these lie spotting theories. Most people believe they can spot a lie, when in fact even those who are adept at lie detection are only about 60% accurate,[12] a statistic that is only slightly better than flipping a coin. Still there are some indicators that may seem more telling than others, and it is helpful to be aware of some of these and how to respond when you believe the other side is using lying as a bargaining trick.[13]

Inconsistent Statements

A negotiator who makes inconsistent or contradictory statements may be lying. For example, at the beginning of a negotiation, if one party says, "I must leave this negotiation at 3:00 PM because I have another appointment." Accordingly, at 3:15 you remind him of his declaration that he had to leave by 3:00, and he answers, "No. I said 4:00." or "No. I never said I had to leave at a specific time." At this point, you may begin to question your own memory of his first statement, but if you are certain your memory is accurate, his inconsistency may point to dishonesty. However, be aware that while your memory may be accurate, perhaps the other side is not lying, but in fact does not remember his prior statement. Therefore, his inconsistency may not be intentional, just forgetful.

When the stakes are higher than simply what time a party is leaving a negotiation, an inconsistent story may point more clearly to lying. For example, if you are negotiating the purchase of a house and you ask the seller if the neighborhood is safe and he answers, "There were a couple of stolen car incidents." Later on in the negotiation, as you are getting closer to making a deal, you repeat the question about crime, and he now says, "There has never been a crime in this neighborhood." His now inconsistent statement may point to dishonesty. Since he is now trying to close the deal, he may want to make his house seem especially desirable to entice the buyer by now claiming there is no crime.

Saying No

"No" is a key word used by negotiators when making misleading or dishonest statements. A negotiator who says "no" after hesitating, or says "no" and changes the subject, may be struggling with the truth. Further, a person who answers a question "no" and refuses to add details may be hesitant to advance a lie with further untruthful details.

Changes in Behavior

A change in a negotiator's behavior may signal lying. For example, a person who begins speaking more formally may be lying. Pay attention to a person who was using contractions such as, "I'd like to hear your proposal" and now says, "I cannot accept your terms." Also, pay attention to how he emphasizes words, changes the tone of his voice, or uses superlatives, such as, "My client DID NOT run the red light. He is an AWESOME driver." A person who is lying may also tend to stumble on words, clear his throat often, or talk too fast. While these are generalized behavior signs, any behavior that is out of the ordinary or a change for that person may indicate lying. Therefore, it is important to establish a baseline for a person if possible. For example, when a person has never raised her voice in previous discussions, and that person is yelling when recounting a detail, she may be lying. However, a person who regularly clears their throat when speaking and who is now clearing her throat when recounting a fact may be not be lying, just in need of a throat lozenge.

Truth Emphasizers

People who are lying often strangely emphasize that they are not. Statements such as "in all honesty," or "to tell you the truth" are sometimes just the opposite. The lying person is so emphatic because he knows his statement is a lie. We should assume that people are telling the truth. Thus, the need to make statements that you are telling the truth may be a cover for the lie that is on the way or in the mix.

Physical Signs

Lying may have some physical manifestations, according to researchers.[14] Liars are more likely to press their lips together, and their smiles often looks forced. Also, their mouth and eye combination may be a giveaway. Truthful people tend to smile with their whole face, exhibiting expressive eyes and crow's feet, if they have them! People tend to fidget when they are not telling the truth. Then again, they just may be nervous. However, if they had been sitting still during the negotiation and then suddenly start fidgeting, this may be a sign that what they are now saying is not truthful. However, one physical sign many once believed to indicate lying has been mostly disproved, namely that liars cannot look the other side in the eye while telling a lie. Apparently, most liars have perfected the technique of looking directly at the person, perhaps in response to hearing that this was a telltale sign of lying.

Responses to Lying

It is difficult to confront someone on a lie during a negotiation, especially where the proof may be lacking. Furthermore, the moment you make the accusation, the tone of the negotiation will change, especially if there has been cooperative behavior by both sides up until the point of the lie. Therefore, you should first analyze if the other side has actually lied, simply misremembered, or is innocently mistaken.

In order for you to determine if a negotiator is really lying, you should ask specific questions concerning the troubling statement and try to zero in the lie. It is helpful to maintain a positive tone and begin with non-threatening questions. For example, in a negotiation about a price dispute over the purchase of a used computer, you might ask "Just to clarify: You said the buyer first offered the seller $3,000 to purchase the item, and now you said the buyer first offered the seller $2,000." Asking questions will highlight inconsistencies in a liar's story. Furthermore, liars who use paltering or lying by omission are often uncovered when asked specific questions. For example, in the house rental problem discussed earlier, when the homeowner answers that he used the grill for his own party last July 4th, an easy follow up question such as, "Is the grill in working condition now?" may have uncovered the truth. However, instead of telling the truth, the homeowner may now choose to make an affirmative lie by answering "yes." If he does confirm his paltering statement with an affirmative lie, and you have your 4th of July party and the grill does not work, it will be much easier to prove your case when you sue the homeowner for misrepresentation as you can recount how the homeowner affirmatively lied as opposed to paltering.

Another response to lying is to give the other side information that will point out that their story cannot be accurate. For example, if a party states that a traffic light was malfunctioning at the time of the accident, you may be able to show a picture taken by a store's street camera that shows the light functioning normally at the time of the accident. However, having a smoking gun picture is often not available, and such a "got you" moment takes place mainly in movies. Therefore, if your attempt to correct lying conduct is not successful, and the lying rises to the level of a material misrepresentation, you may decide to simply say, "I don't think we are making any progress" and end the negotiating session. At this point, if the other side seems confused as to the abrupt end, you may decide to confront the party's lying conduct. Since the negotiation is derailed at this point anyway, confronting him about lying may serve to put him on notice that such conduct will not be tolerated in the negotiation, and perhaps he will correct this behavior.

Exercises 6-1 and 6-2: Ethics

Exercise 6-1. (2-person exercise) (6 minutes—3 minutes each side) The purpose of this exercise is to test your ability to recognize when a party is lying in everyday conversation. You and your partner will take turns and exchange eight points of information about a teacher from your childhood. You can share information about things such as the teacher's name, where and when the teacher taught you, the subject matter, and any other particular information that is pertinent. However, when you reveal the information, two of the items you disclose must be false. As you disclose the information about your teacher, the other side may ask questions, but they are limited to five questions. After you have both taken turns exchanging information, you should each separately write down the two items you disclosed that were false and the two items you believe the other side disclosed that were false. Then exchange papers and see how accurate your assessments were.

Feedback and Discussion: How accurate were your assessments of the other person's lies? If you were accurate, how did you reach the conclusion that the statement (s) was false? If you were not accurate, what would you have done differently to discover the false statements?

When you revealed the false statements, do you think there was any difference between the way you delivered the false and accurate statements? Did you use paltering, omissions, affirmative false statements or a combination of the three methods? If you used different forms of lying, which form, if any, worked best for you? Why?

Exercise 6-2. (2-person exercise) (5 minutes) The purpose of this exercise is to test your ability to recognize if a party is lying during a negotiation. This exercise will consist of a prospective home buyer asking a series of questions to the seller to determine if the buyer can detect false statements made by the seller.

You and your partner will play the role of a buyer and seller of a home. During the negotiation, the buyer will ask the seller the following questions:

1. What is the condition of the roof?
2. What is the condition of the air conditioner?
3. Are the washer/drier and refrigerator in working condition?
4. Is there crime in the neighborhood?
5. Do you know your next-door neighbors? Are they friendly?

Instructions for the seller: If you are playing the role of the seller, before beginning the negotiation, you should write down answers to the above questions as representative of truthful answers. However, when you begin negotiating, you should change your answer to two of these questions and answer falsely (i.e., answer is different from what you wrote down). You may either make an affirmative false statement, engage in paltering, or lie by omission.

Instructions for the buyer: If you are playing the role of the buyer, you may ask these questions in any order you deem appropriate. During the initial questioning, you are not permitted to ask follow up questions.

After receiving initial answers to your questions from the seller, try to determine which two of the seller's answers are false. After making that determination, during the negotiation, you may address your concerns to the seller about the suspected falsehoods using one of the response methods discussed above. You may decide to confront the seller or ask more follow up questions. You may also choose to ignore his false statements. At the end of the 5-minute session, write down which two of the seller's answers you believe are false.

Feedback and Discussion: At the conclusion of the negotiation, the buyer and seller should then exchange papers and see if the buyer correctly determined the seller's untruthful statements. If you were the buyer, and you correctly determined the false statements, how did you come to that determination? If you were the seller, do you

detect any differences in the way you delivered the false answers as opposed to the truthful answers?

Equity

In addition to ethics, the "E" in TABLE requires reflecting on equity. Recognizing and understanding the role of equity in the context of negotiations is important for several reasons. First, as a practical matter, participants are more likely to feel invested in negotiations conducted equitably. This buy-in may result in the participants viewing any subsequently negotiated agreements as legitimate as opposed to unfair or unconscionable. Moreover, certain inequitable or biased behaviors, even if not illegal, can cause significant harm to the participants, their organizations, and to society. Second, alertness to bias can provide tools for thwarting or confronting negative bias actions in ways that may allow negotiations to proceed successfully. Bias during a negotiation can appear in both subtle and overt forms. For example, the other side may interrupt a female speaker more often than a male speaker or address a male in the group more often than the female. More disparagingly, slurs, obscene gestures, or nicknames may be inserted into the negotiation in order to disorient or alter behavior. Being aware of such actions may serve to negate some of their effects, provide necessary information during the negotiation, or signal the likelihood of a viable future relationship. Finally, on a broader level, awareness of bias is the starting point towards challenging conscious or unconscious biases' pernicious effects.

Unconscious biases influence evaluations and decision making in numerous contexts, including in negotiations. Generally, people use unconscious biases to balance competing ideas and make quick decisions. The terms implicit bias and unconscious bias when applied to others are often used as a short hand for ways in which people group others including by race, gender, ethnicity, age, sexual orientation, or other aspects of identity. Cognitive research studies reveal that implicit biases based on cultural and historical beliefs about groups are pervasive and operate "under the scope of human consciousness, and that they influence the ways in which we see and treat others, even when we are determined to be fair and objective."[15] Moreover, scholars on racial bias have observed, "implicit racial biases can influence the behaviors and judgments of even the most consciously egalitarian individuals."[16]

There are powerful studies demonstrating the negative effects of implicit bias in negotiations involving housing and in the criminal justice system.[17] In the context of negotiations for consumer goods, a series of influential studies on the effects of racial and gender bias conducted by Professor Ian Ayers are particularly instructive.[18] One of those studies sent testers of different races and genders posing as potential buyers to hundreds of car dealerships in Chicago. The testers entered new car dealerships separately and bargained to buy similar new cars, using a scripted uniform negotiation strategy. The focus of the study was whether automobile retailers would react differently to this uniform negotiation strategy when the potential car buyers differed only by gender or race. The study revealed systematic negative bias towards African Americans and women. For example, even though the testers used the same negotiating bargaining script, the dealers' salespersons initial sales price offers to the African American buyers and the salespersons' "final offers," which ostensibly represented the lowest prices the salespersons could offer to sell the cars, were much higher for African American potential buyers after several rounds of offers and counter offers. Professor Ayers' studies on racial and gender bias found overwhelming evidence that in a variety of markets—retail car sales, bail bonding, and kidney transplantation—racial minorities are consistently at a disadvantage. More recent studies continue to find implicit racial bias negatively affecting African Americans in negotiations.[19]

There are also significant studies involving bias in negotiations in the employment context. One study demonstrated how employers had different expectations due to unconscious bias regarding how Whites and African Americans would negotiate. The employers expected African Americans to negotiate less forcefully than Whites. In the study, the African Americans reported after the negotiation session that they had negotiated the same in terms of number of offers and counteroffers as the other prospective employees. However, because of the employers' stereotyped expectations, the employers reported that the African American prospective employees negotiated too forcefully with the end result being lower initial salaries for the African American prospective employees.[20]

Many of the identity-based employment negotiation studies focus primarily on gender. These studies analyze the effects of identity not only the outcome of a negotiation, but also on an individual's propensity to initiate a negotiation.[21] Some studies have shown that women often do not initiate compensation discussions, even though these discussions frequently result in higher salaries. One study, focused on graduate students, observed how students who negotiated their initial salaries received on average a 7.4% increase on top of the original offer; however, the same study also observed that only 7% of the female graduate students versus 57% of the male graduate students engaged in salary negotiations.[22]

Studies on gender bias in the negotiation context are instructive and can be used as a guide to studying racial, ethnic, and other types of bias in negotiations. More than thirty years of research have yielded a complex picture. In one of the first studies on gender in negotiations, the researchers observed how the gender of the negotiator affected the negotiations.[23] In their report, they described instances of women being more competitive than men in some contexts, while in other instances, women appeared less competitive. The researchers theorized that the observed differences might occur because women have a greater emphasis on interpersonal relationships, which results in them being more competitive or cooperative depending on their counterparts.

Other gender negotiation studies suggest that women are less positively disposed toward negotiation and more likely to set lower goals.[24] Researchers observed that women often demand and accept less in salary negotiations than do men, are less satisfied with their negotiation performances, and feel lower self-efficacy about their bargaining abilities.[25]

Some studies focus more on the social and institutional processes that might activate gendered behavior rather than gender differences.[26] Studies discussing contextual factors that trigger gender dynamics often rely on characterizing negotiations as either integrative or distributive with different styles of communication associated with each approach.[27] Generally, integrative bargaining is a collaborative approach, where the parties to a negotiation seek solutions that will benefit all parties. The object of the negotiators in integrative bargaining is to increase the total payoff through cooperation—a win-win situation. In an integrative negotiation, parties need to identify and understand their mutual problem, communicate their interests, offer several possible solutions, and then choose a solution that will benefit both parties. To accomplish this result, the parties must avoid interpersonal conflict, thus, communications are usually more inviting and cooperative. In contrast, distributive bargaining is a more competitive and adversarial approach, where each party attempts to maximize their own interests regardless of the other side's loss. This distributive negotiation strategy is often used when distributing or dividing a finite amount of resources such as money, assets, etc. between the parties. The goal under a distributive approach is not a win-win situation, but that one side win as much as possible. In a distributive negotiation, each party is guided mainly by his or her expectations of what the other will accept. In turn, parties usually try to obtain as much information as possible from the other side while at the same time trying to disclose as little accurate information as possible about their own real interests.[28]

Stereotypes would seem to suggest that women would excel at the integrative negotiations, which rely on stereotypical feminine attributes such as cooperation and compassion. In turn, males should stereotypically excel at distributive bargaining, which emphasizes an adversarial approach. However, despite the stereotypes, the results are not that different when the game structure changes between integrative and distributive systems. Interestingly, some studies found that results do change depending on whether the women were negotiating on behalf of themselves or others. One study in particular describes how "women are significantly more effective and aggressive negotiators when negotiating on the behalf of others, rather than for their own benefit."[29]

There are important caveats to gender negotiation analysis. First, gender differences may be overstated.[30] With regard to communications, for example, "many people believe that men and women communicate differently, and, that belief is buoyed by researchers who argue that women's verbal style is best described as supportive, egalitarian, and personal, while characterizing men's as instrumental, competitive, and assertive."[31] Other studies, however, rebut these characterizations. Several studies have shown that there are no differences in outcomes that can be attributed solely to the negotiator's gender and men and women are equally capable of learning and applying effective negotiation strategies.[32] A meta-analysis of numerous studies on gender differences in negotiations found "a bargaining advantage for men under conditions of highest predictive incongruity for women."[33] Examples of such conditions of predictive incongruity for women include "when negotiators are not experienced" and when the laboratory negotiation experiments are designed with "high structural ambiguity." Generally, a negotiation experiment has high structural ambiguity when the negotiators are not provided information to lessen ambiguity, such as the bargaining range, standards for agreement, and values. This meta-analysis also found "a bargaining advantage for women under conditions of lowest predicted role incongruity."[34] Studies with "lowest predicted role incongruity for women" included those where the negotiators had some negotiating practice and experience; where the experiments involved women negotiating on behalf of others; and where information to lessen structural ambiguity, such as bargaining ranges or values, was available.[35]

Additional caveats to gender negotiation studies are in order. First, gender identities can fall outside the male/female dichotomy. Second, individuals have multiple intersecting social identities. For example, a person can identify as African American, female, lesbian, grandmother, and professor and all of these can inform and affect her negotiations.[36] Focusing solely on gender as the difference between men and women fails to account for simultaneous dimensions of identity that may become salient during a negotiation. Moreover, focusing on individuals and their negotiating proclivities misses the cultural and institutional mechanisms and implicit biases that can create identity inequities in negotiations.

As each of us attempt to disrupt our implicit bias by engaging in self-reflection, becoming more culturally competent, and practicing inclusive behaviors, we can help shape our personal and professional lives, our organizations, and our communities. More specifically, in the negotiations context, averting implicit bias and practicing inclusive behaviors may encourage the negotiating parties to hear multiple points of view and allow for innovative solutions.

Recognizing that race and gender, age, sexual orientation, ethnicity, religion and other aspects of identity can affect the outcome of a negotiation, it is important to discuss some of the tools that negotiators can use to lessen these prejudicial effects and negotiate more effectively.

Awareness

The single most important tool against bias in negotiations is awareness. Being aware enables you to have an intention, choose behaviors to implement your intention, monitor your counterpart's reaction, evaluate whether you are achieving the outcome you intended, and if not, change your negotiation behavior.

Mindfulness Meditation

Mindfulness meditation has been shown to help regulate attention and emotions and may help negotiators in stressful negotiations.[37] It may also helpful to reduce bias and increase empathy towards underrepresented or stigmatized persons.

Consider Gendered, Racial, Ethnic and Other Identity-Based Expectations

It is important to consider your own expectations and the expectations of your counterpart about gendered, racial, ethnic, and other identity based stereotypes in negotiation. After identifying your counterpart's expectation, you can decide to either act in conformance with that expectation, deflect it, or defy it. This choice can have risks and benefits.

Preparation

As mentioned in the Chapter 2, on Tactical Planning, being prepared is crucial for any negotiation opportunity. Preparing for the negotiation process involves examining priorities, ranking their importance, and knowing your leverage. Being prepared to reference relevant and objective standards during bargaining situations is especially important. The use of objective measures may provide women and racial minorities with the confidence to initiate a negotiation situation and to ask for an outcome that is in line with that of their co-workers, counterparts, or the market.

Mentors and Social Networks

Having strong ties, as protégés, mentors, or just individuals in social networks can be a strong asset. Having mentors, or being a part of a social network, can open the doors to new opportunities within an organization and provide important information that can be used during negotiations. For example, information gleaned from social networks may serve to provide salary ranges for positions in an organization where such information is otherwise not easily available.

Activate Egalitarian Goals

There is some support for the theory that alerting the other party in the negotiations to fairness and egalitarian goals may help alleviate some negative implicit bias. Suggestions for activating such goals include remarking on the other side's unbiased views or fairness.[38]

Part II

Applying the TABLE Method

Chapter 7

Negotiating Salary Offers & Non-Compete Agreements

"We will waive the non-compete if you agree never to work again."

In this chapter, you will practice negotiating salary offers using the TABLE method. The chapter includes problems for negotiating various components of the offer such as the base salary, bonuses, frequency of reviews, promotion opportunities, job title, benefits, and flexible work schedules. While negotiating salary offers can be stressful, having a negotiating plan ready is empowering and can lead to successful outcomes for both the prospective employee and the employer.

The chapter also includes a discussion of, and problems for, negotiating salary offers that are coupled with employee non-compete agreements. Such employee non-compete agreements can have significant ramifications for both the employee and employer but are less likely to get the same attention as other issues during salary offer negotiations. Often an employee non-compete agreement is presented to a prospective employee at the same time as the new offer of employment. The prospective employee is generally excited about the forthcoming new job and prepared to negotiate salary and benefits, but less ready to focus on the non-compete clause or agreement. Disregarding the terms of a non-compete, however, is ill-advised. A non-compete can have significant ramifications for an employee that proper negotiations can help address. From the employers' perspective, employers want to ensure that they safeguard confidential business information and protect their relationships with their customers, clients, and employees. Accordingly, employers may want to focus on tailoring their restrictive agreements so that they are enforceable and serve their purposes. For these reasons, this chapter includes problems that contain such restrictive agreements. Included in this chapter are some general legal principles on both salary offers and non-compete agreements. This chapter is not intended as a primer on employment, intellectual property, or any other particular areas of the law. Rather, the general laws included here are for use in negotiating the problems contained in this chapter.

Laws Relevant to Salary Offers

There are federal, state, and local laws that are relevant to salary offers. When negotiating salary offers, it is important to research the applicability of all of the various laws. Discussed below are a select few of those laws that may be helpful for negotiating the problems in this chapter.

Federal Laws Relevant to Salary Offers

There are numerous federal laws regarding employment that are relevant to salary offers. For example, Title VII of the Civil Rights Act of 1964 (Title VII) makes it illegal to discriminate against a job applicant or an employee because of the person's race, color, religion, national origin, or sex (including pregnancy).[1] Title VII was amended by the Lilly Ledbetter Fair Pay Act in 2009 (Lily Ledbetter Act).[2] Since the enactment of the Lily Ledbetter Act an employee may bring a legal action for pay discrimination under Title VII after the last pay violation, as opposed to only by the required time after the initial pay disparity. The Lily Ledbetter Act provides that pay discrimination can occur when a pay decision is made, when an employee is subject to that decision, or at any time that an employee is injured by it, and that regardless of when the discrimination began, each paycheck that contains discriminatory compensation is a separate violation.

Case law interpreting Title VII is also critical for understanding the federal laws in this area. For example, the United States Supreme Court, in *Price Waterhouse v. Hopkins,* found that Title VII's prohibition on the basis of sex prohibits employers from discriminating on the basis of the employer's stereotype of the person's respective gender or gender stereotyping.[3] Recently, both the U.S. Court of Appeals for the Second and Seventh Circuits have found that Title VII's prohibition of discrimination on the basis of sex prohibits discrimination on the basis of sexual orientation.[4]

Other relevant anti-discrimination federal laws include Title I of the Americans with Disabilities Act of 1990 (ADA), which makes it illegal to discriminate against a qualified person with a disability and the Genetic Information Nondiscrimination Act of 2008 (GINA), which makes it illegal to discriminate against applicants or employees because of genetic information. Another example is the Age Discrimination in Employment Act of 1967 (ADEA), which protects persons who are 40 or older from discrimination because of their age.[5]

These federal anti-discrimination laws apply to employers with more than 15 employees (more than 20 employees for age discrimination).[6] They apply to numerous types of work situations, including hiring, promotions, wages, and benefits. Prospective employers and applicants should be cognizant that these anti-discrimination protections apply even before an applicant has an offer.[7] Thus, for example, employers should ensure that their questions during the salary offer negotiations, while seemingly innocuous, are in fact compliant with such laws. Along those lines, prospective employees should be mindful in their answers to questions to not inadvertently respond with information that could lead to discussions that would be protected, such as not to chill further discussions.

The Equal Pay Act of 1963 (EPA), another relevant federal law, targets gender discrimination in pay. This law requires employers to pay men and women employees working at the same establishment equal wages "for equal work" on jobs that require "equal skill, effort, and responsibility, and which are performed under similar working conditions."[8] The EPA, however, permits unequal pay for equal work under one of four exceptions: (1) a seniority system; (2) a merit system; (3) a system that measures earnings by quantity or quality of production; or (4) a differential based on any other factor other than sex.[9]

There is extensive case law regarding when various types of jobs meet or do not meet the "equal work" requirement in the EPA. Generally, to initiate a case under the EPA, an employee must show that a coworker of the opposite sex received greater compensation despite performing substantially equal work. The case law interpreting what qualifies as substantially equal work varies, with some courts using a very narrow interpretation while others use a slightly broader interpretation.

There is also considerable case law on the four exceptions in the EPA permitting unequal pay, particularly with regard to the fourth catchall exception for a differential based on "any other factor other than sex." In *Rizo v. Yovino*,[10] the Court of Appeals of the Ninth Circuit recently determined that an employee's salary history no longer satisfies the "any other factor other than sex" EPA exception. The *Rizo* court reasoned that the catchall exception is "limited to legitimate, job-related factors such as a prospective employee's experience, educational background, ability, or prior job performance."[11] The *Rizo* court added the following explanation for its interpretation of the catchall exception in the EPA:

> It is inconceivable that Congress, in an Act the primary purpose of which was to eliminate long-existing "endemic" sex-based wage disparities, would create an exception for basing new hires' salaries on those very disparities—disparities that Congress declared are not only related to sex but caused by sex. To accept the [Employer's] argument would be to perpetuate rather than eliminate the pervasive discrimination at which the Act was aimed.... Allowing prior salary to justify a wage differential ... entrench[es] in salary systems an obvious means of discrimination—the very discrimination that the Act was designed to prohibit and rectify.[12]

Following this decision, an employer at least in the Ninth Circuit (which includes Alaska, Arizona, California, Hawaii, Idaho, Montana Oregon, and Washington) cannot affirmatively defend against an EPA claim by attempting to justify a pay differential between its male and female employees performing equal work on the basis of prior salary.

While the Ninth Circuit Court in *Rizo* clearly found that salary history was not a valid defense for unequal pay under the EPA, it expressly did not address whether a discussion of salary history could play a part in salary negotiations. The *Rizo* Court explained that it was not deciding "whether or under what circumstances, past salary may play a role in the course of an individualized salary negotiation" and would "reserve all questions relating to individualized negotiations for decision in subsequent cases."[13]

State and Local Laws Relevant to Salary Offers

In addition to the federal laws, almost all states have adopted laws that prohibit forms of discrimination against a job applicant or employee.[14] These laws prohibit discrimination in employment based on various factors, such as race, gender, age, marital status, national origin, religion or disability. While several of these state laws track the language in the federal laws, many offer additional protections against employment-related discrimination.

These state laws vary widely with some having few protections against employment discrimination and other states significantly expanding on the protections in the federal laws. Alabama provides an example of a state on the less protective end of the spectrum. While Alabama has a statute prohibiting age discrimination (over age 40), it has no state law prohibiting discrimination in employment because of sex, race, disability, or other factors, and any such claims would have to be addressed by federal law when and if it applies to an employer.[15] Similarly, Georgia has a statute prohibiting discrimination for public workers, but has no state law prohibiting employment discrimination for private employees.[16]

Other states have statutes that expand on the federal laws by covering employers with fewer than 15 employees or by expressly proscribing various types of discrimination. For example, the Connecticut anti-discrimination in employment statute applies to employers with three or more employees (other than religious organizations).[17] Moreover, the Connecticut statute expressly prohibits discrimination on the basis of race, color, religious creed, age, sex, gender identity or expression, marital status, national origin, ancestry, present or past history of mental disability, intellectual disability, learning disability or physical disability, sexual orientation, civil union status, pregnancy, criminal conviction alone, or medical marijuana.[18]

Also, on the broader protection side of the spectrum is Oregon, which has a non-discrimination statute that applies to employers with 1 or more employees and prohibits discrimination on the basis of various factors including race, religion, color, sex, sexual orientation, gender identity, national origin, marital and familial status, disability, expunged juvenile record, pregnancy, childbirth, and related medical conditions, and victims of domestic violence or sexual crimes.[19] In addition to Oregon, several other states' anti-discrimination in employment laws apply to employers with more than one employee. Those states include Arizona, Hawaii, Michigan, Minnesota, Montana, New Jersey, North Dakota, and Vermont.[20]

Despite these federal and state employment anti-discrimination and equal pay laws, the gender, race, and ethnicity pay gap continues to persist. Generally, the gender pay gap (or earnings disparity) is illustrated by the difference in women's annual median earnings relative to men's annual median earnings. Recent studies, using data from 2016 median income, show that in the United States, women working full time had median annual earnings of only 80% the median annual earnings of men working full-time, representing a gender pay gap of 20%.[21] This current pay gap is an improvement over the pay gap several decades ago. For example, in 1981 according to the U.S. Department of Labor, women earned only 59.2% of men's earnings, representing a pay gap of 40%.[22] While the gender pay gap has improved significantly from the 1980s, progress in erasing the gap has actually stalled since 2001. Projections suggest that using the rate of progress seen between 1960 and 2016 for closing the pay gap, women would not reach pay equity with men until the year 2059.[23] If the slower current rate of progress seen since 2001 continues, women will not reach pay equity with men until 2119.[24]

The numbers are even starker for African-American and Hispanic employees. In the United States, recent figures provide that African-American women working full time earn 63% of the earnings of white men working full time, and that Hispanic women earn 54% as much as white men.[25] The racial pay gap appears even within the same gender. In a study of hourly wages, the average black male worker earned just 70% of the hourly wage of the average white male worker and the average black woman earned about 82% of what the average white woman earned.[26] The racial earnings gap persists even at the highest level of educational achievement. In fact, recent trends indicate that the racial earnings gap for black men is actually higher for those with a college degree than it is for high school graduates.[27] Challenges in employment outcomes for women and underrepresented groups appear in various professions, including the law. For example, in law firms, even though women have made up at least half of all law school students for the past 25 years and currently make up 45% of law firm associates, only about 19% of law firm equity partners are women.[28] Women of color make up about 12% of law firm associates and only 2.5% of law firm partners. According to the law firm demographic findings from the National Association for Law Placement (NALP), women and African Americans made small gains in representation at major U.S. law firms in 2016 compared with 2015. However, representation of both these groups remains below 2009 levels.[29]

There are many complex and multifaceted explanations for the pay gap, including job segregation, fewer working hours, or breaks in employment due to caregiving responsibilities, and educational achievement.[30] In addition, some studies attribute part of the gender pay gap to women's propensity to negotiate less frequently than men. Even when taking into account such factors, however, there remains a significant gender and racial pay gap.[31] See the discussion on Equity in Chapter 6.

In order to reduce the pay gap, some states and local governments have enacted laws that go beyond previous measures. For example, Washington State in 2018 passed legislation updating the Washington State's Equal Pay Act of 1943 designed to reduce gender-based workplace discrimination. The Washington State law applies a multimodal approach to the issue. The new law establishes that unequal pay defenses are limited to those "based in good faith on bona fide job-related factors."[32] Additionally, the new law clarifies that an employee's previous salary history will not be deemed valid grounds for unequal compensation. The Washington State legislation also includes provisions on wage transparency. It provides that employers cannot prohibit employees from discussing their current wages with co-workers.

In 2017, Puerto Rico signed the Puerto Rico Act No.16 (Puerto Rico Equal Pay Act).[33] This law expands upon the Federal Equal Pay Act in a similar manner to the laws enacted in Washington State. Puerto Rico's provisions in some respects go even further. The Puerto Rico Equal Pay Act prevents employers from even asking about the employees' former wages unless directly volunteered. This shifts the balance of power and information to the potential or current employee allowing the employee to enter into the negotiations without fear that their previous salaries will affect their future wages. The Puerto Rico law also includes provisions for victims of pay discrimination including double compensatory damages and back pay penalties for employers.

The state of Vermont in 2018 passed a law similar to Puerto Rico's Equal Pay Act. The Vermont law also prevents employers from inquiring about their employee's previous salaries.[34] Additionally, the law also prevents employers from conducting interviews based on the prospective employee's previous salary.

Restrictions on requiring pay history disclosure appears to be a legislative trend. In addition to the states discussed above, other states have also recently passed laws regarding pay history. For example, California's recently enacted law prohibits employers from asking an employee about their previous salary history.[35] In Delaware, an employer may only ask about pay history once an employee has accepted the job offer.[36] In Massachusetts, employers may not assess employees based on their pay history.[37] In Oregon, an employer may not question or request an applicant's pay history.[38] In addition to these various state laws, several local governments have also enacted laws dealing with pay history. For example, New York City, provides that employers may not ask for an applicant's prior salary.[39] In Philadelphia, an employer cannot ask an applicant's pay history or use prior salary to set the salary for a new employee.[40]

The trend restricting inquiries into pay history has extended to the private sector. The White House Equal Pay Pledge, launched at the first United State of Women Summit in June of 2016 had over 100 companies agree to share best practices to develop more equitably based hiring, promotion, and pay policies. Corporate giants from a variety of industries, including AT&T, Colgate-Palmolive Co., Ernst & Young LLP, Gap Inc., General Motors, IBM, Johnson & Johnson, and Target, all promised to conduct annual companywide pay research to determine gender gaps, and review hiring and promotion policies for unconscious bias and structural barriers.[41] By promoting equal-pay efforts across their organizations, these companies are attempting to create opportunities for a more diverse employee base and fostering more inclusive work environments.

Strategies for Employers Negotiations of Salary

Often, experts tend to suggest strategies only for employees in negotiating salaries. However, employers are also in need of strategies for salary negotiations because they have much at stake as well. Employers may have put great time and effort into recruiting potential employees and they do not want to run the risk of losing those employees due to failed salary negotiations. However, it should be comforting to some employers that according to Glassdoor, only 41% of employees even attempt to negotiate their salary.[42] In addition, some employers advertise jobs as non-negotiable, thus trying to alleviate the stressful salary negotiation. However, for many employers it is expected and anticipated that they will negotiate salary with a job candidate.

An employer walks a fine line when negotiating salary. While the employer wants to negotiate the best deal for his company, he does not want to alienate his future employee by taking an overly aggressive position during salary negotiations. It will be a hollow victory for the employer if he gets the deal he wants, but the negotiations have put a strain on the employer-employee relationship, making it difficult for them to work together in the future. In order to avoid such a result, there are certain strategies the employer should implement for a positive negotiation that will help maintain a good working relationship in the future. The following strategies are helpful for the employer engaging in negotiating salaries.[43]

Research Comparable Market Rate Salaries: Before sitting down to negotiate, the employer should conduct research to determine the going rate for the job he is offering. For some entry-level jobs, that rate may be easy to find. There are many salary comparison sites, such as Indeed's Salary Tool, or Salary.com, that collect data from thousands of employers for specific jobs. The Employer is able to narrow his search by location and company. One downside is that many of these sites rely on self-reporting, so the sites' accuracy is only as good as those who are reporting. Yet with thousands of reports, it is easy to glean some meaningful market salary ranges for a particular job.

Make Salary Offers Precise: Employers should consider offering prospective employees precise salary offers rather than round numbers (e.g., "we can offer $121,250" rather than "we can offer $120,000"), because a specific number signals that the employer was very deliberate and careful in arriving at the salary offer number. In order for this to be helpful, the employer should have objective criteria supporting the specific number.

Use Recruiters to Identify Candidates: For certain positions, it may be beneficial for the employer to contact a recruiter. Of course, using a third-party recruiter will result in extra cost, but if a position is somewhat unique or the employer needs more assistance in recruiting, an outside recruiter may be helpful. Once the outside recruiter has identified potential employees and the employer decides on the candidate he wishes to hire, the salary negotiation may run more smoothly with the help of the recruiter. The recruiter will be able to set the stage for the employee and employer as to expectations based on the job and experience of the employee, and the salary discussions may be streamlined due to this outside help.

Carefully Examine a Candidate's Past Work History: Before salary negotiations begin, an employer should take time to review the work history of the candidate. Specifically, make sure references are checked and resumes verified. While some employers leave this task to after salary negotiations, it is helpful to learn as much about the employees' past job history for discussion during salary negotiations. For example, with the candidate's permission, the employer may contact one of the candidate's references who reveals that the candidate prefers to work from home instead of in the office. Of course, the candidate may have revealed this fact himself either at the interview or upcoming salary discussion stage. However, by learning this fact before the negotiations, the employer can factor in how this flexibility in job location may impact salary. If the job requires more in office time, the employer agreeing to allow home office work time may prove a benefit to the candidate that is more important than a salary debate.

Prevent Discriminatory Questions: Part of any tactical planning is the preparation of questions. In negotiating salary offers, employers should be mindful to avoid asking questions that violate or imply violating anti-discrimination laws. For example, an employer should not ask the employee if there is "any situation at home" that will require them to take more time off than is usual for a job of this nature. This type of question could violate both federal and state anti-discrimination laws because it could solicit information on the prospective employee's marital status or family obligations. Another example of a possible discriminatory question may be asking for the employee's salary history. As noted above, various laws prevent employers from inquiring about their prospective employee's past salary.

Be Prepared to Discuss Benefits: As discussed above, an employer should realize that many employees value other benefits alongside money. Therefore, an employer should be prepared to discuss and, if within the framework of their company, offer other benefits to employees in addition to or in lieu of a higher salary. Some of these benefits include health benefits, vacation time, flexible schedules, and the aforementioned ability to work remotely. Thus, when the employer begins the negotiating process, he may wish to discuss the entire benefits package with the candidate, not just money. This is especially important if the employer is somewhat limited in the salary range. If the employer can determine other motivating factors for the employee besides compensation, he will be able to prioritize other parts of a compensation package to keep the negotiations on track.

Be Professional: it should be obvious that the employer should maintain a high level of professionalism during negotiations. The employer should be a role model for the candidate. The employer should recognize that she is a representative of the company. Even if the candidate's demands seem unreasonable, the employer should maintain a calm demeanor and always try to re-focus negotiations that get off track. Professionalism is not simply about good manners. An employer also conveys professionalism by being prepared to discuss all aspects of job compensation, communicating offers and requirements clearly, and having the ability to extend the best offer the company can give.

Knowing when to Let Go and Having Alternatives: In preparing for the salary negotiation, the employer should have planned the minimum acceptable level to make the deal. If the employer reaches that point, and there is no agreement to be made, he must be prepared to walk away. However, before walking away, the employer should try to assess the candidate's other options. A candidate who eagerly shuts down the negotiation likely has many other employment options available, while a candidate who seems to try to reach for a deal may have limited options. If it appears a candidate has limited options, the employer may want to take a break in salary negotiations. Suggesting that the candidate think over the last proposal and get back to the employer in a day or two may result in a better outcome for the employer. This approach not only allows a candidate time to reflect on the offer, but also shows the candidate that the employer is not overly eager to make a deal. However, it should be made clear to the candidate that a day or two delay is not an invitation for the candidate to restart the salary negotiations.

As in any negotiation, determining the minimum acceptable level will also relate to the alternatives available to the employer. In the case of a salary negotiation, the employer should hopefully have other job candidates lined-up in case the salary negotiation fails. The comfort of having other candidates available will allow the employer to walk away more easily.

The more frequently an employer is involved in hiring, the better he will understand the best ways to communicate with candidates for successful outcomes in salary negotiations. However, it is important not to lose sight of the fact that each salary negotiation is unique, and as with any negotiation, preparation is key for an employer to have a successful salary negotiation with a candidate. The better the employer is prepared, the more likely the negotiation will run smoothly, and the employer will be able to maintain a positive relationship with his future employee.

Strategies for Employees Negotiations of Salary

There is no shortage of strategy advice for employees negotiating salaries. Most often, salary negotiations are separate from job offers. Although employers may discuss salary in general during the interview process, often the real salary negotiations take place either during the offer stage or in a separate meeting a short time after the offer has been made. In a single stage process, a prospective employer offers the candidate a job and then discusses salary with the candidate. The prospective employer may offer the candidate the job with a set salary, indicating the job is non-negotiable, or begin salary discussions concurrently with the job offer. In a two-stage process, an employer may offer the prospective candidate the job with a proposed salary and delay salary negotiations if and until the candidate has indicated he is seriously considering accepting the job. Therefore, a prospective employee should be prepared for both scenarios. The following strategies are helpful for employees engaging in salary negotiations.[44]

Research: Prospective employees should always be prepared to discuss salary, and should do their research to find out as much as they can about the salary structure generally for the industry in which they are seeking a job and specifically for the company in which they are interviewing. As noted in strategies for the employer, there are various websites that provide helpful information about comparable salaries for various positions.

List Priorities and Prepare your Offers: In preparing to negotiate salary, a candidate should also include in his ideal salary package including non-monetary items such as vacation time, health coverage, retirement plans, and flex time. The list may be lengthy and will vary depending on the job and industry. A sales position may entail negotiations relating to travel while a corporate office position may be all about the corner office. Once the candidate has made the list and prioritized his items, he is ready to prepare his highest realistic salary goal and his minimum acceptable level.

Delay Salary Negotiations until After Receiving a Job Offer: It may be tempting to try to negotiate salary during the initial interview before getting a job offer. After all, if a job candidate discovers that the prospective employer is not willing to negotiate salary, or the employer proposes a salary that is nowhere near acceptable, why should the candidate waste his time and continue to interview? However, if the candidate has done the thorough research before the interview, he should have some knowledge as to whether the company's salary is within an acceptable range. If not, the candidate should simply pass on the interview. Furthermore, even though the candidate has prepared to discuss salary offers before the interview, if the candidate initiates a salary discussion early on in the interview process, it is almost a sure-fire way not to get an offer. The prospective employer will likely interpret a rigorous approach to discussing salary prior to the offer as premature and wonder if the candidate has any affinity for working with the company beyond getting paid.

Be Enthusiastic: As a prospective employee, an employer looks to see your motivation for the job which can translate to a higher salary offer. Once the candidate has been given an offer, it is important to not only be confident about your ability but to convey that you are excited to be given the opportunity to work for the employer. This enthusiasm ties in with a candidate's likeability factor.

Convince them of your Worth: It is always important in any negotiation to set forth objective criteria as to why you are making an offer. A salary offer is no different. A salary request should always be coupled with the reasons why you are worth that number.

Collaboration not Competition: Receiving a job offer and its subsequent salary negotiation begins as an arms-length discussion. Except if you are being hired by family or a friend, you likely have had no prior relationship with your potential employer before salary negotiations. However, if you ultimately accept the job, this relationship has the potential of becoming an arms-open relationship, in a business sense. Therefore, the candidate should do everything possible to keep the negotiations friendly and respectful. Even though you want to advocate for your salary request, if you ultimately take the job, this discussion is just a first in a series of future negotiations. How you set the tone during this negotiation may set a precedent for future negotiations.

Walk away Politely and Respectfully: If discussions do not produce your desired salary and you have decided to decline the job because your alternative is preferable to the offer on the table, your exit strategy is important. Although this job may not have worked out for you, you never know in the future if your paths may cross again with this employer. Therefore, it is always desirable to keep the door open, especially within the same industry. If the negotiations do not result in your employment, you should express your thanks for the offer.

Laws for Non-Compete

It is helpful to distinguish a non-compete clause from related employee provisions. While the term *non-compete* agreement is often used as a catchall for various employee restrictions, a *non-compete* should be distinguished from two related agreements: *non-solicitation* agreements and *confidentiality* agreements.

Non-compete agreements are generally agreements between employers and employees that delay or limit the activities that the departing employee can engage in and that block the departing employee from working for competing firms.

Non-solicitation agreements, while often included within non-compete agreements, are distinct from them and address different concerns. Very generally, a *non-solicitation* agreement restricts an employee from soliciting an employer's other employees or an employer's customers or clients when the employee leaves the company.

Confidentiality agreements also are often included within non-compete agreements but differ from them. Basically, confidentiality agreements are designed to protect the employer's trade secrets or other confidential information.

Federal Laws Relevant to Trade Secrets

Most of the laws governing non-compete, non-solicitation, and confidentiality agreements are state laws. There is, however, an important federal law providing federal protection for intellectual property deemed trade secrets. The federal Defend Trade Secrets Act (DTSA) is similar in many ways to the Uniform Trade Secrets Act, which was adopted by 47 states. DTSA, however, provides a federal claim for trade secret misappropriation. DTSA allows an opportunity for employers to litigate trade secret misappropriation in federal courts and provides them an alternative to state laws on misappropriation of trade secrets. The DTSA provides protection for misappropriation of financial, scientific, business, economic, technical, or engineering information in the form of "patterns, plans, compilations, program devices, formulas, designs, prototypes, methods, techniques, processes, procedures, programs, or codes, whether tangible or intangible, and whether or how stored, compiled, or memorialized physically, electronically, graphically, photographically, or in writing" as long as reasonable measures are taken to protect the secrecy of the information and the employer can prove that economic value is derived from that secrecy.[45]

State Laws on Non-Compete, Non-Solicitation, and Confidentiality Agreements

State laws governing non-compete agreements differ significantly among jurisdictions. In some states, non-compete clauses are significantly limited by legislation or difficult to enforce in their courts. Other states are more accepting of non-compete agreements and their courts may agree to enforce certain portions of a non-compete even when other portions are unenforceable.

California

In California, all non-compete or other contracts that prohibit or restrain anyone from engaging in trade, business, or lawful profession are deemed void except for three limited stated exceptions. These exceptions involve the sale of a business or its goodwill, the disassociation of a partnership, or the expected dissolving of ownership. Even for these limited exceptions for non-compete restrictions, California law requires the non-compete to specify the geographic area of the non-compete restrictions and to limit it to the area where the entity had transacted business. Additionally, California courts will not reform a void and unenforceable non-compete covenant in the employment context. California's exceptions do not apply to non-compete agreements ancillary to employment agreements. Accordingly, employee non-compete agreements would not be enforced. California law does, however, appear to allow an employer to protect its trade secrets from misappropriation and the federal DTSA would apply in cases of trade secret misappropriation. Whether California will uphold a non-solicitation provision preventing an employee from hiring or soliciting other employees is unclear and depends on "whether the contract is as lawful as reasonably possible and the potential impact if the agreement is upheld or invalidated."[46] Accordingly, employers "looking to utilize non-solicitation agreements should look to keep them narrow in term and scope."[47]

Oregon

Oregon, unlike California, will enforce employee non-compete agreements, but it is fairly protective of employees. Under the Oregon statute, a covenant not to compete in the employment context is voidable and unenforceable unless four requirements are met. [48] First, the employer must tell the employee in a written job offer at least two weeks before the employee starts work that the non-compete is required, or the non-compete is entered into upon a "bona fide advancement." Second, the employee must be exempt from Oregon minimum wage and overtime laws. Third, the employer must have a "protectable interest," which is interpreted as the employee having access to the employer's trade secrets or competitively sensitive confidential information. Fourth, the employee's annual gross salary must be more than the median family income for a family of four as calculated by the Census Bureau.

The Oregon law does, however, allow a non-compete agreement to be enforced for a non-exempt employee or an employee who does not meet the salary threshold, if the employer pays the former employee the greater of 50% of the employee's salary or 50% of the median family income for a family of four during the restrictive period of the non-compete.[49] If the non-compete restrictive period exceeds eighteen months from the date the employee left the employment, any period after the initial eighteen months would be unenforceable. Oregon law enforces non-solicitation agreements and also enforces rights to protect confidential business information and trade secrets.

It may be helpful to review the relevant Oregon statute, excerpted here:

> **O.R.S. § 653.295. Noncompetition agreements; bonus restriction agreements; applicability of restrictions.**
>
> (1) A noncompetition agreement entered into between an employer and employee is voidable and may not be enforced by a court of this state unless:
>
> (a)(A) The employer informs the employee in a written employment offer received by the employee at least two weeks before the first day of the employee's employment that a noncompetition agreement is required as a condition of employment; or
>
> (B) The noncompetition agreement is entered into upon a subsequent bona fide advancement of the employee by the employer;

(b) The employee is a person described in ORS 653.020 (3);

(c) The employer has a protectable interest. As used in this paragraph, an employer has a protectable interest when the employee:

(A) Has access to trade secrets, as that term is defined in ORS 646.461;

(B) Has access to competitively sensitive confidential business or professional information that otherwise would not qualify as a trade secret, including product development plans, product launch plans, marketing strategy or sales plans; or

(C) Is employed as an on-air talent by an employer in the business of broadcasting and the employer:

(i) In the year preceding the termination of the employee's employment, expended resources equal to or exceeding 10 percent of the employee's annual salary to develop, improve, train or publicly promote the employee, provided that the resources expended by the employer were expended on media that the employer does not own or control; and

(ii) Provides the employee, for the time the employee is restricted from working, the greater of compensation equal to at least 50 percent of the employee's annual gross base salary and commissions at the time of the employee's termination or 50 percent of the median family income for a four-person family, as determined by the United States Census Bureau for the most recent year available at the time of the employee's termination; and

(d) The total amount of the employee's annual gross salary and commissions, calculated on an annual basis, at the time of the employee's termination exceeds the median family income for a four-person family, as determined by the United States Census Bureau for the most recent year available at the time of the employee's termination. This paragraph does not apply to an employee described in paragraph (c)(C) of this subsection.

(2) The term of a noncompetition agreement may not exceed 18 months from the date of the employee's termination. The remainder of a term of a noncompetition agreement in excess of 18 months is voidable and may not be enforced by a court of this state.

(3) Subsections (1) and (2) of this section apply only to noncompetition agreements made in the context of an employment relationship or contract and not otherwise.

(4) Subsections (1) and (2) of this section do not apply to:

(a) Bonus restriction agreements, which are lawful agreements that may be enforced by the courts in this state; or

(b) A covenant not to solicit employees of the employer or solicit or transact business with customers of the employer.

(5) Nothing in this section restricts the right of any person to protect trade secrets or other proprietary information by injunction or any other lawful means under other applicable laws.

(6) Notwithstanding subsection (1)(b) and (d) of this section, a noncompetition agreement is enforceable for the full term of the agreement, for up to 18 months, if the employer provides the employee, for the time the employee is restricted from working, the greater of:

(a) Compensation equal to at least 50 percent of the employee's annual gross base salary and commissions at the time of the employee's termination; or

(b) Fifty percent of the median family income for a four-person family, as determined by the United States Census Bureau for the most recent year available at the time of the employee's termination.

(7) As used in this section:

(a) "Bonus restriction agreement" means an agreement, written or oral, express or implied, between an employer and employee under which:

(A) Competition by the employee with the employer is limited or restrained after termination of employment, but the restraint is limited to a period of time, a geographic area and specified activities, all of which are reasonable in relation to the services described in subparagraph (B) of this paragraph;

(B) The services performed by the employee pursuant to the agreement include substantial involvement in management of the employer's business, personal contact with customers, knowledge of customer requirements related to the employer's business or knowledge of trade secrets or other proprietary information of the employer; and

(C) The penalty imposed on the employee for competition against the employer is limited to forfeiture of profit sharing or other bonus compensation that has not yet been paid to the employee.

(b) "Broadcasting" means the activity of transmitting of any one-way electronic signal by radio waves, microwaves, wires, coaxial cables, wave guides or other conduits of communications.

(c) "Employee" and "employer" have the meanings given those terms in ORS 652.310.

(d) "Noncompetition agreement" means an agreement, written or oral, express or implied, between an employer and employee under which the employee agrees that the employee, either alone or as an employee of another person, will not compete with the employer in providing products, processes or services that are similar to the employer's products, processes or services for a period of time or within a specified geographic area after termination of employment.[50]

Florida

In Florida, non-compete agreements and non-solicitation agreements are governed by the same statute, and are characterized as "valid restraints of trade or commerce."[51] Much like Oregon, Florida courts will enforce employee non-compete and non-solicitation agreements. However, unlike Oregon, Florida law appears to favor employers' interest over employees' interest.[52] The Florida statute that governs covenants not to compete in the employment context requires that contracts meet three elements to be enforceable. First, the covenant not to compete must be *in writing*, signed by the employee. Second, the employer must be using the non-compete agreement to protect "legitimate business interests." Some statutorily permissible legitimate business interests include: trade secrets, customer, patient, or client goodwill, and substantial relationships with specific prospective or existing customers. Third, the Florida statute requires that the covenant not to compete be "reasonable in time, area, and line of business." Florida's reasonableness in time, area, and line of business requirement is determinate on what legitimate business interest is being protected. Generally, if the legitimate business interest is *not* trade secret related, a former employee or independent contract is presumptively reasonable if 6 months or shorter and unreasonable if longer than two years. In determining the reasonableness in time of a non-compete agreement predicated upon the protection of trade secrets, a court shall presume a restraint of 5 years or less is reasonable, and a restraint 10 years or more is unreasonable. Under Florida law, a *trade secret* is defined as "information, including a formula, pattern, compilation, program, device, method, technique, or process that derives independent economic value, actual or potential, from not being generally known to, and not being readily ascertainable by proper means by, other persons who can obtain economic value from its disclosure or use; and is the subject of efforts that are reasonable under the circumstances to maintain its secrecy."[53] Florida's laws on covenants not to compete prevent courts from considering potential economic hardship to the employee when determining the reasonableness of a non-compete agreement.[54] The statute does, however, allow Florida courts to (1) consider the health, safety, and public welfare of the restrictive covenant, (2) specify a particular public policy that will be impacted, and (3) permit a court to weigh that public interest against the legitimate business interest.[55] The combination of these two rules, results most often in more favorable outcomes for the employer.[56]

It may be helpful to review the relevant Florida statute, excerpted here:

Fla. Stat. § 542.335—Valid restraints of trade or commerce.

(1) Notwithstanding § 542.18 and subsection (2), enforcement of contracts that restrict or prohibit competition during or after the term of restrictive covenants, so long as such contracts are reasonable in time, area, and line of business, is not prohibited. In any action concerning enforcement of a restrictive covenant:

(a) A court shall not enforce a restrictive covenant unless it is set forth in a writing signed by the person against whom enforcement is sought.

(b) The person seeking enforcement of a restrictive covenant shall plead and prove the existence of one or more legitimate business interests justifying the restrictive covenant. The term "legitimate business interest" includes, but is not limited to:

1. Trade secrets, as defined in §688.002(4).
2. Valuable confidential business or professional information that otherwise does not qualify as trade secrets.
3. Substantial relationships with specific prospective or existing customers, patients, or clients.
4. Customer, patient, or client goodwill associated with:
    a. An ongoing business or professional practice, by way of trade name, trademark, service mark, or "trade dress";
    b. A specific geographic location; or
    c. A specific marketing or trade area.
5. Extraordinary or specialized training.

Any restrictive covenant not supported by a legitimate business interest is unlawful and is void and unenforceable.

(c) A person seeking enforcement of a restrictive covenant also shall plead and prove that the contractually specified restraint is reasonably necessary to protect the legitimate business interest or interests justifying the restriction. If a person seeking enforcement of the restrictive covenant establishes prima facie that the restraint is reasonably necessary, the person opposing enforcement has the burden of establishing that the contractually specified restraint is overbroad, overlong, or otherwise not reasonably necessary to protect the established legitimate business interest or interests. If a contractually specified restraint is overbroad, overlong, or otherwise not reasonably necessary to protect the legitimate business interest or interests, a court shall modify the restraint and grant only the relief reasonably necessary to protect such interest or interests.

(d) In determining the reasonableness in time of a post term restrictive covenant not predicated upon the protection of trade secrets, a court shall apply the following rebuttable presumptions:

1. In the case of a restrictive covenant sought to be enforced against a former employee, agent, or independent contractor, and not associated with the sale of all or a part of:
    a. The assets of a business or professional practice, or
    b. The shares of a corporation, or

c. A partnership interest, or

d. A limited liability company membership, or

e. An equity interest, of any other type, in a business or professional practice,

a court shall presume reasonable in time any restraint 6 months or less in duration and shall presume unreasonable in time any restraint more than 2 years in duration.

2. In the case of a restrictive covenant sought to be enforced against a former distributor, dealer, franchisee, or licensee of a trademark or service mark and not associated with the sale of all or a part of:

a. The assets of a business or professional practice, or

b. The shares of a corporation, or

c. A partnership interest, or

d. A limited liability company membership, or

e. An equity interest, of any other type, in a business or professional practice,

a court shall presume reasonable in time any restraint 1 year or less in duration and shall presume unreasonable in time any restraint more than 3 years in duration.

3. In the case of a restrictive covenant sought to be enforced against the seller of all or a part of:

a. The assets of a business or professional practice, or

b. The shares of a corporation, or

c. A partnership interest, or

d. A limited liability company membership, or

e. An equity interest, of any other type, in a business or professional practice,

a court shall presume reasonable in time any restraint 3 years or less in duration and shall presume unreasonable in time any restraint more than 7 years in duration.

(e) An equity interest, of any other type, in a business or professional practice, a court shall presume reasonable in time any restraint 6 months or less in duration and shall presume unreasonable in time any restraint more than 2 years in duration.

(f) The court shall not refuse enforcement of a restrictive covenant on the ground that the person seeking enforcement is a third-party beneficiary of such contract or is an assignee or successor to a party to such contract, provided:

1. In the case of a third-party beneficiary, the restrictive covenant expressly identified the person as a third-party beneficiary of the contract and expressly stated that the restrictive covenant was intended for the benefit of such person.
2. In the case of an assignee or successor, the restrictive covenant expressly authorized enforcement by a party's assignee or successor.

(g) In determining the enforceability of a restrictive covenant, a court:

1. Shall not consider any individualized economic or other hardship that might be caused to the person against whom enforcement is sought.
2. May consider as a defense the fact that the person seeking enforcement no longer continues in business in the area or line of business that is the subject of the action to enforce the restrictive covenant only if such discontinuance of business is not the result of a violation of the restriction.
3. Shall consider all other pertinent legal and equitable defenses.
4. Shall consider the effect of enforcement upon the public health, safety, and welfare.

(h) A court shall construe a restrictive covenant in favor of providing reasonable protection to all legitimate business interests established by the person seeking enforcement. A court shall not employ any rule of contract construction that requires the court to construe a restrictive covenant narrowly, against the restraint, or against the drafter of the contract.

(i) No court may refuse enforcement of an otherwise enforceable restrictive covenant on the ground that the contract violates public policy unless such public policy is articulated specifically by the court and the court finds that the specified public policy requirements substantially outweigh the need to protect the legitimate business interest or interests established by the person seeking enforcement of the restraint.

(j) A court shall enforce a restrictive covenant by any appropriate and effective remedy, including, but not limited to, temporary and permanent injunctions. The violation of an enforceable restrictive covenant creates a presumption of irreparable injury to the person seeking enforcement of a restrictive covenant. No temporary injunction shall be entered unless the person seeking enforcement of a restrictive covenant gives a proper bond, and the court shall not enforce any contractual provision waiving the requirement of an injunction bond or limiting the amount of such bond.

(k) In the absence of a contractual provision authorizing an award of attorney's fees and costs to the prevailing party, a court may award attorney's fees and costs to the prevailing party in any action seeking enforcement of, or challenging the enforceability of, a restrictive covenant. A court shall not enforce any contractual provision limiting the court's authority under this section.

(2) Nothing in this section shall be construed or interpreted to legalize or make enforceable any restraint of trade or commerce otherwise illegal or unenforceable under the laws of the United States or of this state.

(3) This act shall apply prospectively, and it shall not apply in actions determining the enforceability of restrictive covenants entered into before July 1, 1996.

Delaware

Unlike Florida and Oregon, Delaware does not have a statute that governs the enforcement of non-compete or non-solicitation contracts, but rather relies on Delaware common law. Under Delaware law, a contract restricting competition or solicitation is enforceable only if it is reasonable in scope and duration, advances a legitimate economic interest of the party enforcing the contract, and can survive a fairness analysis by the Delaware courts.[57] In determining the reasonableness of the duration of a non-compete agreement, Delaware courts consider several factors including the nature of the employee's position; the nature of the interest to be protected; the geographic scope of the agreement; and the duration of the restriction.[58] Generally, a one or two year covenant is presumed reasonable for employees in an upper or mid-level management position.[59] Delaware courts have determined that a reasonable geographic area should be consistent with and extend only as far as the employer's legitimate business interests.[60] Courts have also permitted non-competes without geographic limits in specific situations, so long as the limitations prescribed by the agreement are reasonable.[61] Delaware courts determine what constitutes a legitimate business interest. Delaware courts have previously held that employers' goodwill and employers' confidential information qualify as legitimate business interests that can be protected by a non-compete agreement.[62] Additionally, Delaware courts will permit non-compete contracts characterizing an employee's knowledge of customer lists, trade secrets, and proprietary information as a legitimate business interest.[63]

In a recent case, governed by Delaware law, Walmart, Inc. sued their former Chief Tax Advisor claiming that her move to Amazon, Inc. would violate her existing non-compete contract with Walmart.[64] The Chief Tax Advisor informed Walmart that she had been offered a senior global tax position at Amazon.com, Inc., one of Walmart's significant competitors. Walmart brought an action to enforce its non-compete agreement claiming it needed to enforce the agreement in order to protect its sensitive and proprietary business information from being shared by their former Chief Tax Advisor. Walmart alleged that the executive was bound by a non-compete provision, and that her new employment with Amazon would directly violate the terms of that non-compete agreement with Walmart. Walmart claims that its Tax Advisor's move to another company "eviscerates the contractual terms that Walmart bargained for" in its employment agreement with the executive. As part of the case, Walmart filed with the court the entire non-compete agreement at issue as an exhibit to its court filings. The non-compete from the case is attached as Exhibit 7-A at the end of this chapter.[65]

Texas

Texas law will treat a non-compete agreement as enforceable as long as it is ancillary to an otherwise enforceable agreement.[66] With regard to ancillary employment agreements, Texas law demarcates a difference between information and training given post and prior to the execution of any non-compete agreement. Specifically, any information and training prior to employment cannot be supported or included in a non-compete covenant. Texas state law also places the burden of proving the validity and necessity of the non-compete agreement on the employer. Under Texas law, the employer must show the non-compete agreement has reasonable limitations regarding length, area, and scope and protects the business interests of the employer. Generally, customer non-solicitation agreements in Texas are interpreted as having the same restrictions on enforceability as non-compete agreements and must be reasonable. Texas law also protects confidential business information and trade secrets.

Ohio

Ohio provides that a non-compete is only enforceable if it does not go beyond what is necessary to protect the employer, does not impose any unnecessary hardships upon the former employee, nor cause any harm on the public.[67] Ohio law allows courts to reform and enforce those necessary portions of non-compete when the original covenant is deemed unreasonable in order to protect the employer's legitimate interests. Ohio has adopted the Uniform Trade Secrets Act.

Salary, Non-Compete Problems

Instructions

After reading the legal principles and strategies in this chapter, you are now ready to apply those principles and strategies for negotiating practice problems using the TABLE method. Below are three problems involving individuals who are negotiating issues concerning salary and non-compete agreements. Each problem contains general information followed by confidential information in which each negotiator will choose a bargaining position on key issues. While the general information will be known by both sides, your bargaining position is confidential, although you may disclose it, or some of it, during the negotiation session if you choose to do so. Following the confidential information, you are given guidelines and suggestions as to how to approach the negotiations using the TABLE method.

After reviewing the information, you should complete the Tactical Planning Worksheet (provided in Appendix A). Each problem provides the law to use in completing your worksheet. Also, be sure to include your bargaining positions on your worksheets. After completing a Tactical Planning Worksheet for each problem, you and your counterpart are ready to conduct a negotiation in which you attempt to reach an agreement. While there is no time limit set for each problem, you should be able to complete the initial negotiations for each problem within 30 minutes.

After you complete each negotiation, you and your negotiating counterpart should exchange planning worksheets so that you can analyze the bargaining positions you and your counterpart planned for the negotiation. Finally, you should complete the Post Negotiation Self-Reflection Worksheet (found in Appendix B).

For further explanation of the methodology for negotiating the problems, please refer to the Authors' Notes in the Chapter 1, Introduction.

Overview of Problems 7-1, 7-2, and 7-3

Problem 7-1 is a two-person salary negotiation in which a prospective employee is negotiating with the CEO of a company concerning future employment. The focus of the negotiation is on the salary offer and a proposed non-compete agreement offered by the employer.

Problem 7-2 is a two-person negotiation based on the same parties and facts as Problem 7-1. However, you are asked to apply the laws of a different state to those facts.

Problem 7-3 is a two-person negotiation involving negotiating the enforcement of an executed non-compete agreement. In this problem, attorneys are negotiating on behalf of a current employee and her employer. The employer wishes to fire the employee but has given the employee the option of resigning instead of being fired. The boss also informs the employee that she will enforce the non-compete agreement the employee had signed prior to starting her job.

Problem 7-1

General Information

Assume for purposes of this negotiation that the Florida laws discussed above apply.

Alina is a 28-year-old who has interviewed and been offered several jobs. She is a highly sought-after recruit in the technology field. She has narrowed her search down to two prospective employers: Howe from Company 1 offered her a job with a salary of $70,000. Company 2 offered her a job with a slightly higher salary, but Company 2 is a start-up company and has only been in the technology field for a short time. Company 1 is willing to discuss her salary offer. Howe, of Company 1, gave her an employment agreement and a non-compete agreement for her review.

Company 1 has interviewed 35 candidates for this position and Alina is the top candidate. However, Howe believes he has several qualified candidates to choose from if Alina does not accept their offer. Howe is willing to discuss the offer as he believes Alina is a good fit for the position. Further, both Alina and Howe are aware that the typical starting salary for an entry level job in his field is between $70,000 and $80,000.

Alina prefers to work at Company 1. Company 1 is well established in the technology industry. After reviewing the employment agreement and non-compete agreement, from Company 1, Alina telephoned Howe and told him she was interested in the position but would like to discuss the salary and bonus provisions. In addition to salary, Alina told Howe that she is concerned with the non-compete agreement and would likely not take the job with the non-compete as currently drafted. Howe said he has some flexibility with the salary offer and with the non-compete agreement. Howe then set up a meeting with Alina to discuss her concerns.

The salary provisions and non-compete agreement are excerpted below:

Compensation

1. As full compensation for all services provided, the employee shall be paid at the rate of $70,000 per year. Such payments shall be subject to such normal statutory deductions by the Employer. Bonuses may be awarded at the discretion of employer.
2. The salary mentioned in paragraph (l) shall be reviewed on an annual basis.

Non-Competition Agreement

1. In consideration of the training to be provided by Employer to the Employee, Employee will not, either during employment with Employer or for a period of one year thereafter, directly or indirectly, for himself/herself or any third party, accept employment or engage in any business or activity, which is directly or indirectly in competition with Employer.
2. Employee will not solicit any current customer or potential customer of Employer identified during the course of employment with Employer, or otherwise divert or attempt to divert any existing business of Employer. Employee will not, either during employment with Employer or for a period of one year thereafter, either directly or indirectly, for Employee or any third party, solicit, induce, recruit, or cause another person in the employ of Employer to terminate his/her employment for the purpose of joining, associating or becoming employed with any business or activity which is in competition with any products and/or services sold, marketed, or provided by Employer.
3. The geographical area to which this non-competition agreement applies is any area in which Employer currently solicits or conducts business, and/or any area in which Employer plans to solicit or conduct business for a period of one year after Employee leaves employment with Employer. Both parties agree that the time and scope of this Non-Competition agreement are reasonable.

Confidential Information

Both Alina and Howe will prepare planning worksheets for the upcoming negotiation. Each party's planning worksheet is confidential. It includes bargaining positions on the issues involved in the negotiation in the role of the Employee (Alina) or the Employer (Howe). This information should not be shared with the other party prior to the negotiation. For purposes of this problem, in addition to the other components of your Tactical Planning Worksheet, your planning worksheet needs to include your bargaining position on these issues:

A. For Howe: the maximum salary and non-monetary benefits he is willing to offer.

B. For Alina: the minimum salary and non-monetary benefits she is willing to accept.

C. For Alina and Howe: determining the bonus provisions.

D. For Alina and Howe: the terms of the non-compete agreement.

Tactical Planning

In planning the negotiation, both the employee and employer should carefully consider the balance of power. An employer typically has more power than a prospective employee, in that the employer makes the hiring decision and often may choose from a number of candidates. However, be aware of situations, such as this problem, where the prospective employee is a highly recruited candidate for the job, and thus, the employee's uniqueness may prove to reallocate some of the power.

Refer to Chapter 2 to guide you through the steps in preparing your Tactical Planning Worksheet (Appendix A) for this problem. Be sure to refer to the strategy guidelines for Employers and Employees discussed in this chapter and the information contained in the general information and confidential information above for this problem.

Arranging the Negotiation

For purposes of this negotiation, you may assume the negotiation will take place in-person, at Howe's office.

Bargaining

In a traditional salary negotiation, the employer and employee should begin with some ice-breaking. In this instance, it is important for the parties to establish a rapport not only to set the tone for a positive negotiation, but also to establish a foundation for a future working relationship.

As the parties move to bargaining, the parties are benefitted from the fact that the opening offer has already been made prior to the negotiation, because Howe has offered Alina $70,000 as a starting salary. At this point, either Howe or Alina should acknowledge this offer as the starting point, begin to exchange offers and counteroffers, and make concessions. Both parties will likely have questions, and those questions should be interspersed throughout the negotiation in order for each party to gain information and perhaps adjust the goals they have outlined on their planning worksheets. Since there is also the issue of the non-compete, that issue may either be discussed in conjunction with the salary offer or separately from that discussion.

Letting go or Resolving & Executing the Agreement

As the bargaining phase concludes, there are likely three possible outcomes: 1) Alina and Howe reach a mutually acceptable agreement; 2) they do not reach an agreement and Howe and Alina decide to part ways; or 3) final offers are made and Howe and/or Alina decide to think it over and come back with a decision a short time in the future.

It is unlikely the negotiation would continue beyond this session. However, one scenario where the negotiations may continue is if Alina and Howe came to a tentative agreement on an issue, but Howe was unable to complete the deal because he did not have the authority. For example, if Howe did not have the authority to change the terms of the non-compete, he may have to consult with the company's lawyers and obtain approval to make the agreed changes with Alina. However, if the company lawyers do not give their approval, negotiations may need to continue, or this may be a deal breaker.

If Alina and Howe come to terms on the salary and non-compete, the employment agreement will reflect those changes. At this point, Alina and Howe will sign the agreement and, hopefully, this will be the start of a great working relationship.

Ethics and Equity

Both Alina and Howe are aware of the salary range for this position in this field. Therefore, neither Alina nor Howe should make a claim that the range is higher or lower. However, Alina should be aware that employers may not be forthcoming as to the highest salary they can offer. Just like a settlement negotiation in a litigation context, an employer likely does not want to offer his highest authority initially when negotiating salary offers. However, Howe should be careful not to misrepresent that the salary he can offer is the highest, if it is not. As in any negotiation, this type of lie can not only derail the negotiation, but if discovered, also set up future problems not only to his credibility but also to that of the company.

Alina should also be mindful of not overselling her value, and in the course of doing so, make misrepresentations as well. Unfortunately, it is somewhat typical for job candidates to inflate the number of salary offers they have been offered, in an effort to raise the stakes in the present negotiation. Playing the "I've got better offers game" may backfire. For example, in this case, Alina does have a legitimate other offer and she may wish to use that offer as a negotiating point. However, if she should misrepresent that she has other additional offers from other companies, her lie may be quickly discovered, as many industries are like small communities, and shared information is not uncommon. Even if Alina does not reveal the names of the companies that gave her these made-up offers, Howe may be well aware that her alleged salary offers do not sound legitimate, given the current market in that industry. Further, if Alina oversells herself, she may find Howe withdrawing his offer, and she has now eliminated her number one choice for a job.

Howe, as an employer, should also be mindful of recent laws that do not allow an employer to ask a candidate about salary history. If he attempts to violate these laws, he would not only be engaging in unethical behavior, but also positioning his company to be the subject of a lawsuit. It is expected that Howe would also act ethically and not discriminate against Alina during salary negotiations based on such factors as race, gender, age, marital status, national origin, religion or disability. It is difficult to determine during a negotiation if discriminatory conduct is occurring. However, if proven after the fact, Howe could be in violation of numerous state and federal laws.

Tactical Planning Worksheet Reveal

After concluding the negotiations, you and your counterpart should exchange your individual Tactical Planning Worksheets so that you both can see the bargaining positions you had planned to use during the negotiation. You should compare the two worksheets and see how far apart you were initially. Also, you should analyze whether and why you strayed from your worksheet, especially in the areas of offers and counteroffers. What positive aspects from your counterpart's worksheet do you wish you had included in yours?

Post-Negotiation Self-Reflection Worksheet

At the conclusion of the reveal session for this problem, be sure to complete the Post-Negotiation Self-Reflection Worksheet (found in Appendix B). Your Post-Negotiation Self-Reflection Worksheet should be completed individually and optimally within a short period of time after the Tactical Planning Worksheet reveal, while the negotiation session is fresh in your mind.

Problem 7-2

Assume for purposes of this negotiation that the Oregon laws discussed above apply.

Using the same facts as in Problem 7-1, negotiate the problem using Oregon law (as excerpted above) rather than Florida law. After completing the Oregon version of the negotiation, in addition to completing the Post-Negotiation Self-Reflection Worksheet (found in Appendix B) compare your results using Oregon law versus Florida law. Was there a difference in the results? Why or why not?

Problem 7-3

General Information

Assume for purposes of this negotiation that the Delaware laws discussed above apply.

Tara Elliot works as a dental assistant for Dr. Evelyn Montes. Dr. Montes has had a solo dental practice for ten years. Tara has worked for Dr. Montes for the past eight years. When Tara was hired, Dr. Montes's required her to sign a non-compete agreement. The non-compete agreement states in part:

Non-Compete Agreement

In consideration of the employment opportunity provided by Dr. Montes (Employer) and Tara Elliot (Employee), agree to the following:

1. **Term of Agreement.** This Agreement is effective on the date executed by both parties and shall remain in effect throughout the term of Employee's employment with the Company and for a period of one year thereafter.
2. **Limitations of this Agreement.** This Agreement is not a contract of employment. Neither Employee nor Employer is obligated to any specific term of employment. This Agreement is limited to the subject matter of covenants not to compete or solicit as described in this Agreement.
3. **Covenant Not to Compete.** Employee agrees that at no time during the term of her employment with Employer will she engage in any business activity which is competitive with Employer nor work for any company which competes with Employer. For a period of one (1) year immediately following the termination of her employment, Employee will not, for herself, or on behalf of any other person or business enterprise, engage in any business activity, which competes with Employer within 5 miles of the office in which Employee was employed.
4. **Soliciting Customers After Termination of Agreement.** For a period of one (1) year following the termination of employment with Employer, Employee shall not, directly or indirectly, disclose to any person, firm or corporation the names or addresses of any of the customers or clients of Employer or any other information pertaining to them. Neither shall Employee solicit, or attempt to solicit, any customer of Employer on whom Employee became acquainted during the term of employment, as the direct or indirect result of employment with the Employer.
5. **Injunctive Relief.** Employee hereby acknowledges that (1) Employer will suffer irreparable harm if Employee breaches her obligations under this Agreement; and that (2) monetary damages will be inadequate to compensate Employer for such a breach. Therefore, if Employee breaches any of such provisions, then Employer shall be entitled to injunctive relief, in addition to any other remedies at law or equity, to enforce such provisions.
6. **Severable Provisions.** The provisions of this Agreement are severable, and if any one or more provisions may be determined to be illegal or otherwise unenforceable, in whole or in part, the remaining provisions and any partially unenforceable provisions to the extent enforceable shall nevertheless be binding and enforceable.

Tara is a very popular dental assistant, and Dr. Montes clients request dental cleanings from Tara twice as often than from Dr. Montes's other assistant. Tara is booked with appointments three months in advance, and Dr. Montes is well aware of her popularity. However, in the last year, her relationship with Tara has soured. Dr. Montes learned through several clients that Tara often gives her opinions as to whether a client's teeth need dental treatment, and even recommends that the client should not waste their time or money getting their teeth examined by Dr. Montes since Tara knows that they have no cavities or other dental problems that require a checkup. By Tara giving such advice, she is not only directly violating office policy, but more importantly, she is, in essence, practicing dental medicine without a license, which could potentially subject Dr. Montes to a malpractice claim or disciplinary action by the dental board. Dr. Montes has spoken to Tara several times about refraining from giving any advice. Tara denied giving any such advice. However, Dr. Montes is aware through her patients that Tara has continued to give such advice. Further, due to Tara telling patients that they do not need a check-up, Dr. Montes has lost revenue from those patients who have relied on Tara's opinion instead of Dr. Montes's opinion.

In addition to the advice giving over the past year, Tara has arrived late to work on many occasions, and has taken fourteen additional personal days off than she was allotted for her vacation/personal days. Tara claims that although she has been late to work on some occasions, that even if she is late with a patient appointment, she is extremely efficient and always completes her schedule of patients on time. Further, she stated that she had to take off more time the past year to help her mother who was recovering from a lengthy illness. Tara also noted that she did not get paid for the extra days she missed during the past year. Dr. Montes is aware of Tara's explanation about her late arrivals and time off, but her erratic schedule has caused numerous conflicts with the rest of the office staff, who feel they have to work extra hours to cover for her absences and late schedule. The increased tension between office staff and Tara is resulting in a toxic work environment.

Due to the continuing problems with Tara, Dr. Montes decided she could no longer work with Tara and asked that she leave within 30 days. Dr. Montes stated that she is not sure if she would give Tara a letter of recommendation, although she would be willing to discuss a letter with Tara. Dr. Montes also stated that she plans to enforce the non-compete agreement, because of Tara's popularity with her patients and her concern that Tara may try to solicit some of Dr. Montes's patients for any new position she obtains. Dr. Montes told her that since Tara was bound by her non-compete agreement, she would pay Tara her full salary of $5,000 per month for four months and continue her health care benefits as well for those four months. Of course, Dr. Montes reminds Tara that under the non-compete, Tara could obtain a job right away (and not have to wait one year) as long as the new job is outside of the 5-mile radius.

Tara was quite upset and told Dr. Montes that she had been a loyal employee. Tara also told Dr. Montes that Dr. Kaminski, a long-time friend of hers, has told her that if she ever wants to leave Dr. Montes' practice, he always has a job for her. Dr. Kaminski's dental office is within three miles of Dr. Montes' offices. Tara also told Dr. Montes that she was consulting with a lawyer and that her counsel would be in touch. After hearing this from Tara, Dr. Montes has also retained an attorney to handle Tara's departure from the office.

Confidential Information

After consulting with their respective clients, both Tara's attorney and Dr. Montes's attorney will prepare Tactical Planning Worksheets for the upcoming negotiation. Each party's planning worksheet is confidential. It includes bargaining positions on the issues involved in the negotiation in the role of the Employee (Tara) or the Employer (Dr. Montes). This information should not be shared with the other party prior to the negotiation. For purposes of this problem, in addition to the other components of your Tactical Planning Worksheet, your planning worksheet needs to include your bargaining position on these issues:

A) For Tara and Dr. Montes: the enforcement or modification of the non-compete restriction and of the non-solicitation provisions.

B) For Tara and Dr. Montes: severance pay and health coverage.

C) For Tara and Dr. Montes: their reputations in the community and the letter of recommendation.

Tactical Planning

In the context of this problem, be especially aware that this is an employer/employee relationship that is fractured beyond repair. The parties, who at one time shared what could be described as an arms-open relationship, now have entered into what is in effect an arms-length relationship. The fact that the employer has asked the employee to leave, as well as the parties hiring attorneys to negotiate, is evidence of the adversarial nature of their relationship. Neither party wishes to maintain a relationship to any extent, a factor that allows the attorneys to be more aggressive in their negotiating positions. However, the attorneys should never lose sight of their professionalism, even as they are acting as adversaries and advocates for their clients.

Refer to Chapter 2 to guide you through the steps in preparing your Tactical Planning Worksheet (Appendix A) for this problem. Be sure to refer to the strategy guidelines for Employers and Employees discussed in this chapter and the information contained in the general information and confidential information above for this problem.

Arranging the Negotiation

Since this negotiation involves attorneys negotiating on behalf of their clients, for purposes of this problem, assume the negotiation takes place in one of the attorney's offices. However, in an actual negotiation, for the convenience of the attorneys, they may decide to negotiate by telephone, Skype, or any of the other formats discussed in Chapter 3, that is conducive to this type of negotiation.

Bargaining

The attorneys should begin the negotiation with some ice-breaking and set the agenda. These negotiations may take place over several sessions, as the matters are somewhat complex. Therefore, the parties should establish a time frame for the initial negotiation. They should also communicate any upcoming conflicts they may have that would prevent a continuation of the negotiating process if they do not reach an agreement in the initial negotiation.

After a brief ice-breaking and an agenda setting discussion, the attorneys should begin negotiating the terms of Tara's departure from her job with Dr. Montes. Having consulted with their clients prior to the negotiation, the attorneys' worksheets should reflect their clients' goals, and the attorneys should set forth their offers, counteroffers, and concessions. They should also be prepared to make reasonable adjustments to their prepared bargaining positions based on information they may receive during the negotiation. This information may either be offered by the attorneys or result from answers to questions posed by the attorneys.

In this case, Dr. Montes has a real concern that due to Tara's popularity with her clients, her clients may well decide to follow Tara to her new job, especially if prompted by Tara to do so. Dr. Montes's attorney should be able to use the fact of Tara's popularity to stress the importance of enforcing the non-compete agreement. Yet the non-compete agreement Tara signed may be unduly restrictive, in that it prevents her from working as a dental assistant within a five-mile radius for one year. Given that Tara is not a dentist like Dr. Montes and does not run a dental business but is a dental assistant who will need to work under the supervision of a dentist, this provision may be too restrictive. Tara's attorney should be able to make an effective argument regarding this provision. Dr. Montes' attorney should stress, however, that she is offering Tara four months' severance to soften the effect of the non-compete. However, the non-solicitation provision may carry more weight, even though Tara's attorney should work toward softening the stringent no solicitation terms contained in the agreement.

Even though their clients may no longer want a relationship, it is important in the context of the negotiation that the attorneys not only advocate for their clients but are also willing to seek compromise. The attorneys need to be mindful that although their clients have a contentious relationship, they will need to work together to come to a mutually acceptable settlement.

Letting Go or Resolving

As noted above, the attorneys may not be able to complete a successful negotiation in one session. In fact, as discussed in Chapter 4 on Bargaining, if the discussion appears to be non-productive, they may want to break and plan another session. This break may also give them an opportunity to regroup with their clients and perhaps revise their goals and demands in advance of the next negotiating session.

If the attorneys are unable to reach a settlement, the next step may well involve litigation. Unless there is some reconsideration that Tara will continue to work for Dr. Montes, if the attorneys cannot work out an agreement, the parties may ultimately decide to let a court resolve this dispute.

If the attorneys reach a settlement on behalf of their clients, they should draft an agreement that sets forth all the terms of Tara's departure from Dr. Montes's employment. The clients will then review and sign the agreement. At this point, the parties will go their separate ways. Hopefully, the parties will abide by the terms of the agreement and attorneys will not be needed to enforce the terms down the road.

Ethics and Equity

Non-compete agreements are fraught with potential ethical issues. Because one of the purposes of these agreements is to prevent employees from stealing clients when they leave their employment, as in this problem, these agreements presume employees will engage in sabotaging their employer by taking the employers' clients with them. In addition, this non-compete agreement not only restrains solicitation but also restrains Tara from working in her field for a period of time. A non-compete agreement has to have some balance, however, in that the employee cannot be so constrained by the agreement such that the employee is no longer employable.

The attorneys must remember to avoid using unethical tactics in a negotiation such as this. It would be easy to imagine Tara's attorney would be eager to misrepresent her popularity by downplaying the willingness of Dr. Montes' clients to leave with Tara in an effort to get Dr. Montes not to enforce the agreement. Similarly, it would also be tempting for Dr. Montes' attorney to exaggerate Tara's incompetence in giving medical advice to her clients, to support her initial hesitancy to provide Tara a letter of recommendation.

Tactical Planning Worksheet Reveal

After concluding the negotiations, you and your counterpart should exchange your individual Tactical Planning Worksheets so that you both can see the bargaining positions you had planned to use during the negotiation. You should compare the two worksheets and see how far apart you were initially. Also, you should analyze whether and why you strayed from your worksheet, especially in the areas of offers and counteroffers. What positive aspects from your counterpart's worksheet do you wish you had included in yours?

Post-Negotiation Self-Reflection Worksheet

At the conclusion of the reveal session for this problem, be sure to complete the Post-Negotiation Self-Reflection Worksheet (found in Appendix B). Your Post-Negotiation Self-Reflection Worksheet should be completed individually and optimally within a short period of time after the Tactical Planning Worksheet reveal, while the negotiation session is fresh in your mind.

EFiled: Jun 06 2018 09:12PM EDT
Transaction ID 62109409
Case No. 2018-0414-

Exhibit 7-A

EXHIBIT A

RLF1 5331231v.1

POST-TERMINATION AGREEMENT
AND COVENANT NOT TO COMPETE

This Post-Termination Agreement and Covenant Not to Compete (this "Agreement") is entered into as of February 28, 2014 by and between Wal-Mart Stores, Inc., its subsidiaries and affiliates (collectively, "Walmart") and Lisa Wadlin ("Associate").

RECITALS

WHEREAS, Walmart proposes that Associate: (a) be permitted to continue Associate's at will employment with Walmart; and (b) be promoted from the Associate's existing position of Vice President, International Tax, to become Senior Vice President, Global Tax (the "Promotion"); and

WHEREAS, as consideration for and as a condition of: (a) Associate continuing Associate's at will employment with Walmart; and (b) receiving the Promotion (collectively, the "Special Items"), Associate is required to execute and deliver this Agreement to Walmart;

AGREEMENT

NOW, THEREFORE, in consideration of the premises and the acknowledgments, covenants, representations, warranties and agreements contained herein and for other good and valuable consideration, including but not limited to the Special Items being conveyed to Associate by Walmart, the receipt and sufficiency of which is hereby acknowledged, the parties hereto agree as follows:

1. ACKNOWLEDGMENTS. As part of this Agreement, the parties specifically acknowledge that:

(A) Walmart is a major retail operation, with stores located throughout the United States, territories of the United States, and in certain foreign countries;

(B) Associate has served as Vice President, International Tax, which appointment was made by the Walmart Board of Directors and which position is a key officer position and Associate will become Senior Vice President, Global Tax, which is a promotion and a key officer position appointed by the Walmart Board of Directors;

(C) As an essential part of its business, Walmart has cultivated, established and maintained long-term customer and vendor relationships and goodwill and competitive advantages, which are difficult to develop and maintain, have required and continue to require a significant investment of time, effort, and expense, and that can suffer significantly and irreparably upon the departure of key officers, regardless of whether the officer has been personally involved in developing or maintaining the relationships, goodwill or competitive advantages;

(D) In the development of its business, Walmart has expended a significant amount of time, money, and effort in developing, maintaining, and protecting private, sensitive, confidential, proprietary, and trade secret information including but not limited to, information regarding Walmart's products or services, strategies, research and development efforts, logistics, transportation, selling and delivery plans, geographic markets, developing or potential geographic markets, developing or potential product markets, mergers, acquisitions, divestitures, data, business methods, computer programs and related source and object code, supplier and customer relationships, contacts and information, methods or sources of product manufacture, know-how, product or service cost or pricing, personnel allocation or organizational structure, business, marketing, development and expansion or contraction plans, information concerning the legal or financial affairs of Walmart, any other non-public information, and any other information protected by the most recent Nondisclosure and Restricted Use Agreement executed by Associate (collectively, "Confidential Information"), the disclosure or misuse of which could cause irreparable harm to Walmart's business, anticipated business, and its competitive position in the retail marketplace;

(E) Associate has had access to such Confidential Information in Associate's current key officer position that would be of considerable value to Walmart's global and domestic competitors and potential competitors and as Senior Vice President, Global Tax, Associate will continue to have access to Confidential Information that would be of considerable value to Walmart's global and domestic competitors and potential competitors; and

(F) Associate acknowledges that Walmart is entitled to take appropriate steps to ensure: (i) that its associates do not misappropriate or make any other improper use of Confidential Information; (ii) that no individual associate, competitor or potential competitor gains an unfair, competitive advantage over Walmart; and (iii) that its competitors and potential competitors do not improperly gain access to or make any use of Confidential Information in their efforts to compete against, or cause harm to, Walmart.

2. TRANSITION PAYMENTS. For purposes of this Agreement, the term "Transition Period" means a period of two (2) years from the effective date of Associate's termination of employment with Walmart. If Walmart terminates Associate's employment, Walmart will pay Associate during the Transition Period an amount equal to Associate's base salary at the rate in effect on the date of termination ("Transition Payments"), subject to such withholding as may be required by law and subject to the conditions set forth in this Section 2. Transition Payments will commence and be paid at the times and in the amounts provided in Section 2(E).

(A) Transition Payments will not be paid if Associate is terminated as the result of Associate's violation of any Walmart policy.

(B) No Transition Payments will be paid if Associate voluntarily resigns or retires from employment with Walmart.

(C) Given the availability of other programs designed to provide financial protection in such circumstances, Transition Payments will not be paid under this Agreement if Associate dies or becomes disabled. If Associate dies during the Transition Period, Transition Payments will cease, and Associate's heirs will not be entitled to the continuation of such payments. Transition Payments will not be affected by Associate's disability during the Transition Period.

(D) Associate's violation of the obligations under Sections 4, 5 or 6, below, or any other act that is materially harmful to Walmart's business interests during the Transition Period, will result in the immediate termination of the Transition Payments, the recovery of the Transition Payments already made, and any other remedies that may be available to Walmart. Any future employment by Associate that does not violate Sections 4, 5, or 6 below will not result in the termination or reduction of the Transition Payments.

(E) Transition Payments will be paid as follows:

(i) The first Transition Payment shall be an amount equal to six months of the Associate's base salary, less applicable withholding, and shall be paid within thirty (30) days following termination; and

(ii) Subsequent Transition Payments shall commence on the first regularly scheduled pay period following six (6) months after Associate's termination and shall be made during each regularly scheduled pay period thereafter during the Transition Period. Each Transition Payment shall be the amount which would have continued as part of Associate's regular base salary, less applicable withholding, and shall be made in the regularly scheduled payroll cycle, subject to the terms and conditions of this Agreement.

(F) Receipt of Transition Payments will not entitle Associate to participate during the Transition Period in any other incentive, restricted stock, performance share, stock option, stock incentive, profit sharing, management incentive or other associate benefit plans or programs maintained by Walmart; except, that, Associate will be entitled to participate in such plans or programs to the extent that the terms of the plan or program provide for participation by former associates. Such participation, if any, shall be governed by the terms of the applicable plan or program.

3. **BENEFITS.** Associate will be eligible for all other payments and benefits accrued and owing at the time of termination. Participation in all other benefit programs available to current associates will end on the effective date of Associate's termination, subject to Associate's rights under COBRA to continue group medical and dental coverage for eighteen (18) months, pursuant to the terms of COBRA, which are currently extended to terminating Walmart associates.

4. **COVENANT NOT TO COMPETE.** Due to the strategic, sensitive and far-reaching nature of the Associate's current and former positions at Walmart, and the Confidential Information to which the Associate is and has been exposed, Associate agrees, promises, and covenants that:

(A) For a period of two (2) years from the date on which Associate's employment with Walmart terminates, and regardless of the cause or reason for such termination, Associate will not directly or indirectly:

(i) own, manage, operate, finance, join, control, advise, consult, render services to, have a current or future interest in, or participate in the ownership, management, operation, financing, or control of, or be employed by or connected in any manner with, any Competing Business as defined below in Section 4(B)(i) and/or any Global Retail Business as defined below in Section 4(B)(ii); and/or

(ii) participate in any other activity that risks the use or disclosure of Confidential Information either overtly by the Associate or inevitably through the performance of such activity by the Associate; and/or

(ii) solicit for employment, hire or offer employment to, or otherwise aid or assist any person or entity other than Walmart in soliciting for employment, hiring, or offering employment to, any Officer, Officer Equivalent or Management Associate of Walmart, or any of its subsidiaries or affiliates.

(B)(i) For purposes of this Agreement, the term "Competing Business" shall include any general or specialty retail, grocery, wholesale membership club, or merchandising business, inclusive of its respective parent companies, subsidiaries and/or affiliates that: (a) sells goods or merchandise at retail to consumers and/or businesses (whether through physical locations, via the internet or combined) or has plans to sell goods or merchandise at retail to consumers and/or businesses (whether through physical locations, via the internet or combined) within twelve (12) months following Associate's last day of employment with Walmart in the United States; and (b) has gross annual consolidated sales volume or revenues attributable to its retail operations (whether through physical locations, via the internet or combined) equal to or in excess of U.S.D. $5 billion.

(ii) For purposes of this Agreement, the term "Global Retail Business" shall include any general or specialty retail, grocery, wholesale membership club, or merchandising business, inclusive of its respective parent companies, subsidiaries and/or affiliates, that: (a) in any country or countries outside of the United States in which Walmart conducts business or intends to conduct business in the twelve (12) months following Associate's last day of employment with Walmart, sells goods or merchandise at retail to consumers and/or businesses (whether through physical locations, via the internet or combined); and (b) has gross annual consolidated sales volume or revenues attributable to its retail operations (whether through physical locations, via the internet or combined) equal to or in excess of U.S.D. $5 billion in any country pursuant to (B)(ii)(a) or in the aggregate equal to or in excess of U.S.D. $5 billion in any countries taken together pursuant to (B)(ii)(a) when no

DM 4666831 4

business in any one country has annual consolidated sales volume or revenues attributable to its retail operations equal to or in excess of U.S.D. $5 billion.

(iii) For purposes of this Agreement, the term "Management Associate" shall mean any domestic or international associate holding the title of "manager" or above.

(iv) For purposes of this Agreement, the term "Officer" shall mean any domestic Walmart associate who holds a title of Vice President or above.

(v) For purposes of this Agreement, the term "Officer Equivalent" shall mean any non-U.S. Walmart associate who Walmart views as holding a position equivalent to an officer position, such as managers and directors in international markets, irrespective of whether such managers and directors are on assignment in the U.S.

(C) Ownership of an investment of less than the greater of $25,000 or 1% of any class of equity or debt security of a Competing Business and/or a Global Retail Business will not be deemed ownership or participation in ownership of a Competing Business and/or a Global Retail Business for purposes of this Agreement.

(D) The covenant not to compete contained in this Section 4 shall bind Associate, and shall remain in full force and effect, regardless of whether Associate qualifies, or continues to remain eligible, for the Transition Payments described in Section 2 above. Termination of the Transition Payments pursuant to Section 2 will not release Associate from Associate's obligations under this Section 4.

5. FUTURE ASSISTANCE. Associate agrees to provide reasonable assistance and cooperation to Walmart in connection with any agency investigation, litigation or similar proceedings that may exist or may arise regarding events as to which Associate has knowledge by virtue of Associate's employment with Walmart. Walmart will compensate Associate for reasonable travel, materials, and other expenses incidental to any such support Associate may provide to Walmart, at Walmart's request.

6. PRESERVATION OF CONFIDENTIAL INFORMATION. Associate will not at any time, directly or indirectly, use or disclose any Confidential Information obtained during the course of Associate's employment with Walmart and following the Associate's termination of employment with Walmart, except as may be authorized by Walmart.

7. REMEDIES FOR BREACH. The parties shall each be entitled to pursue all legal and equitable rights and remedies to secure performance of their respective obligations and duties under this Agreement, and enforcement of one or more of these rights and remedies will not preclude the parties from pursuing any other rights and remedies. Associate acknowledges that a breach of the provisions of Sections 4 through 6, above, could result in substantial and irreparable damage to Walmart's business, and that the restrictions contained in Sections 4 through 6 are a reasonable attempt by Walmart to protect its rights and to safeguard its Confidential Information. Associate expressly agrees that upon a breach or a threatened breach of the provisions of Sections 4 through 6,

DM 4666831 5

Walmart shall be entitled to injunctive relief to restrain such violation, and Associate hereby expressly consents to the entry of such temporary, preliminary, and/or permanent injunctive relief, as may be necessary to enjoin the violation or threatened violation of Sections 4 through 6. With respect to any breach of this Agreement by Associate, Associate agrees to indemnify and hold Walmart harmless from and against any and all loss, cost, damage, or expense, including, but not limited to, attorneys' fees, incurred by Walmart, and to return immediately to Walmart all of the monies previously paid to Associate by Walmart under this Agreement; provided, however, that such repayment shall not constitute a waiver by Walmart of any other remedies available under this Section or by law, including injunctive relief.

8. SEVERABILITY. In the event that a court of competent jurisdiction shall determine that any portion of this Agreement is invalid or otherwise unenforceable, the parties agree that the remaining portions of the Agreement shall remain in full force and effect. The parties also expressly agree that if any portion of the covenant not to compete set forth in Section 4 shall be deemed unenforceable, then the Agreement shall automatically be deemed to have been amended to incorporate such terms as will render the covenant enforceable to the maximum extent permitted by law.

9. NATURE OF THE RELATIONSHIP. Nothing contained in this Agreement shall be deemed or construed to constitute a contract of employment for a definite term. The parties acknowledge that Associate is not employed by Walmart for a definite term, and that either party may sever the employment relationship at any time and for any reason not otherwise prohibited by law.

10. ENTIRE AGREEMENT. This document, along with the most recent Non-Disclosure and Restricted Use Agreement executed by and between the parties (the "Ancillary Agreement"), contain the entire understanding and agreement between Associate and Walmart regarding the subject matter of this Agreement and the Ancillary Agreement. This Agreement, together with the Ancillary Agreement, supersede and replace any and all prior understandings or agreements between the parties regarding this subject, and no representations or statements by either party shall be deemed binding unless contained herein or therein.

11. MODIFICATION. This Agreement may not be amended, modified, or altered except in a writing signed by both parties or their designated representatives.

12. SUCCESSORS AND ASSIGNS. This Agreement will inure to the benefit of, and will be binding upon, Walmart, its successors and permitted assigns, and on Associate and Associate's heirs, successors, and permitted assigns. No rights or obligations under this Agreement may be assigned to any other person without the express written consent of all parties hereto.

13. COUNTERPARTS. This Agreement may be executed in counterparts, in which case each of the two counterparts will be deemed to be an original.

DM 4666831 6

14. GOVERNING LAW AND VENUE. This Agreement shall be governed by, and construed in accordance with, the laws of the State of Delaware, without regard to Delaware law concerning the conflicts of law. The parties agree that any action relating to the interpretation, validity, or enforcement of this Agreement shall be brought in the courts of the State of Delaware, County of New Castle, or in the United States District Court of Delaware, and the parties hereby expressly consent to the jurisdiction of such courts and agree that venue is proper in those courts. The parties do hereby irrevocably: (a) submit themselves to the personal jurisdiction of such courts; (b) agree to service of such courts' process upon them with respect to any such proceeding; (c) waive any objection to venue laid therein; and (d) consent to service of process by registered mail, return receipt requested. Associate further agrees that in any claim or action involving the execution, interpretation, validity, or enforcement of this Agreement, Associate will seek satisfaction exclusively from the assets of Walmart and will hold harmless all of Walmart's individual directors, officers, employees, and representatives. The parties also agree that they will first attempt to resolve any disputes arising under this Agreement through good faith negotiations.

15. STATEMENT OF UNDERSTANDING. By signing below, Associate acknowledges: (i) that Associate has received a copy of this Agreement, (ii) that Associate has read the Agreement carefully before signing it, (iii) that Associate has had ample opportunity to ask questions concerning the Agreement and has had the opportunity to discuss the Agreement with legal counsel of Associate's own choosing, and (iv) that Associate understands the rights and obligations under this Agreement and enters into this Agreement voluntarily.

16. SECTION 409A. The payments made under this Agreement are intended to comply with section 409A of the Internal Revenue Code of 1986, as amended, and applicable guidance issued thereunder ("Section 409A"). Although Walmart intends to administer this Agreement so that it will comply with the requirements of Section 409A, Walmart does not represent or warrant that this Agreement will comply with Section 409A or any other provision of federal, state, local, or non-United States law. Walmart, or either of its directors, officers, employees or advisers shall not be liable to the Associate (or any other individual claiming a benefit through the Associate) for any tax, interest, or penalties the Associate may owe as a result of compensation paid under this Agreement, and shall have no obligation to indemnify or otherwise protect the Associate from the obligation to pay any taxes pursuant to Section 409A.

IN WITNESS WHEREOF, the parties hereto have executed this Agreement on the date first above written.

WAL-MART STORES, INC.	LISA WADLIN
By: ______________________	______________________
Name: Jackie L. Telfair	
Title: Vice President, Executive and Corporate Compensation	

Chapter 8

Prenuptial Agreements

"So you can achieve your goal of making me happy, I'll let you give me everything I want."

The four simple words, "I want a prenup" spoken by one future spouse to the other often strikes fear in the recipient and has a dramatic effect. Many future spouses when hearing these words are immediately offended, and respond with a resounding "No." After the "No" often comes proclamations of "If you loved me you wouldn't want a prenup," or "you don't think our marriage is going to last." These statements by a future spouse are often spoken due to a lack of knowledge and understanding about the purpose and benefits of a prenuptial agreement and the positive role it can play for both spouses in a marriage. These fears are often based on preconceived myths that surround prenuptial agreements, mainly that these agreements are used by the wealthy to deprive a future spouse of receiving any assets from the marriage. However, today's prenuptial agreements, if negotiated properly, can be an effective way for both spouses to manage and direct their lives together.

This chapter allows for practicing the TABLE method in its entirety, that is, from soup to nuts, for negotiating a prenuptial agreement. A prenuptial agreement (prenup), also referred to as a premarital or antenuptial agreement, is a contract between a couple contemplating marriage that allows the couple to define and convey their expectations, especially with regard to their finances and property, for the upcoming marriage, and to determine their legal rights during the marriage and in the event of divorce and at death. A prenup serves as a handy vehicle for applying the principles of TABLE for several reasons. First, it involves a clear example of an arms-open negotiation, where the parties have a prior relationship and are intent on maintaining the relationship after the negotiations are complete. Second, negotiating a prenuptial agreement generally requires the parties to confront various difficult and sometimes emotionally fraught issues including death or ill health. This chapter demonstrates how using the TABLE method alleviates some of the stress involved in such sensitive negotiations. Finally, and perhaps most importantly, a prenuptial agreement demonstrates in starkest terms the power of negotiations. Negotiating a prenuptial agreement allows the couple to determine many of their own terms for their upcoming marital relationship, instead of leaving the terms to the default provisions of state laws. This chapter describes some general legal principles regarding prenuptial agreements. Recall that this book, however, is not intended as a primer on any particular area of the law nor intended to provide legal advice. Rather, the general legal principles included in this chapter are for use in practicing negotiation skills through the problems. Also, note that the statutes and cases cited are subject to revision, and local rules may somewhat vary the analysis.

If a couple decides not to have a prenup, they are choosing to have a state's laws governing marriage supply the terms and conditions of their marriage. In effect, a couple marrying without a prenup enters into a contract whose terms are determined by an automatic default state legal system.[1] Often the couple contemplating marriage without a prenup is not even aware of the parameters of their state's default contractual laws regarding marriage. To illustrate this, Exhibit 8-A at the end of this chapter sets forth what a *fictional no-prenup marital contract* could look like based on an unknown underlying state law. Notice the *fictional no-prenup marital contract* is extremely unpredictable in its application, partly because the couple's married legal relationship would generally be subject to the laws of the state, or foreign country, where the married couple ultimately wind up residing as such laws may exist at the time. In a highly mobile society, this unpredictability often provides an impetus for the couple to negotiate the terms of their marriage themselves, instead of leaving the terms of their marriage to the vagaries of the various state law systems. Before a couple enters into a marriage, with or without negotiating a prenup, they should have some awareness of the contractual nature of a marriage and the legal consequences of entering into the marital relationship. Moreover, a couple contemplating negotiating a prenup should familiarize themselves with the likely default laws that would apply if they do not enter into a prenup, so they have some understanding of what they would obtain, or give up, if they enter into a negotiated prenuptial agreement.

Overview of Different Default Legal Systems Absent a Prenup

The laws governing spousal rights and obligations vary tremendously from country to country and, within the United States, from state to state. As seen from the *fictional no-prenup marital contract* in Exhibit 8-A, without a prenuptial agreement the laws that apply to marital property division, support, or distribution will generally be the laws of the state where the couple eventually reside, which may not be the state where they got married. For example, a couple who flies to Las Vegas for their wedding, but who live their entire marriage in Florida will be subject to the laws of Florida in the case of divorce or death. Moreover, even if a couple gets married in the state where they have been living, absent a prenuptial agreement, they cannot simply rely on that state's laws. For example, a couple who marries in Florida where they live at the time but then move to California and live there would generally be subject to the laws of California in the case of divorce or death.[2]

Common Law States and Community Property States

The United States has two general legal systems of marital property ownership: (1) common law and (2) community property. The vast majority of U.S. states (41 of the 50) are common law states. These common law states derived their legal system of marital property from the English common law legal system. The remaining nine states are community property states. Those states are Arizona, California, Idaho, Louisiana, Nevada, New Mexico, Texas, Washington, and Wisconsin.[3] Although only nine of the fifty U.S. states are community property states, two of those states (California and Texas) are particularly populous states. Accordingly, approximately one-third of the U.S. population resides under a community property regime. The community property regime derives from the civil law system and came to the U.S. primarily by way of French and Spanish settlers.

Common Law States

In the forty-one common law states, marital status alone does not affect ownership of property earned during an ongoing intact marriage. Rather, during the marriage, in common law states, each spouse is the separate owner of all he or she earns during the marriage and the person whose sole name appears on the title of property (e.g., name on deed to a vacation house or the title to a car), is deemed the owner of that property even if that person is married.[4] Assume Sam and Sally are married and reside in a common law state. Sam receives a substantial holiday bonus at work. As he is leaving his office, he notices a car sale at the dealership next door. He sees a little sports car, purchases it with his bonus check, and puts the title to the car solely in his name. In a common law state, Sam is deemed the sole owner of the car during their marriage. Also, in common law states, each spouse is the separate owner of all he or she earns during the marriage. In the event of a divorce, however, ownership and title do not control division of property in a common law state. This separate title-based ownership system only applies during the ongoing marriage. If the couple divorces in a common law state, the state's divorce laws generally determine the ownership of the property. Also, upon death, the common law states generally provide rights to the surviving spouse beyond his or her separate property.

Common Law States— Equitable Distribution upon Divorce

The laws for dividing property at divorce in common law states vary from state to state, but they all use the general notion of *equitable distribution*, whereby the courts have authority to divide property equitably between the spouses getting divorced. While all of the common law states use *equitable distribution* for divorce, the common law states apply two very different systems for equitable distribution, namely, the *all property* and the *dual property* systems. As the name implies, under the *all property* system, used in a few common law states, upon divorce, the court divides any property owned by either spouse. That is, in *all property* equitable distribution jurisdictions, the divorce courts take into account all of the property of the two spouses, regardless of when or how it was acquired or which spouse held title to the property, and attempt to divide that total equitably between the spouses. By contrast, under the *dual property* system, property is categorized as either *non-marital property* or *marital property* and only *marital property* is subject to equitable distribution.[5] Generally, in *dual property* states, property acquired prior to the marriage by either spouse and property acquired by gift or inheritance by either spouse, is deemed *non-marital* property and is not subject to equitable distribution. On the other hand, property purchased or earned during the marriage is *marital property* to be divided equitably upon divorce. In some of the dual property states, however, *non-marital* property could still be divided between the couple, if the court finds that fairness (equity) requires it.

The underlying nuances for equitable distribution are complex and vary significantly among the common law states. For example, under the dual property system of equitable distribution, questions often arise as to when property is actually *marital property* and when it is *non-marital property*. In some dual property states, for example, potential future earnings tied to professional licenses (e.g., medical or legal licenses) or educational degrees are deemed marital property.[6] In other dual property states, such professional licenses are not deemed marital property. Also, although the property one of the spouses had before the marriage is usually not considered marital property, some pre-marital property could be considered marital property. For example, when marital earnings were used to improve or repair the pre-marital property, or to pay debts on the property, or even if the couple lived in or otherwise used the pre-marital property during their marriage, such property, or a portion of it, could be considered marital property.[7] In addition, non-marital property could become marital property by commingling the property in a way such that it cannot be distinguished from other marital property. For example, if a wife received an inheritance of $500,000 from her mother, and instead of keeping the amount in a separate account, deposited it in a joint account with her husband or combined it with marital funds to purchase property or pay marital debts or expenses, the inheritance could become marital property. The percentage of the pre-marital property deemed to be marital property and subject to division varies by state and would ultimately be determined by a court. Issues also arise in determining whether property is marital or non-marital, for property obtained after the couple separates but before divorce. For example, in some states a married couple continues to accumulate marital property until they divorce, but in other states a separation stops the accumulation of marital property.[8]

The equitable distribution system is also somewhat difficult to predict because the system is intended to divide the marital property fairly (*equitably*), which may, but may not, be equally between the two. Courts often take several factors into consideration in making the determination as to the equitable distribution. The factors may include the:

- Length of the marriage;
- Age, health, and mental fitness of each party;
- Standard of living established during the marriage;
- Future earning power of the parties;
- Financial condition of each party;
- Contributions to the marriage of each party;
- Needs of the children (if any); and
- Any other factors the court may feel is relevant.[9]

Diagram - Common Law States

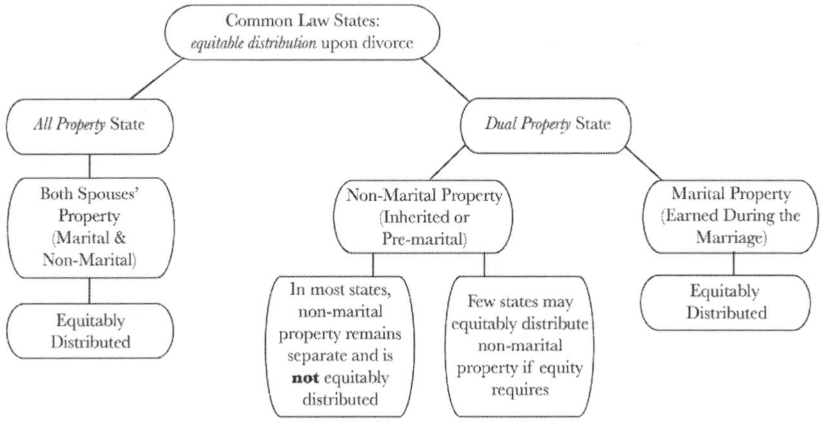

Common Law States— Surviving Spouse's Rights upon Death

When one of the spouses dies in a common law state, absent a prenuptial agreement, the state's intricate rules regarding a surviving spouse's rights to the other's property at death would apply. All common law states allow a spouse to leave his or her property by validly executed will to the other. Without a valid will, the state's laws regarding dying without a will (referred to as dying intestate) apply. Surviving spouses have favored status in most states when their spouse dies intestate. In many states, if the children of the decedent and of the surviving spouse are children of both, the surviving spouse of an intestate estate inherits the entire estate.

Issues arise, however, when a spouse would prefer to leave some or all of his or her property at death to someone other than the surviving spouse. What happens, for example, when a spouse chooses to leave some, or all, of her property to her children from a prior marriage or to her parents instead of to her surviving spouse? All U.S. common law states, except for Georgia, provide that a spouse who was disinherited or who was not satisfied with the property distribution in their deceased spouse's estate plan can choose to receive a surviving spouse's elective share of the deceased spouse's property as provided by state law. The state laws vary as to what percentage (e.g., 50%, 1/3rd, 30%, etc.) a surviving spouse might be entitled to and which assets are included in determining the decedent's estate for spousal elective share purposes. In addition to the right to claim a spousal elective share (sometimes referred to as a forced share), a surviving spouse in many common law states also has significant other rights upon death of a spouse. For example, a surviving spouse could claim a share of the deceased spouse's estate as a pretermitted spouse when the deceased spouse had written a will before marrying the surviving spouse. In addition, surviving spouses often have rights to homestead (usually the right to remain for life in the family home), and to certain exempt property, and family allowance under state laws. The laws governing these various rights differ from state to state.

Often couples enter into a marriage with children from a prior relationship. These couples may mistakenly believe that they can ensure their children's interests in their estates simply by drafting a will. Absent a prenuptial agreement, however, the state's default laws on death may provide a very different result. For example, assume Alice, a financial analyst, has two children from her prior marriage. She marries Bob, who has not been previously married and has no children. Bob has a steady job as an accountant and is financially independent. After the marriage, Alice and Bob agree, but do not put the agreement in writing, that if Alice should die her property should go to her two children. Alice writes a will leaving her property to her children. At Alice's death, despite Alice's faith in him and despite Alice's will, Bob could change his mind about Alice's children and legally take his spousal elective share of her estate as provided under state law. The amount Bob could get varies from state to state but could be as much as half of Alice's estate, which she planned would go to her children.

Community Property States

There are numerous differences among the community property states, but some generalizations are available. Generally, the nine community property states agree that a spouse's *separate property* includes (1) property owned prior to the marriage and (2) property acquired during the marriage by gift or inheritance. Similarly, the *community* property states commonly define "community property" as a catchall of all property acquired during the marriage that is *not* separate property.[10]

Significant consequences flow from this categorization. In a community property state, upon the marriage each spouse acquires an ownership interest in one-half of the property the other spouse earns during the marriage, regardless of how the property is nominally titled. For example, if one spouse earns an annual salary of $200,000, the other spouse is deemed to own one-half of those earnings, $100,000, by virtue of the marriage.

Similarly, property purchased with marital earnings is community property and owned one-half each. For example, assume Sam and Sally, the couple we met before, were married in and resided in a community property state. Sam still wants that little sports car. He purchases it with his bonus from work and puts title in his sole name. In a community property state, since the purchase was after they were married and from his earnings, Sam and Sally are deemed one-half owners each automatically even though Sam alone paid for it and only Sam's name is on the title.

The theory often used to explain the community property regime is the partnership theory of marriage. The partnership theory recognizes that the economic success of a partnership is due to the efforts and contributions of both partners in the partnership, whether or not both are earning wages.[11] Even if one spouse is not earning wages, that spouse's non-monetary contributions are just as significant to the success of the partnership as the wage-earning spouse's contributions. For example, Morgan is a stay at home parent whose primary responsibility is care of the children and managing the household. Her spouse, Dylan, works in an engineering firm. The partnership theory of community property deems each spouse's efforts as contributing equally to the economic success of the partnership. In its best light, the community property regime allows the spouses the flexibility to determine their roles in the marriage in ways that are optimal to the success of the family, even when such a division might otherwise be economically detrimental to one of the spouses (e.g., the one who taking a break from a career).

Community Property States— Division of Property on Divorce

Generally, the various community property states provide that upon divorce each spouse keeps his or her *separate* property but divide *community property.* Where the community property states differ, however, is in how they divide the *community* property upon divorce. In some community property states upon divorce, the *community property* is split equally, such that each spouse obtains one-half.[12] In the other community property states upon divorce, however, instead of splitting the community property one-half each, the courts in those states divide the community property based on *equitable division.* Thus, in those community property states there could be an unequal disposition of the community property, if the court determines that an unequal split of the community property is equitable.[13]

Diagram - Community Property States

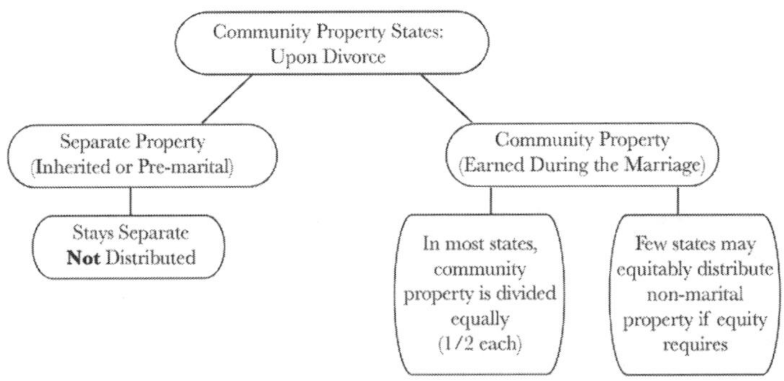

Death—Community Property States

The death of a spouse ends the marriage and therefore the community. Generally, in community property states at death a spouse can dispose of (1) his or her separate property and (2) one-half of the community property. Recall that in a community property state immediately upon the marriage each spouse acquires an ownership interest in one-half of the marital property.[14] Because a surviving spouse in a community property state was already recognized as a partner in the marriage by virtue of obtaining his or her one-half of the community property, the surviving spouse does not also have any rights to elect against the deceased spouse's will.

Moving from Community Property States to Common Law States

Spouses who acquired property while living in a community property state (e.g., California) might later move to a common law state (e.g., Florida). Even though the couple is moving to a common law state, some of their property may retain its community property status.[15] Several common law states have enacted statutes based on the Uniform Disposition of Community Property Rights at Death Act. Generally, these statutes serve to maintain each spouse's legal rights in the property that was community property before the couple moved to a common law state. The idea behind these statutes is that most persons who move from one state to another do so for reasons that have nothing to do with the community property system or common law system (e.g., they move for job opportunities or family reasons) and they did not intend to change the community property characteristics of their previously acquired properties when they moved. Generally, these statutes presume that property purchased during marriage while a spouse was resident in a community property state remains community property even though the spouses move to a separate property state. If a spouse in such a separate property state owned such original community property at death, one-half of such community property would generally be distributed pursuant to the decedent's will or the laws of intestacy. The other one-half of the original community property would be deemed to be the property of the surviving spouse. There are instances, however, in which property loses its community property status.

Moving from Common Law States to Community Property States

A move from a common law state (e.g., New York) to a community property state (e.g., Arizona) may create significant issues for a surviving spouse. Unlike common law states, the community property states do not give the surviving spouse the right to a spousal elective share at death. A couple who spent most of their marriage in a common law state and only a couple of months or years in a community property state may have little community property. At death, the surviving spouse in that scenario would have little community property and yet no right to take against the deceased spouse's will.

Other Issues Involving Community Property

While earned income is considered community property, the nine community property states differ in their rules on many other significant issues, some of which are noted below. The following discussion is helpful in two ways: (1) if a couple decides not to negotiate a prenup they should recognize that these issues would be addressed by their states' default law in instances of divorce or death and (2) if the couple decides to negotiate a prenup they could look at these topics and determine if and how they want to agree on their resolution.

Income from Separate Property: There are two different rules among the community property states for whether income, such as dividends, interest, or rent, derived during the marriage from otherwise separate property remains separate or is deemed community. For example, assume one of the spouses had owned stock prior to the marriage and that separate property stock generated dividends during the marriage. Some community property states would treat the dividend income that was generated during the marriage from that separate property as still generally deemed separate. By contrast, if the spouses resided in other community property states, the dividend income that arose during the marriage from that separate property is treated as community property.

Comingled Property: In a community property state, there is a strong presumption that property acquired during a marriage is community and is owned one-half each. On the other hand, if one spouse has separate property prior to the marriage and sells that property during the marriage the proceeds from the sale of the separate property would continue to be separate as long as the spouse does not combine the proceeds with community property. Issues arise, however, when separate and community property are combined, commonly referred to as comingled property. The community property states have developed varying laws for determining when property is deemed comingled and the consequences of such characterization.

Debt Payments on Separate Property: If separate property was burdened with a debt and community property was used to pay down the debt, many community property states provide that the separate property remains separate, but that the community property used to pay the debt must be reimbursed. Other community property states, however, would not deem the property as remaining separate but instead apportion the property pursuant to their state laws.

Life Insurance Proceeds: When community property is used to pay premiums on a life insurance contract purchased before the marriage, in some community property states the proceeds of the life insurance policy would remain separate, but the community would be entitled to reimbursement for the amount paid as premiums.[16] In other community property states, the insurance policy proceeds would be divided pro rata based on the allocation of monies used to pay the premiums. If the life insurance policy is a term life policy, many of the community property states characterize the proceeds by focusing on whether the premiums for the most recent term were paid from community or separate funds.

Creditors: The community property states differ on when creditors can reach community property. In some community property states a creditor of one spouse can reach the community property, even if the debt was incurred by one of the spouses prior to the marriage. Separate property is generally, however, not subject to the creditors of the other spouse. In some states, debts incurred during the marriage are presumed to be community debt.[17]

Personal Injury Recovery: In some community property states the amounts recovered from a claim or judgment for a personal injury sustained during the marriage are deemed separate property except for amounts designated to compensate for lost earnings. In other community property states, the amounts received in satisfaction of a claim or judgment from a personal injury is community property, if the injury occurred during the marriage.

Management: Generally, during an ongoing marriage, each spouse has equal rights to manage, control, and dispose of the community property. In some community property states, however, gifts of community property (other than to the other spouse) require the other spouse's consent.[18]

Alimony and Spousal Support in Common Law and Community Property States

Both community property and common law states could award alimony or maintenance. Generally, the law of the state where the couple resides determines the type of alimony available to the parties. Several states have structured their laws on alimony in part on the Uniform Marriage and Divorce Act (UMDA). Generally, under the UMDA alimony awards are in the amounts and for the periods of time the court deems appropriate and fair after considering all relevant factors including:

- The financial resources of the spouse requesting the support;
- The time the requesting spouse needs to obtain education or job training in order to find employment;
- The standard of living during the marriage;
- The age, health, and mental fitness of the spouse seeking the amount;
- The length of the marriage; and
- The ability of the other spouse to make the maintenance payments.[19]

Courts have great flexibility in applying these factors. Moreover, while equitable distribution of property and alimony are distinct concepts, in some states the courts combine the concepts. For example, where the equitable distribution of marital property results in a fairly sizeable estate for each party, the courts might decide that each is adequately self-sufficient and that there is no need for an award of alimony or maintenance.

Prenuptial Agreements

After reading through the overview of the state default laws and discovering that they are not well tailored to their marriage goals, a couple might decide to enter into a prenuptial agreement.

Enforceability of Prenuptial Agreements

Prenuptial agreements are enforceable in every state and rarely set aside by a court. In the early days of prenuptial agreements, when they were not as common, the courts often held them invalid under the theory that most prenups were simply tools the rich used to take advantage of a less financially secure spouse. It was believed that the wealthier spouse was able to coerce his partner into signing a prenup and that these agreements effectively promoted divorce. However, today, with full recognition of prenups by all states, prenups are looked upon more favorably, as a planning mechanism for the couple, not only if they divorce but also in the event of death of a spouse.

Nevertheless, prenups are not impenetrable and are subject to being set aside under certain conditions. For example, a prenup is subject to being set aside for the following reasons.[20]

No fair and reasonable financial disclosure: Best practices would have both parties fully disclose all of their income, assets, and liabilities. Without proper disclosure, the agreement is subject to being set aside by a court.[21] False information or misleading information will not constitute proper disclosure.

Not properly executed: A prenup must be in writing and signed by both parties. It is best for the parties to hire separate attorneys to draft their prenup, so as to avoid a future claim by a spouse that there was a lack of independent advice or a conflict of interest.

Illegal or invalid provisions or provisions against public policy: Provisions that are illegal or against public policy should not be included in a prenuptial agreement. For example, a provision in the agreement stating that the couple will not accurately report their earnings in order to avoid their income tax obligations would be illegal and unenforceable. A provision that would be against public policy would be a prenuptial agreement provision that restricts child support, custody or visitation rights.

Time pressure: Both parties should have time to properly consider and review a prenuptial agreement. A prenuptial agreement signed right before walking down the aisle is subject to being set aside for duress. A spouse may be able to make an argument that her spouse pressured her to sign the prenup or he would cancel the wedding. However, if the parties were represented by separate counsel who had advised their clients thoroughly as to the contents of the agreement, the last-minute signing may not have much effect in invalidating the agreement.

Unconscionable: If the prenuptial agreement basically allows one spouse to prosper while the other spouse suffers great harm, the agreement may be set aside as unconscionable. Generally, finding that a prenup agreement is unconscionable is difficult, since the agreement is entered into in part for the purpose of spouses giving up certain rights. However, even if the initial agreement was permissible, a court may consider a material change in circumstance after the agreement is entered into that may cause unanticipated economic hardship to a party. In this circumstance, a court may set aside certain provisions or the entire agreement.

Benefits of Prenuptial Agreements

A prenup may be beneficial for many couples depending on their circumstances. For example, for spouses who contemplate that they might move to another state, or another country, with a different set of laws, a prenuptial agreement provides some certainty against changes in the marital laws of the place where they currently reside and the places where they may move. Additionally, couples may want to have a prenuptial agreement, if they happen to fall into any of these following common scenarios.

1) One or both of the future spouses have children from prior relationships and want to provide for them;
2) The future spouses have assets acquired prior to their marriage or anticipated through inheritance;
3) A business partnership or company agreement requires a future spouse to have a prenuptial agreement in place so the business can maintain business confidences during divorce actions;
4) A future spouse already has substantial retirement benefits, stock options, profit sharing, or other employee benefits;
5) One of the future spouses has significant outstanding debt;
6) One or both of the future spouses have been so traumatized by drawn-out divorce proceedings (either their own or a family member's) that only a thoughtfully negotiated prenuptial agreement with their prospective spouse will ease their concerns about entering into a marriage;
7) A family trust requires a future spouse to have a prenuptial agreement in place as a condition to receiving the benefits from that trust; and
8) A future spouse expects to become, or is already, involved in a family-owned business or already has a business.

While most of these common scenarios are straightforward, both the family trust and the family-owned business as an impetus for a prenup, require more explanation. While the newly engaged couple may not want to consider the possibility of divorce or death, their parents may be well aware of the risks. Parents (on one or both sides) may insist on setting up some financial protection for their child before the wedding. Even if the parents are excited about the upcoming marriage and thrilled to be welcoming their future son or daughter-in-law into their family, they may be wise enough to know that life sometimes does not always go as planned or hoped.

Parents who worry about the possibility that their child might divorce may decide that they should not simply leave that child an inheritance outright through their wills.[22] The parents might instead set up a family trust for that child with prenuptial requirements included in the trust document.[23] The parents could, for example, set up a family trust naming their child as the trust beneficiary but provide that the beneficiary could obtain trust assets only if he or she has a prenuptial agreement in place. The family trust could contain language such as the following:

> Notwithstanding the foregoing distribution provisions, if a beneficiary under the trust marries after the trust is established or is married when the trust is established, the Trustee shall not distribute income or principal from the trust to or for the benefit of the beneficiary until the Trustee is provided a copy of a valid prenuptial, postnuptial, or similar agreement whereby the spouse or intended spouse has waived rights to income and principal from the beneficiary's trust.

Notice that this example prenuptial-agreement-trust-clause is not very strict. In this example, the trust document only requires that the marital agreement contain language waiving the spouse's interest, if any, in the family trust property itself. It does not require the agreement to have the spouse waive rights to the trust beneficiary's non-trust property. If the parents prefer, they could tailor the family trust language to say that the trust beneficiary only benefits from the family trust if the beneficiary shows the trustee a copy of a broadly worded and executed prenuptial agreement where the trust beneficiary's spouse has waived *all rights*. The family trust could even include a sample prenuptial agreement and provide that the beneficiary's prenuptial agreement should substantially conform to the sample. A middle ground might have the family trust provide that the trust beneficiary show the trustee that the spouse has waived rights to the trust and waived rights to elect against the trust beneficiary's estate.

This approach of having a family trust with an embedded prenuptial agreement requirement may seem somewhat elaborate. It is becoming more popular, however, because parents are increasingly finding that can no longer rely on the family trust system alone to protect their children's inheritance in the event their children get divorced. In the past, parents focusing on estate planning thought that as long as they did not include their prospective son or daughter-in-law as a trust beneficiary, their children's beneficial interests in the family trust could not be reached by a former son or daughter-in-law in cases of divorce. Until fairly recently, this assumption may have been correct. In the past, if a family trust did not name the children's spouses as beneficiaries, and the trust document gave the trustee discretion on when and how to distribute trust assets to a trust beneficiary, the beneficiary's interest in the family trust while the assets were still in the trust,[24] would, in most states, have been protected from the beneficiary's creditors, including the beneficiary's former spouse's claims.

Recently, however, the laws surrounding a former spouse's access to family trusts at divorce have become much murkier, even in states with laws once viewed as designed to protect such discretionary beneficial trust interests.[25]

Moreover, if a state uses an *all property* approach to equitable distribution, then the beneficiary's interest in the trust could be subject to division. Some courts may count the beneficiary's interest in the trust as the beneficiary's property, even if that beneficiary's interest in the trust is dependent on the discretion of a trustee. Even states that use a *dual property* approach may look at the beneficiary's interest in the family trust in determining how to divide property upon divorce of that beneficiary. While most states using the *dual property* system for equitable distribution continue to treat inherited wealth as separate and not subject to equitable division during divorce, courts may look at assets in a family trust in deciding how to divide marital non-trust assets.

A family trust with a prenuptial agreement requirement serves several purposes. First, it increases the likelihood that upon a divorce the trust beneficiary will be able to keep the trust assets. Second, it may help to protect the parents and their estate plans from being dragged into their child's messy divorce litigation. Even if a former daughter or son-in-law could not ultimately reach assets in the family trust under state law, absent a prenuptial agreement waiver, a divorce court might issue subpoenas for the parent's estate planning documents or otherwise try to delve into the parents' assets during a divorce. Finally, perhaps the most important benefit of the prenuptial requirement being embedded in the parent's trust is that it allows the about-to-be-married child to raise the topic of a prenuptial agreement with his or her fiancé and blame the idea on the folks.

Another impetus for a prenup includes protecting a family business. Parents and other owners of a closely held business may want to protect disruption of an ongoing business by insisting that any equity owners have prenuptial agreements in place. Although a buy-sell agreement itself would probably give the company a right of first refusal in cases of involuntary stock transfers (such as in a divorce), the added feature of the prenup might help to prevent involving the company in divorce litigation.

The above list of scenarios for prenups is not exhaustive. There are, of course, numerous other reasons why couples may wish to negotiate a prenup, including simply facilitating open discussions and nurturing healthy communications.

Standard Coverage of a Prenup

Prenuptial agreements can be relatively simple or quite complex but generally include provisions for determining each spouse's rights in the event of divorce, separation, or death. See Exhibit 8-B at the end of this chapter for a sample prenuptial agreement. In their prenup, the couple could agree not to seek a share in each other's property in those events or to only seek a share that is different from the one they could claim under their state's default rules. For example, the agreement could provide that certain property, such as a future spouse's pre-marital home or business will remain separate even if the couple divorced. They may agree that income or appreciation on separate property should stay separate or alternatively that income or appreciation should be deemed marital. They might agree to keep separate all life insurance proceeds, even if the premiums were paid by marital earnings. They may wish to borrow the community property concept that one-half of all marital earnings belong to each spouse, regardless of who earns the property or how it is titled.

With regard to death, the prenuptial agreement could cover property passing by will, property passing if a spouse dies without a will (intestate), or property passing in other ways including by trust or by rights of survivorship. A future spouse could agree to waive rights to spousal elective share, intestate share, pretermitted share, homestead, exempt property, and family allowance. Waivers of these death-type rights are more common when one or both of the future spouses have children from a prior relationship. A spouse who wants to preserve property for children of the first marriage may ask the other spouse to waive some or all of these rights.

In addition to handling property division at death or divorce, the future spouses could in most states waive or determine support in their prenuptial agreement. They could, for example, waive any rights to such support, particularly if both spouses are capable of and expect to continue working. Alternatively, the future spouses could agree to certain support, especially if one spouse might not be earning income for some years.

It is important to note that state laws vary on what they permit to be included in prenups and how they must be executed. The Uniform Premarital and Marital Property Act ("Act") has been adopted in a majority of states in whole or in part. Its purpose is to bring "clarity and consistency" to the prenuptial agreements made between couples that modify or waive rights at death or divorce. The Act recognizes that prenuptial agreements may contain many different legal terms and formats, and since courts will strive to enforce them, it is beneficial to have some uniformity. The Act defines certain legal terms and provides what is generally permitted and prohibited in such agreements.

Other Provisions in a Pre-Nuptial Agreement

In addition to the standard provisions, couples may wish to tailor their prenup to address their particular goals and objectives. These additional provisions, such as lifestyle provisions, may be outside the scope of typical contracts and, accordingly, they may be subject to more scrutiny by a court and harder to enforce.

Lifestyle Provisions in Prenuptial Agreements

Prenuptial agreements are very effective in solidifying a couple's expectations concerning issues such as the allocation of finances, inheritance, and business-related interests. However, couples may also find it tempting to include conduct requirements for their married life through a prenuptial agreement. They may think, "As long as we're drafting this document, let's put everything we can think of that may become a problem in our marriage. Then we will know exactly what is expected of each other." This kind of sentiment is probably the reason behind so-called lifestyle provisions in prenuptial agreements. These provisions are meant to control behavior. Some of these lifestyle provisions may be unenforceable in court, but some couples believe that by putting the provisions in writing, the effect will be that a future spouse may, at least, stop and think before engaging in the specific conduct. Some typical lifestyle provisions include the following.

Infidelity Provisions: A very popular lifestyle provision, the infidelity provision, requires a spouse to pay a fine or other penalty if unfaithful.[26] Reportedly, actor Catherine Zeta-Jones has such a clause in her prenuptial agreement with her husband and fellow actor Michael Douglas, providing a $5 million dollar bonus to her for each time he is unfaithful.[27] These provisions are usually included in circumstances where a future spouse has a known history of infidelity.

Weight Provisions: Prenuptial agreements have been known to contain provisions assessing monetary penalties if a spouse gains weight during the marriage. Some agreements penalize the spouse based on the amount of the gain (e.g., over 10 lbs.). Other provisions seek to have the spouse maintain a certain maximum weight and penalizes weight gain over that amount (e.g., 120 lbs.). The weight limit provisions may even specify the dates and times for the weigh-ins. Hopefully, a spouse will not have to weigh-in immediately following Thanksgiving dinner.

In-law Provision: Prenuptial agreements may attempt to limit or restrict the time a couple spends with their in-laws. For example, a provision may bar a mother-in-law from sleepovers. Another provision might limit a couple's visits with their in-laws to no more than two consecutive days. Presumably, in-law jokes are still permitted. Similar provisions may also limit the time a future spouse could spend with certain family or friends.

Drug Testing Provision: For a spouse with a known or suspected drug problem, the random drug testing clause is a common addition to the prenuptial agreement. Typically, if the test is positive, a monetary penalty is imposed. The sample collecting procedure is usually left up the couple.

Social Media Provisions: Rapidly gaining popularity, social media provisions typically restrict spouses from disparaging each other on social media. Other social media provisions restrict posting of nude or unflattering photos of a spouse or forbid posting anything about the spouse without prior approval by the spouse.[28]

Baby Payout Provision: In this type of provision, a baby boom means a big payout for one of the spouses. This clause provides a monetary reward for each child born. Beyoncé and Jay-Z presumably had such a clause. In the event of divorce, Beyoncé would allegedly collect five million dollars for each child born of the marriage. [29] While this clause sounds like child support, determining child custody and support issues are decided by a judge and prohibited in prenuptial agreements. These provisions are typically meant to promote procreation, but the monetary incentive may not accomplish the goal and may in fact backfire. For example, if one spouse wants more children and the other spouse thinks one is enough because the payout is just too expensive, would that spouse stop "trying" to procreate? It would be better for the couple to have a discussion about having children before marriage, and hopefully they will both put forth the necessary effort.

No Children Provision: The no children provision is the opposite of a pay per child provision. In this provision, the couple agrees not to have children. Enforcing this clause is difficult if not impossible.[30] Parents are legally responsible for the welfare of their children whether they "wanted" the child or not. Trying to assess a penalty for having a child may violate public policy.[31] Furthermore, it does not quite create a Hallmark memory for the child. While it is disheartening for a child to find out he or she was not wanted, it is devastating for the child to find out that mom or dad has to pay a penalty for the child being born. If one party truly desires not to have children, and the other does, the couple should sit down and discuss the matter thoroughly before deciding to get married. A prenup may not be the appropriate vehicle to address the issue of their issue.

Religious Provisions: Couples may wish to put in the prenuptial agreement a provision about their religious practices or the practices of their children. This may be especially desirable in marriages of mixed faiths, or in marriages where one spouse is more devout in their religious practice than the other. For example, in a marriage where one spouse is Jewish and the other spouse is Christian, the couple may include a clause that their children will be raised in the Jewish faith. In that clause would be an explanation as to what "being raised in the Jewish faith" would entail. Specifically, the couple may agree that the children will attend temple services or religious school. While adults may include in a prenuptial agreement what religious holidays they wish to celebrate, such restrictions on children are typically unenforceable. Courts have deemed such provisions as imposing an unconstitutional restraint on the religious freedom of the child, reasoning that a preference for a certain religion is too restrictive on a child's right to choose how or if they want to engage in religious practice.[32]

Pet Provisions: Pets are considered by many couples as members of the family. As such, it is easy to see that a dispute as to where their "child" may reside after a divorce is a real concern. Although prenuptial agreements cannot decide custody and child support for human children, a couple can decide what to do about their animal child in case of divorce through a clause in the prenuptial agreement. Without a couple deciding custody of their pet in their prenuptial agreement, a court would likely award the pet to a spouse along the same terms as other property (e.g., one spouse gets the dog and the other spouse gets the smart TV). Furthermore, a pet could get caught up in a contentious divorce and the battle over custody could turn ugly. It may not be wise for couples to leave Fido's future up to a judge or to battle over their pet's future at the time of a divorce. Instead, it is best for the couple to decide their pet's future themselves while they are in a loving relationship.

In drafting a pet prenuptial agreement provision, the couple should determine with whom the pet will live, and who will pay for the medical and food costs associated with the pet. It is possible to have a shared custody clause, in which the couple agrees not only to split the costs associated with the pet, but also for the pet to be a part-time resident of both homes in case of divorce.

The prenuptial agreement clause works best if the couple owns the pet before marriage because it will be easier to decide that specific pet's fate should the couple divorce. However, if the couple anticipates obtaining a pet after marriage, the couple could draft a clause concerning any future pets.

Caution on Lifestyle Provision

When negotiating a prenup, it may be tempting to include some of these lifestyle provisions. However, a couple should consider whether they really want to live their married life monitoring their spouse's conduct and enforcing penalties or rewards as set forth in the prenuptial agreement. The couple should talk about these issues and decide before marriage if their lifestyles are compatible.

Attorney's Fees in Prenuptial

Once a couple has agreed upon the terms in a prenuptial agreement, they are hopeful that in the event of divorce, the agreement will be enforced and divorce proceedings will be a formality rather than a battle. In order to ensure that the agreement is enforced and unchallenged, some couples include a clause, which uses payment of attorney's fees as a disincentive for challenging the agreement. One method would be to have a clause stating that any party challenging the prenup will have to pay both spouses' attorney's fees. Another less restrictive clause would reward a spouse who successfully wins a challenge to a prenup by having the losing spouse pay the winning spouse's attorney's fees.

While state law will dictate whether such provisions are enforceable, generally the losing spouse pays provisions are likely to be upheld. However, an agreement that restricts either party from challenging the prenuptial agreement by punishing the challenger is likely to be found by a court to be a restraint on a party's due process right of access to the courts.

Mediation or Arbitration Provisions

As with many negotiations, couples may choose to limit or avoid courts as much as possible by having their divorce resolved through mediation or binding arbitration. Although often used interchangeably, mediation and binding arbitration are not the same procedure. In mediation, parties jointly hire a neutral third party, called a mediator, to hear their dispute.[33] The mediator then offers recommendations on how the parties may resolve the dispute. However, the parties can ultimately decide whether to follow the mediator's recommendations or not, and then proceed to court to finalize the divorce. In binding arbitration, a neutral third party called an arbitrator, hears the parties' dispute, and then makes a binding decision as to the resolution of the divorce, much like a judge would do in a court of law.

There are benefits to including a mediation or arbitration clause. First, these procedures allow the parties to decide on a mediator and arbitrator, whereas a judge is randomly assigned to their case. Second, the costs associated with hiring mediators and arbitrators are usually much less than those associated with a lengthy court battle. Third, an effective mediator or arbitrator will be skilled at hearing both sides of a dispute, making efficient use of time, and keeping the peace. A court proceeding is often a formalized, time-consuming process whereby the judge has little time to sort through a myriad of issues. In fact, many courts recommend or require a couple to go through mediation before the court renders a final decision.

These alternative systems may even be combined. A couple may choose to include both mediation and arbitration in their prenuptial agreement. For example, a couple may have a clause agreeing to first go to mediation, and if that process does not work, to then go to binding arbitration. Of course, while mediation or arbitration may be a more efficient process, there is no guarantee that the process will run smoothly or that the mediator or arbitrator will be as skilled as a judge. These alternative dispute resolution provisions in prenuptial agreements are typically upheld as providing the couple alternatives to lengthy court proceedings.

Sunset and Escalator Provisions

One reason a couple may be eager to have a prenuptial agreement is because of a nagging doubt that their marriage may not last "until death do them part." Couples might believe, however, that if their marriage lasts a certain number of years (e.g., 5 or 10 years) the prenuptial agreement would no longer be necessary. A sunset clause is basically an expiration date for the prenuptial agreement. Chris Rock reportedly had such a clause in his prenuptial agreement with his spouse, Malaak Compton Rock.[34] Under the terms of their sunset clause, their prenuptial agreement would "sunset" on the couple's 18th wedding anniversary. But unfortunately, they did not ride off into the sunset on a road of marital bliss. After 20 years of marriage, Chris filed for divorce. Both Chris and Malaak agreed the prenuptial agreement was no longer valid due to the sunset clause. Subsequently, Malaak sought a division of Chris Rock's purportedly $70 million net worth. Malaak alleged she had given up her career to care for their children and that he should pay her a significant amount of that $70 million so that she can maintain her lifestyle. The battle led to a messy tabloid divorce.

Chris Rock's divorce is not a typical outcome of having a sunset provision. In the best of cases, the sunset clause terminates the prenuptial agreement but the long-term marriage is stable and the couple stays married. In other cases, the sunset clause could have the perverse effect of accelerating divorce. For example, a sunset clause effective in year five of the marriage may encourage a divorce in year four so that the prenuptial agreement is still valid.

There are many variations on sunset provisions. Some provisions, frequently called escalator provisions, do not offer a complete sunset of the agreement but reward a spouse for staying in the marriage over time.[35] Perhaps a better name for these provisions would be sunrise provisions, because they provide monetary rewards, or a greater division of assets, at designated years in the marriage.

Sunset provisions and their variations are attempts to reward longevity in a marriage. Unfortunately, they often encourage ending the marriage before the sunset date. It would be better for a couple to review their prenuptial agreement at various times during the marriage, or, if or when, circumstances change in their marriage to see if the prenup they entered into still reflects their wishes. A prenuptial agreement can always be amended or revoked by agreement of the couple. Placing a random time frame for altering or revoking the agreement is artificial. The sunset clause often becomes a total eclipse of the marriage.

Companion Documents

Couples negotiating prenups may realize that in addition to the prenup they want to execute additional documents to round out their marital or estate planning goals. Often the process of negotiating the prenup serves as the impetus for couples to also enter into related, or companion, agreements.

Trust Created by Fiancé

The previous discussion on trusts focused on trusts created by parents, grandparents, or other family members of the couple planning to wed. In other words, those were trusts created by a third party (e.g., the parents or grandparents). This section addresses trusts created by one of the two prospective spouses themselves. Before going any further, it helps to clarify that if a prospective spouse puts premarital assets into a trust and names himself or herself a trust beneficiary, that trust is generally referred to as a self-settled trust. In the vast majority of states, such a self-settled trust does not provide any more creditor protection (from future creditors including former spouses upon divorce), than not having the assets in a trust.[36] This section is not referring to such self-settled trusts. Rather, it discusses the possibility of one of the future spouses setting up a trust for the benefit of other people.

A future spouse may want to create a trust prior to the wedding with his or her own pre-marital assets and name third parties as beneficiaries. For example, a future spouse with children from a prior relationship may want to set up a trust with some separate assets prior to the wedding for the benefit of his or her children. This trust could be revocable or irrevocable. If the person setting up the trust (settlor) can change his or her mind about the trust (that is, if the trust is revocable) then, the assets could still count during equitable distribution particularly if the state uses an *all property* approach.[37] Even if the state does not use the *all property* approach, the assets in the revocable trust could be subject to equitable distribution to the extent they were comingled with marital funds. Setting up such a revocable trust, however, might help to create discipline in keeping the assets in the trust separate from marital assets. To reduce the risk that the assets in the trust for the children could be reached during a divorce, it helps to combine the trust with a prenuptial agreement whereby the new spouse waives any right to assets in the pre-marital children's trust.

Wills, Health Care Proxies, and Durable Powers of Attorney

In the process of negotiating their prenups, prospective spouses should consider the benefits of also executing needed companion documents such as wills, health care proxies, and durable powers of attorney. It is important that there is consistency and clarity among these related documents.

Prenuptial Agreement Problems

Instructions

After reading the legal principles and strategies in this chapter, you are now ready to apply those principles and strategies in negotiating practice problems using the TABLE method. Below are three problems involving couples negotiating prenuptial agreements. Each problem contains general information followed by confidential information in which each negotiator will choose a bargaining position on key issues. While the general information will be known by both sides, your bargaining position is confidential, although you may disclose it, or some of it, during the negotiation session if you choose to do so. Following the confidential information, you are given guidelines and suggestions as to how to approach the negotiations using the TABLE method.

After reviewing the information, you should complete the Tactical Planning Worksheet for the problem (found in Appendix A). For completing the worksheet, you are given the state in which the problem takes place to use as the basis for your legal research. Also, be sure to include your bargaining positions on your worksheets. After completing a Tactical Planning Worksheet for each problem, you and your counterpart are ready to conduct a negotiation in which you attempt to reach an agreement. While there is no time limit set for each problem, you should be able to complete the initial negotiations for each problem within 30 minutes.

After you complete each negotiation, you and your negotiating counterpart should exchange planning worksheets so that you can analyze the bargaining positions you and your counterpart planned for the negotiation. Finally, you should complete the Post-Negotiation Self-Reflection Worksheet (found in Appendix B).

For further explanation of the methodology for negotiating the problems, please refer to the Authors' Notes in Chapter 1 Introduction.

Overview of Problems 8-1, 8-2, and 8-3

Problem 8-1 is a two-person negotiation in which an engaged couple is attempting to negotiate the preliminary terms for their prenuptial agreement.

Problem 8-2 is a two-person negotiation based on the same parties and facts as Problem 8-1. However, you are asked to apply a different jurisdiction's laws than in Problem 8-1.

Problem 8-3 is a two-person negotiation involving attorneys negotiating on behalf of the engaged couple.

Problem 8-1

General Information

Assume for this problem that the couple resides in a common law, all property equitable distribution state for purposes of divorce. Also, assume that the state's law provides that at death the surviving spouse would be entitled to elect one-third of all the decedent's estate.

Isabella and Jake are engaged to be married. They are in their late 20's, both currently employed, and it is the first marriage for both. He earns $90,000 per year as a software engineer and she earns $110,000 as a financial analyst. They have no children from prior relationships. They have a dog that they adopted from an animal rescue group six months ago. Jake currently rents an apartment for $2,000 per month. Isabella lives in a condo valued at $500,000. She inherited the condo from her grandmother several years ago debt free. The condo maintenance fee is $150 per month, and the utilities are $250 per month. Carrying costs for the condo (real property taxes and insurance) are $4,000 per year. Jake plans to move into Isabella's condo after their wedding. In addition, Jake and Isabella have the following major assets:

Isabella	Jake
$75,000 in stocks	$50,000 in stocks
Engagement ring valued at $20,000	

Jake is expecting an inheritance of $1,000,000 from his grandfather. His grandfather is 90 years old and in poor health. Neither Jake nor Isabella have student loan debt or other debt.

Jake and Isabella have fully disclosed their assets to each other. Jake and Isabella both hope to have one child. Jake has expressed a preference to take a few years off from work when they have their child. Isabella prefers to continue working after the child is born because she is in line for a series of promotions at her job and is concerned that she would lose the opportunity for promotion if she takes time off.

Jake's parents and Isabella's parents are both divorced. They both witnessed the stress and emotional toll placed on their respective families during the divorce process. Neither of their parents had a prenuptial agreement and thus their respective divorces were time consuming and involved lengthy court proceedings. While Jake and Isabella believe their marriage will not end in divorce, they have decided to discuss entering into a prenuptial agreement, which will allow them to plan the distribution of their assets and property in the event of divorce or death. Although they believe that a prenuptial agreement is best to protect them in case their marriage is short term, they do not want the prenuptial agreement to last forever. Therefore, they have preliminarily decided to include a sunset clause in the prenuptial agreement and wish to negotiate the specifics of that clause.

They hope to be able to negotiate the preliminary terms of their prenuptial agreement before hiring lawyers. After they have reached consensus on the major issues, they have agreed to obtain separate lawyers to formalize the agreement and to work out any remaining issues. They also want to make sure that the agreement complies with the law and has full legal effect.

Confidential Information

The information contained in your planning worksheet is confidential. It includes your bargaining positions on the issues involved in the negotiations. This information should not be shared with the other party prior to the negotiation. For purposes of this problem, your planning worksheet should include your bargaining position on each of these issues:

A. The custody of the dog

B. The ownership (title) and disposition of the condominium

C. Jake's inheritance from his grandfather

D. Division of assets during and post marriage

E. Division of expenses during marriage

F. Time off from outside employment after birth of a child

G. The sunset clause

Although Jake and Isabella agreed to "discuss" the matter, they are realistically attempting to negotiate a prenuptial agreement.

Tactical Planning

Use the Tactical Planning Worksheet (Appendix A) to plan for the negotiation. Also, for guidance, see Exhibit 8-C, a sample worksheet for dissolution of marriage, at the end of this chapter. Although Exhibit 8-C would be used in a simplified divorce where the parties do not have a prenup, it provides a worksheet for listing assets and liabilities similar to a worksheet you may want to use in planning for a prenup negotiation.

Arranging the Negotiation

Jake and Isabella would need to arrange the logistics for negotiating their prenuptial agreement. They would need to decide where and when to meet and how much time to allocate to their initial discussion. For purposes of this negotiation, you can assume that Jake and Isabella have chosen an in-person, informal, setting such as his apartment or her condominium for the initial discussion.

Bargaining

Jake and Isabella, as an engaged couple, do not require traditional ice-breaking for their negotiation. It would seem somewhat awkward for Jake to begin the negotiation by asking ice-breaking questions such as, "How about that football game last night," or "We have been having some hot weather lately." However, they should avoid the temptation to jump right in with the first offers. Instead, they should spend some time communicating their hope that a prenuptial agreement will further strengthen their relationship and that their goal is to have a prenuptial agreement that is mutually beneficial.

Jake and Isabella should also make full use of their planning worksheet during the bargaining phase. However, neither of them should feel the other is "hiding" something on the worksheet for several reasons. First, in an arms-open negotiation such as this, engaged couples should feel that they are participating in an open discussion and there is no secret hidden agenda in the worksheets. Second, in the prenuptial agreement arena, as noted above, full disclosure is generally required for the agreement to be enforceable. If a partner appears to be hiding the worksheet, the other partner may interpret this conduct as attempting to hide assets.

Once the couple begins the process of exchanging offers, counteroffers, and concessions, it may be tempting for Jake or Isabella to quickly reject each other's proposals without due consideration under the belief that "no holds barred" responses will move the negotiations along. However, they may find that this approach can derail this negotiation in the same manner as any other negotiations. For example, if Jake or Isabella act dismissive in rejecting an offer, this behavior may quickly dissolve their collaborative approach.

In addition, the couple should stay calm, as the more emotional they get, the less likely they will be able to agree on matters. They should try not to interrupt each other and really listen to concerns expressed by the other. As in any other negotiation, they should feel free to ask questions, especially about their partner's concerns or objections. Jake and Isabella should also keep in mind that this is a collaborative process, not an adversarial one. In other words, they should think of this negotiation as if they are putting together a business, the business of husband and wife. They should not think of this negotiation as attempting to settle a lawsuit, as in husband v. wife. Further, just because they are engaged does not obviate the need for each of them to provide objective criteria to support their offers, counteroffers, and concessions. Providing the reasons and explanations supporting their offers will only encourage reciprocal communication facilitate working toward solutions.

Letting Go or Resolving

If Jake and Isabella come to an agreement on all or major issues, they should make an informal list of the terms they have agreed upon while it is fresh on their minds. They should next make an appointment to see their separate attorneys to formalize the agreement soon.

Although unlikely, if their negotiation has been a failure and they are deadlocked on all issues, it may be time for them to end the negotiation. This may occur after one discussion, or several discussions. It is best if Jake and Isabella try and work out their differences and take as much time as necessary to do so, but at some point, these negotiations may become non-productive and even destructive, especially if they begin to argue more than discuss. It should be their top priority to preserve their relationship.

If Jake and Isabella are deadlocked and believe further discussion on remaining issues would be more harmful than helpful, they may want to meet together with an attorney or a mediator to try and work out the remaining issues and formalize the agreement. They should end the negotiation by making a list of what is agreed upon, if anything, what is disputed and their positions on these disputed issues, and a list of questions they have for their attorneys. Their meeting with the attorney or mediator should be a collaborative approach to resolving the issues on the table, hopefully in a productive and amicable manner. If they do come to a basic agreement with the attorney or mediator, they should then consult separate attorneys to formalize the agreement as noted below.

If consulting with an attorney or mediator does not help to resolve their issues, they will need to consider the alternatives they have outlined in their planning worksheet. Most likely, their worksheets reflect two alternatives: 1) forgoing the prenuptial agreement and getting married or 2) forgoing the marriage for lack of a prenuptial agreement. While these alternatives seem quite drastic, if the prenuptial agreement is of utmost importance to either of them, and they are unable to come to an agreement, they will need to choose their best alternative.

Jake and Isabella should hire separate attorneys to execute the final agreement. Hiring an attorney to formalize the prenuptial agreement is required in some states, but, even if not required, it is important to have the expertise of an attorney to make sure the agreement complies with the law. Also, each party hiring their own attorney is evidence that this agreement was entered into independently and without coercion or outside influence from the other party. Having each party meet with an attorney will also be beneficial in that each will have the opportunity to ask questions of their attorney about the agreement and obtain the attorney's legal opinion about the terms preliminarily agreed upon. However, certainly by Jake and Isabella doing the initial negotiation, the visit to their attorneys will be much easier and less stressful than if they had begun the process of negotiating the prenup at their respective attorneys' offices.

Hopefully, their attorneys will hammer out the details, provide advice, and draft an agreement that will be acceptable to both parties. Once the agreement is formalized, Jake and Isabella can put the agreement away along with any stress endured with the process and continue planning their wedding.

Ethics and Equity

In this very arms-open relationship, one would expect the couple to act ethically and equitably in negotiating their prenuptial agreement. However, the manner in which they relate to each other has probably already been established, and thus each may believe they can predict if they will receive fair treatment from their spouse to be. The purpose of this book, however, is not to psychoanalyze their relationship, but to offer guidance in negotiating skills. The couple should keep in mind that if the past history of their relationship involves instances of dishonesty, they must be particularly diligent in pursuing honesty in prenup negotiations. Honesty is a key ingredient in drafting a prenuptial agreement, in that these agreements require proper disclosure of assets from both parties to be enforced. However, some couples may be tempted not to disclose all of their assets or to undervalue their assets, especially if one person has more assets. Even though they will pledge their love to their fiancé, money is a different issue for some and they want to maintain control of a portion of their assets by hiding it from their spouse. Or, they simply do not want to go through the meticulous preparation required to list and disclose all the assets. Whatever the reasons behind non-disclosure, parties who fail to fairly and reasonably disclose their finances, will likely be discovered and any protection they sought from a prenup could be lost. In essence, the nondisclosure may result in their worst fear. During divorce proceedings, all the hidden assets will likely be uncovered and when revealed, the prenuptial agreement may be set aside, leaving a court to decide how the assets would be distributed.

Couples should also make a great effort to treat each other equitably during this negotiating process. For example, if the couple's dynamic is for one of them to take control and make all decisions, that person should take a step back from their usual course of conduct in the negotiations. Because this is a negotiation, and the terms of the prenup must be mutually acceptable and agreed upon willingly by both parties, any suggestion to a court that one party was bullied into accepting terms may result in that agreement not being enforced due to coercion or duress.

Tactical Planning Worksheet Reveal

After concluding the negotiations, you and your counterpart should exchange your individual Tactical Planning Worksheets so that you both can see the bargaining positions you had planned to use during the negotiation. You should compare the two worksheets and see how far apart you were initially. Also, you should analyze whether and why you strayed from your worksheet, especially in the areas of offers and counteroffers. What positive aspects from your counterpart's worksheet do you wish you had included in yours?

Post-Negotiation Self-Reflection Worksheet

At the conclusion of the reveal session for this problem, be sure to complete the Post-Negotiation Self-Reflection Worksheet (found in Appendix B). Your Post-Negotiation Self-Reflection Worksheet should be completed individually and optimally within a short period of time after the Tactical Planning Worksheet reveal, while the negotiation session is fresh in your mind.

Problem 8-2

For this negotiation, assume the same facts and parties as in Problem 8-1. For this problem, however, assume that the couple resides in a common law, *dual property* equitable distribution state. Also, assume that the state's law for this problem provides that at death the surviving spouse is entitled to a one-third of all the decedent's estate.

How would this change the negotiation strategy for each party?

Problem 8-3

General Information

Assume for this problem that the couple resides in a community property state that divides community property equally.

Carl and Sharon are engaged to be married. They both have been married previously. Carl is 66 years old and has one child from his previous marriage. Sharon is 65 years old and has two children from her previous marriage. They wish to enter into a prenuptial agreement. Carl wishes to keep their assets separate and share the expenses jointly during their marriage. Sharon tentatively supports this plan, but believes there should be some distribution of Carl's assets to her since he is much wealthier than Sharon. However, they both agree that the bulk of their assets should be preserved for their children in the event of death or divorce.

Carl and Sharon currently live in separate apartments. Sharon rents her apartment and Carl owns his apartment. Sharon's lease is up in two months. At that time, they plan to marry and live in Carl's apartment. They have agreed that if Carl should predecease Sharon, Sharon will remain in the apartment rent free until her death if she wishes. Sharon has long-term health care coverage, at a cost of $7,000 per year in premiums. If she becomes incapacitated, she will be able to use her insurance to take care of her health needs. At Sharon's death, the apartment would pass to Carl's children. Carl and Sharon also have the following assets:

Carl	Sharon
Stock funds valued at $6,000,000	Stock funds valued at $1,000,000
Bond Funds valued at $3,000,000	Pension valued at $2,000,000
Apartment valued at $1,200,000	

Carl and Sharon have decided to have their respective attorneys work out the details and draft the prenuptial agreement. Therefore, you and your partner will assume the role of the attorneys who will negotiate the prenuptial agreement on behalf of their clients.

Confidential Information

You should assume that you have met with your client prior to the negotiation and have determined their bargaining positions on the following issues.

The bargaining positions on these issues are confidential and should not be shared with the other party prior to the negotiation. Please include your client's bargaining position on each of these issues on your planning worksheet.

A. Carl and Sharon's alternatives if they do not agree on a prenuptial agreement

B. Division of expenses

C. Division of assets

Tactical Planning

The attorneys should complete the Tactical Planning Worksheet (Appendix A) based on the attorney's discussion with the client prior to the negotiation as noted in the Confidential Information above.

Arranging the Negotiation

In arranging the negotiation, it is possible that the fiancés, given their experience with previous marriages, will want to attend and participate in the negotiation along with the attorneys. This is an exceptionally bad idea. In general, clients attending negotiations with their attorneys may cause disruption making the negotiation process more difficult. In the case of fiancés attending a prenuptial agreement negotiation with the attorneys, the potential for a disastrous result is high. The attorneys will want to be strong advocates for their clients, yet the fiancé may be caught between wanting to get the best result for himself and worrying about hurting the person he loves. The attorneys will be placed in extremely sensitive positions. Therefore, in arranging the negotiation, it is important to reassure the client that the attorneys should handle the prenuptial discussions but will keep them informed of all the details throughout the process. In any negotiation, attorneys are ethically bound to keep clients reasonably informed about their case so this is a requirement and not a special accommodation.

After having, hopefully, convinced the fiancés to allow the attorneys to handle the negotiation, the next step is to arrange where and when the negotiation will take place. Since this is a more formalized negotiation involving attorneys, the first negotiation meeting may likely be in person, in a setting such as in an office conference room. However, it is possible to use alternative formats, such as the telephone or skype to start the negotiation. It will likely depend on the accessibility and convenience of the attorneys.

The negotiation should be scheduled promptly. Many couples wait until shortly before the wedding, some even days before the wedding, to consult attorneys to negotiate prenups. Perhaps it is a reluctance to initiate what they perceive will be a tedious and stressful event that disrupts the joyous wedding planning, or they believe that the negotiating and drafting of the agreement is a simple procedure, which can be accomplished in a few hours, like the wedding rehearsal.

In the case of a second marriage as with Sharon and Carl, they may not be planning a grand ceremony with months of planning, and will want to marry without delay. However, a prenuptial agreement drafted hastily due to time constraints gives ammunition to a party to have it set aside later down the road. Attorneys should be reminded that the more time the attorneys have to negotiate and draft the agreement before the wedding, the more time they will have to work out potential roadblocks. Generally, attorneys should have at least six months prior to the wedding to negotiate and execute a prenup. Therefore, as soon as they are retained, they should get down to the business of negotiating the prenup. Attorneys should also feel comfortable rejecting potential clients who have not allocated sufficient time before the wedding for the attorneys to thoroughly negotiate and draft a prenuptial agreement.

Bargaining

In a formalized setting, there will be a need for ice-breaking and setting the agenda. It is important for the attorneys to establish a rapport that will facilitate a productive negotiation. Also, setting the agenda, especially as to the time allotted for the initial negotiation, will be helpful in that attorneys may be bound by other obligations or appointments that will limit the amount of available time to negotiate. If the attorneys learn of these time constraints at the beginning of the negotiation, they can better allocate their time for discussion. If there is no discussion as to a time allotment, the attorney may suddenly jump up from the table and say, "I gotta go." This sudden exit may harm the rapport established, as the other attorney may find this conduct unprofessional or simply just a trick or tactic.

It is also important for the attorneys to make statements initially that they will strive to come to a fair and equitable agreement for their clients. They should be sensitive to the fact that their clients entrusted many of their life decisions as a married couple to these attorneys and guard against letting negotiations get out of hand. Nothing would be more difficult than reporting to the fiancés that they were unable to work amicably with the attorney and negotiations broke down due to personality conflicts.

The attorneys should bring their worksheet to the negotiation. Since they are negotiating in a representative capacity, they will likely need to refer to the worksheet when making offers, counteroffers, and concessions. They may also need to refer to research during the negotiation to support their objective criteria. Attorneys are advocates for their clients, and as such, have a duty of loyalty and confidentiality that will require them to protect information received from their clients.

Letting Go or Resolving

Hopefully, the negotiation is successful, and the attorneys will arrive at a preliminary agreement. At this point, each attorney will need to take the agreement to their respective clients for final approval, since it is the client, not the attorney, who has the final authority to accept or reject all proposals. While the attorney should have preliminary approval to make and reject offers on behalf of clients during the negotiations, the final agreements must be approved by the client before it is put in contract form.

If the attorneys were unable to come to an agreement during the negotiation, they should adjourn and go back to their clients and discuss the next step. It may be likely there was agreement on some issues but not others. By discussing the outcome with their clients, attorneys can offer their advice as to what should occur from this point forward. Of course, it is important for the attorneys to remember that this is a couple, and if no mutually satisfactory agreement is reached, there will be a definite chill in the air when the couple discusses the outcome outside of the presence of their attorneys. In order to minimize the chilling effect, the attorneys should offer solutions to their clients consistent with their client's goals but should also discuss alternatives with their clients. It is likely that clients will not get everything they want, as in most negotiations. However, the attorney should not bully the client into accepting the agreement by making a statement such as, "Well, if you don't sign, there goes your dreams of marrying your fiancé." Presenting an alternative in this way is not only insensitive but may allow the client to potentially raise the defense of coercion or duress if the client tries to set aside the agreement during a divorce proceeding in the future. Since no lawyer wants to become a witness or a defendant in a malpractice action, it is important to calmly and professionally discuss alternatives if the parties fail to reach an agreement.

If the fiancés agree to the proposed terms of the prenuptial agreement negotiated by their attorneys, the attorneys will then formalize the agreement and begin the drafting process. Once the attorneys have completed the drafting to their satisfaction, the attorneys will show the final draft form to their respective clients. The attorneys should draft the agreement using language that the couple can understand completely. The attorneys should also take the time to go over the agreement in its entirety with their clients to make sure there is no confusion.

Once the couple approves the prenuptial agreement, they should sign and witness the document with their attorneys present and as with any prenup, put it away for safekeeping along with your other "insurance" policies.

Ethics and Equity

As noted in Problem 8-1, parties must properly disclose their assets for the prenuptial agreement to be enforceable. In this case, since Carl and Sharon are represented by attorneys, their attorneys are ethically bound to require their clients to properly disclose assets and not offer advice to them on ways to conceal assets. If, in fact, an attorney aids a party in hiding assets, the attorney will not only be subject to discipline by the bar but could also be charged with fraud.

During the course of negotiations, their attorneys should advocate on their behalf but guard against creating animosity that may negatively impact the couple's relationship. The attorneys must try and strike a balance between advocating their clients' bargaining positions and preserving the couple's relationship. If they do reach an agreement for their clients, the attorneys will hopefully be able to report to the couple that these negotiations were collaborative, and the result is fair and balanced for both of them.

Attorneys must be sure that prenuptial agreements are not one sided. Prenuptial agreements that give one party everything and the other party nothing, may be set aside as unconscionable.

Tactical Planning Worksheet Reveal

After concluding the negotiations, you and your counterpart should exchange your individual Tactical Planning Worksheets so that you both can see the bargaining positions you had planned to use during the negotiation. You should compare the two worksheets and see how far apart you were initially. Also, you should analyze whether and why you strayed from your worksheet, especially in the areas of offers and counteroffers. What positive aspects from your counterpart's worksheet do you wish you had included in yours?

Post-Negotiation Self-Reflection Worksheet

At the conclusion of the reveal session for this problem, be sure to complete the Post-Negotiation Self-Reflection Worksheet (found in Appendix B). Your Post-Negotiation Self-Reflection Worksheet should be completed individually and optimally within a short period of time after the Tactical Planning Worksheet reveal, while the negotiation session is fresh in your mind.

Exhibit 8-A

Fictional No-Prenup Marital Contract

This Agreement is made this day ____ of _____, 20__, by and between _________, ("Spouse 1"), and _______________, ("Spouse 2"); who **by virtue of signing their marriage license and participating in their wedding ceremony today** have entered into a legal binding relationship.

RECITALS

1. By getting married the parties have entered into a legally binding relationship.

2. The Parties agree to the following:

    a. In the event of divorce or separation, the parties want the laws of the State where they happen to be domiciled or residing in at that time to apply to them, including its laws on spousal support, property division, and division of fees and costs relating to separation and divorce.

    b. At the time of the death of the first spouse to die, the parties want the laws of the State where they happen to be domiciled or residing in at the time to apply its laws to the distribution of that deceased spouse's property, whether or not that deceased spouse has written a Will or has children, and without taking into account the property or financial obligations of the surviving spouse.

IN CONSIDERATION of the parties getting married, the parties agree as follows:

1. **Property Rights.** In the event of the parties' separation, as defined under the State laws of whichever State the parties happen to be domiciled at the time, each party shall have the right to make such claims or demands of the other party for transfer, monetary award, equitable distribution award, equitable lien, or community property award, or division of any kind under any applicable statute or law of that applicable State that may govern the disposition of property upon separation or divorce, as such laws now exist or may hereafter be enacted or amended. Each party shall be entitled to receive the amount or value of property and be charged with the such debt, secured or unsecured, as determined by such law of that applicable State that may govern the disposition of marital or community property upon separation or divorce, as such laws now exist or may hereafter be enacted or amended.

2. **Spousal Support**. Each party has whatever rights he or she may have to receive alimony, maintenance, or spousal support from the other, including temporary, rehabilitative, indefinite and permanent, both periodic and lump

sum, whether such right or claim results from common law, statutory law, or by way of equitable rights as may be applicable under the laws that now exist or may hereafter may be enacted of the State where the couple happens to be domiciled.

PROPERTY RIGHTS UPON DEATH OF A PARTY

3. **Rights of Surviving Spouse**. Whether or not a spouse writes a will, the surviving spouse has the rights available under the laws of the State where the deceased spouse was domiciled or owned property at death, including all of his or her property rights, claims, and interests as a surviving spouse to the other party's property, including but not limited to, dower, curtesy, the right of election regarding the estate of the other or to renounce and take against the will of the other, interest in augmented estate, right to inheritance in the event of intestacy, family allowance, homestead rights, exempt property, and all other similar or related rights under applicable law, including the law of any state or foreign jurisdiction where the deceased spouse may be domiciled or own property at death, and further including any rights resulting from changes in law that may take effect after execution of this Agreement.

ATTORNEY'S FEES AND COSTS

4. **Fees and Costs Relating to Separation or Divorce or in Connection with the Administration of the Estate of a Deceased Party**. The parties acknowledge that, in the event of a marital separation, or upon the death of a party, they may each incur attorney's fees to represent their interests. Each party agrees that the State law where the parties reside shall govern whether each party is solely responsible for any such attorney's fees or costs incurred by him or her and any fees and costs incurred in connection with any suit for divorce, or that a party (or his or her estate) may incur in connection with the administration of the estate of a deceased party, or whether the party may also be responsible for some of the costs of the other party, including the other party's claim for any attorney's fees and costs associated with any future separation or divorce action, including, but not limited to, fees and costs awarded during the pendency of such action.

Signature of Spouse 1: NOT REQUIRED – DEEMED SIGNED BY VIRTUE OF MARRIAGE LICENSE AND PARTICIPATING IN MARRIAGE CEREMONY

Signature of Spouse 2: NOT REQUIRED – DEEMED SIGNED BY VIRTUE OF MARRIAGE LICENSE AND PARTICIPATING IN MARRIAGE CEREMONY

Exhibit 8-B

§ 50:57. Sample Prenuptial Agreement
8A Conn. Prac., Family Law & Prac. § 50:57 (3d ed.)

AGREEMENT

This Agreement in contemplation of marriage is made by and between __________________ *[name of party 1]* and __________________ *[name of party 2]*, who will be referred to in this Agreement as the parties, as of *[date of agreement]*.

WHEREAS, *[name of party 1]* and *[name of party 2]* are both single and legally free to marry each other; and

WHEREAS, each party recognizes that in the absence of an agreement such as this, certain interests, rights and claims may accrue to each of them in the property and interests of the other as a result of marriage to each other; and

WHEREAS, *[[name of party 1]/[name of party 2]/the parties] [has/have] [a child/children]* from a prior marriage for whom they desire to make appropriate arrangements through lifetime transfers and/or testamentary provisions; and

WHEREAS, the parties, to promote marital tranquility, desire to fix, limit, and determine by this Agreement the interest, rights, and claims that may accrue to each of them in the property and estate of the other by reason of their marriage or in the event of marital difficulties herein referred to, and to accept the provisions of this Agreement in lieu and in full discharge, settlement, and satisfaction, of any and all interests, rights, and claims that otherwise each might or could have under the law, in and to the property and estate of the other, both before and after the other's death.

NOW THEREFORE, in consideration of the anticipated marriage between the parties, and the mutual covenants and promises set forth herein, the parties agree as follows:

Article I. FINANCIAL DISCLOSURE

1.1 *[Name of party 1]* has disclosed to *[name of party 2]* the nature and extent of *[his/her]* assets and liabilities and the sources and amounts of *[his/her]* present income. Said disclosure included both earned and unearned income, whether or not the same is taxable for federal tax purposes. Such information is also set forth on Schedule *[designation of schedule]* attached hereto.

1.2 *[Name of party 2]* has disclosed to *[name of party 1]* the nature and extent of *[his/her]* assets and liabilities and the sources and amounts of *[his/her]* present income. Said disclosure included both earned and unearned income, whether or not the same is taxable for federal tax purposes. Such information is also set forth on Schedule *[designation of schedule]* attached hereto.

1.3 Each party has carefully examined the other's financial condition and position. Each party has had the opportunity to make further inquiries about the other's financial position, and each party acknowledges receipt of satisfactory information and responses to all such inquiries. Each party further acknowledges that he or she had ample time to conduct such inquiries prior to the execution of this Agreement.

1.4 Each party acknowledges that he or she has been fully informed as to the financial circumstances of the other party. The purpose of such financial disclosure is to enable each party, prior to entering into this Agreement, to fully understand the specific nature and extent of the assets, income and other property interests to which this Agreement applies.

Article 2. DEFINITION OF SEPARATE PROPERTY

2.1. Notwithstanding the contemplated marriage of the parties, and notwithstanding any periods of cohabitation prior to said marriage, each party agrees that the property described hereafter shall remain the separate property of the other party:

(1) All property, whether real or personal, belonging to the other party at the time of the signing of this Agreement; and

(2) All property acquired or to be acquired by the other party by gift, devise, bequest or inheritance, including gifts from one party to the other; and

(3) All property acquired by the other party in his or her separate name while living together outside the marital relationship; and

(4) Any recovery or claim arising from a personal injury suffered by the other party; and

(5) All interest, dividends, rents, profits or other income acquired from the aforestated separate property, or acquired from property purchased with separate property; and

(6) All appreciation in value of the aforestated separate property, whether attributable to market conditions or to the skills and efforts of the owner thereof or any other individuals or entities; and

(7) All proceeds (whether in money or in kind) from any sale, exchange or other transfer of separate property; and

(8) All insurance proceeds attributable to any loss, destruction or other damage to any separate property; and

(9) Any patents, trademarks, copyrights, licenses, licensing agreements or the like which either party holds at the time of this Agreement or subsequently acquires.

(10) All property purchased with the proceeds of the separate property or the interest, dividends, rents, profits or other income acquired from the aforestated separate property.

2.2. The parties specifically agree that the following events, without limitation, shall under no circumstances be evidence of any intention or agreement by either party to change their respective separate property interests into joint property, marital property or community property as those terms may be defined under the terms of the laws of any state which may have or acquire jurisdiction over either party:

(1) The filing of joint federal or state tax returns;

(2) The taking of title to other property, whether real or personal, in joint tenancy or in any other joint or common form;

(3) The designation of one party by the other as a beneficiary of his or her estate or as trustee or as any other form of a fiduciary;

(4) The commingling by one party of his or her separate funds or property with the separate funds or property of the other party, including the time, toil, and talent of either of the parties and the pledging of joint, separate, or community credit for the benefit of the other's separate estate;

(5) Any oral statement by either party;

(6) The use and payment of funds derived from said separate property or the interest, dividends, rents, profits or other income from property purchased with separate property for debts and obligations of the marriage or for the purchase of assets for either party or for the marital estate;

(7) Any written statement by either party other than any expressed written agreement changing separately owned property into jointly owned property or a written statement designating a particular piece of property as a gift to the other;

(8) The payment from the funds of either of any obligations, including but not limited to, the payment of mortgages, interest or real property taxes, repairs or improvements on a separately or jointly held residence;

(9) The joint occupation of a separately owned residence, even though designated as a homestead;

(10) The birth or adoption of one or more children to the parties of the marriage; and

(11) Any other event not included above.

Article 3. SEPARATE PROPERTY RIGHTS

3.1 All properties presently owned by *[name of party 1]*, including those properties listed in Schedule *[designation of schedule]* and such property as defined in Article 2, are now *[his/her]* sole and separate property and shall remain the separate property of *[name of party 1]* together with all mutations, changes, increases, and appreciation in the value of said properties, and all of said properties shall be restored to *[his/her]* in the event the parties separate or in the event of a court ordered declaration of invalidity, annulment, or dissolution, or to *[his/her]* estate in the event of *[his/her]* death. *[Name of party 2]* does hereby waive and forever disclaim all marital and other rights in such property, and *[name of party 2]* agrees that *[name of party 1]* shall have the exclusive right to control and manage such property.

3.2 All properties presently owned by *[name of party 2]*, including those properties listed in Schedule *[designation of schedule]* and such property as defined in Article 2, are now *[his/her]* sole and separate property and shall remain the separate property of *[name of party 2]* together with all mutations, changes, increases, and appreciation in the value of said properties, and all of said properties shall be restored to *[him/her]* in the event the parties separate or in the event of a court ordered declaration of voidness, annulment, or dissolution, or to *[his/her]* estate in the event of *[his/her]* death. *[Name of party 1]* does hereby waive and forever disclaim all marital and other rights in such property, and *[name of party 1]* agrees that *[name of party 2]* shall have the exclusive right to control and manage such property.

3.3 Each party has the sole and exclusive right at all times to manage and control his or her separate property, the same as if he or she were unmarried.

3.4 Each party has the sole and exclusive right at all times to dispose of any part of his or her separate property by deed, will, or otherwise, on his or her sole signature, without any involvement or control by the other party, and the other party hereby ratifies and consents on his or her part to any such disposition.

3.5 Each party acknowledges that the right of the other to retain, manage and control his or her separate property as granted above extends not merely for the duration of the marriage, but additionally in the event the marriage ends by decree of dissolution, annulment or legal separation, including pendente lite proceedings, or at the death of either party.

3.6 Notwithstanding any other provision of this Agreement, either party may, only by appropriate, notarized written instrument, transfer, give, convey, devise, or bequeath any property to the other party. Neither party intends by this Agreement to limit or restrict in any way the right to receive any such transfer, gift, conveyance, devise, or bequest from the other, except as stated in this Agreement.

3.7 In the event one party voluntarily conveys to the other any interest in any property which is declared by this Agreement to be the separate property of such party, either by will or by instrument of conveyance or document of title signed by the transferring party, then the provisions of said will or instrument of conveyance or documents of title shall control over the provisions of this Agreement to the extent of any conflict between such documents regarding such property.

3.8 Each party acknowledges that no promises or other representations have been made by the other party or by any third person as to any future transfers of separate property.

3.9 Except as otherwise specifically provided in this Agreement, any property, funds or other assets now owned or hereafter acquired by the parties that are classified as the separate property of one of them can become the separate property of the other or the parties' joint property only by a written instrument executed and acknowledged with the same formalities as this Agreement by the party whose separate property is to be transferred or reclassified.

Article 4. INHERITANCES AND GIFTS

DURING THE MARRIAGE

4.1 *[Name of party 1]* has a number of relatives who have apparently accumulated substantial wealth consisting of several million dollars. Due to the relationship and the love and affection between *[name of party 1]* and such individuals, it is anticipated that *[he/she]* will inherit substantial wealth from one or more of such individuals. It is further anticipated that *[name of party 1]* may receive substantial lifetime gifts from such individuals, that *[he/she]* is or may be designated, without *[his/her]* knowledge, as the beneficiary of one or more trusts, and/or that *[he/she]* is or may be, without *[his/her]* knowledge, a beneficiary of insurance on the life of one or more relatives. Any bequest, trust interest, inheritance, gift, insurance benefits or the like received by *[name of party 1]* prior to, during or after the marriage shall be *[his/her]* separate property free of any claim of *[name of party 2]*.

4.2 It is similarly anticipated that *[name of party 2]* may receive funds or assets during the marriage by way of gift, trust, inheritance, life insurance proceeds or the like. All such funds and assets shall be *[his/her]* separate property free and clear of any claim by *[name of party 1]*.

4.3 Each party has included in his or her financial disclosure any gifts, trust interest, inheritance or like benefits already received. Each has also included in his or her financial disclosure any gift, trust interest, inheritance, or similar benefit known to him or her which is absolutely vested at the present time. Apart from the disclosures already provided, both parties acknowledge that contingencies and circumstances beyond their control make it impossible to project or disclose at the present time the exact nature, amount, timing or other details of any gift, inheritance, trust interest, insurance proceeds or other similar benefits which he or she may receive in the future from any third party, and such impossibility shall not be a basis for any attack on this Agreement by separate legal proceeding or in any action for divorce, dissolution of marriage, legal separation or annulment.

Article 5. PROPERTY ACQUIRED JOINTLY

DURING THE MARRIAGE

5.1 The parties contemplate that during the marriage they may jointly acquire a residence and other real and/or personal property.

5.2 In the absence of an express written agreement to the contrary, any jointly acquired property, whether real or personal, shall be owned by the parties in proportions equal to their respective contributions to the purchase price.

5.3 In the event jointly acquired real or personal property is financed through a mortgage or other loan, in the absence of any express written agreement to the contrary, it shall be owned by the parties in proportions equal to their respective contributions to the down payment.

5.4 All mortgage or loan payments, insurance, property taxes, maintenance expenses and other carrying charges and costs associated with the purchase, ownership, or upkeep of jointly owned property shall be paid by the parties in proportions equal to their respective ownership interests therein.

5.5 Upon any sale, exchange or other transfer of jointly owned property, each party shall be entitled to any resulting proceeds and shall be responsible for any resulting liability in proportions equal to their respective ownership interests therein.

5.6 Upon any termination of the marriage, whether by the death of one of the parties or by a judicial decree of annulment, legal separation or dissolution, the parties (and/or their respective estates) shall divide and distribute any jointly owned property in proportion to the parties' respective ownership interests therein.

5.7 Nothing contained herein shall preclude either party from transferring to the other, by will, deed or similar written instrument, his or her interest in any jointly owned property, nor shall anything contained in this Agreement constitute a waiver or rejection of such a transfer. Each party acknowledges that no representations or promises of any kind whatsoever have been made by the other or by any third person with respect to any such transfer or bequest.

5.8 In the event that either party transfers his or her interest in jointly owned property to the other, from and after the date of such transfer, the property in question shall be treated as the separate property of the recipient for purposes of this Agreement.

Article 6. INCOME AND EXPENSES

DURING THE MARRIAGE

6.1 All earnings and accumulations resulting from the personal services, skills, efforts and work of *[name of party 1]*, together with all property acquired or further income derived therefrom shall be the separate property and income of *[name of party 1]*.

6.2 All the earnings and accumulations resulting from the personal services, skills, efforts and work of *[name of party 2]*, together with all property acquired or further income derived therefrom shall be the separate property and income of *[name of party 2]*.

6.3 During the marriage, each of the parties shall be responsible for the payment of his or her own personal expenses, including such items as clothing, medical and health care, separate travel and entertainment and the like. Neither party shall be obligated to make any contribution of any kind toward the living expenses or support of any child born to or adopted by the other prior to the marriage of *[name of party 1]* to *[name of party 2]*.

6.4 During the marriage, each party shall contribute equally to the parties' joint-living expenses, including groceries, joint travel and entertainment, and the utilities for the home(s) in which the parties reside.

6.5 Notwithstanding the foregoing, any funds expended by either party for the benefit of the other shall be presumed to be a gift, and not a payment for which reimbursement or repayment is later expected, unless the parties agree to the contrary in writing. The parties acknowledge that no promises or representations of any kind have been made by either party or by any third party as to any future gifts or other payments by either party on behalf of the other.

6.6 It is foreseeable that the parties may, from time to time, jointly occupy a residence solely owned by one of them, or may jointly use some other separately owned asset. It is the intent of this Article to create a joint obligation for the payment of operating expenses associated with such joint use. However, no such payment by the nonowner party shall create any right of ownership, right to reimbursement or other property right.

Article 7. PRESENT AND FUTURE

LIABILITIES AND CREDIT

7.1 *[Name of party 2]* agrees that all liabilities, indebtedness, encumbrances, liens, debts, and obligations in *[his/her]* name, guaranteed by *[him/her]*, assessed against any property listed in Schedule *[designation of schedule]* of this Agreement, or for which *[he/she]* is otherwise liable (whether personal or contingent) are *[his/her]* sole liabilities and obligations, to be satisfied and paid solely from *[his/her]* separate estate and from which *[he/she]* will forever hold harmless, indemnify, and defend *[name of party 1]* from any claim.

7.2 *[Name of party 1]* agrees that all liabilities, indebtedness, encumbrances, liens, debts, and obligations in *[his/her]* name, guaranteed by *[him/her]*, assessed against *[his/her]* separate property listed in Schedule *[designation of schedule]* of this Agreement, or for which *[he/she]* is otherwise liable (whether personal or contingent) are *[his/her]* sole liabilities and obligations, to be satisfied and paid solely from *[his/her]* separate estate and from which *[he/she]* will forever hold harmless, indemnify, and defend *[name of party 2]* from any claim.

7.3 The parties agree that the property described in this Agreement as being the separate property of or belonging to the separate estate of *[name of party 1]* shall never be liable for the debts or obligations of *[name of party 2]*, except upon advance written agreement of the parties executed with the same formalities as this Agreement.

7.4 The parties agree that the property described in this Agreement as being the separate property of or belonging to the separate estate of *[name of party 2]* shall never be liable for the debts or obligations of *[name of party 1]*, except upon advance written agreement of the parties executed with the same formalities as this Agreement.

7.5 Notwithstanding the foregoing, either party may voluntarily elect to contribute toward the payment of a separate liability of the other. However, such payment shall not constitute an assumption of the liability by the contributing party nor shall such payment constitute an admission of responsibility for the liability by the contributing party. Both parties acknowledge that no promises or other representations have been made by either party or by any third person as to any future contributions of either toward the separate liabilities of the other. In addition, the payment of a liability by one party associated with separate property of the other party shall not constitute any degree of ownership in the separate property.

7.6 *[Name of party 1]* shall not have any authority to deal with the separate property or income or credit of *[name of party 2]* in any fashion with any third persons for any purposes, except by the prior written consent of *[name of party 2]*.

7.7 *[Name of party 2]* shall not have any authority to deal with the separate property, or income or credit of *[name of party 1]* in any fashion with any third persons for any purposes, except by the prior written consent of *[name of party 1]*.

7.8 The parties recognize the complexity of modern business credit transactions and each desires to allow the other to enter into such transactions without regard to his or her approval or joinder. If either party enters into a transaction wherein credit is extended to that party or that party becomes liable or obligated for the repayment, contingent or otherwise, of credit extended to any third party, whether or not the transaction is expressly denominated as a "separate-property" transaction, and unless a contrary intent is specifically and expressly stated, then that obligation will be satisfied by the party incurring it wholly from his or her separate property, and the party incurring the obligation will hold the other party harmless from that obligation and indemnify him or her if he or she is ever required for any reason to satisfy that obligation. The assets, if any, acquired through any such credit transaction will be and remain the separate property of the party obligating his or her separate property for the credit extended in acquiring the assets or resulting in the acquisition of the assets. Similarly, any business failure of one of the parties or any bankruptcy, reorganization, composition, arrangement, or other debtor/creditor action of or against a party will in no way affect the other party, and neither party is relying or will rely on the other party for any credits, accommodation, or indulgence in these regards.

Article 8. TAX LIABILITY

8.1 Any taxes, interest, or penalties that *[name of party 1]* may owe for income or gains received or accrued by *[his/her]* or that is otherwise attributable to *[his/her]* separate property or income as defined in this Agreement shall be *[his/her]* sole liabilities and obligations to be paid solely from *[his/her]* separate funds.

8.2 *[Name of party 1]* shall forever hold harmless, indemnify and defend *[name of party 2]* from any claims, liability and any and all tax liens that might hereafter arise through the filing of a joint return or the failure to file proper returns or to pay the required taxes with respect to *[his/her]* separate taxable income and/or gains as defined in this Agreement.

8.3 Any taxes, interest, or penalties that *[name of party 2]* may owe for income or gains received or accrued by *[him/her]* or that is otherwise attributable to *[his/her]* separate property or income as defined in this Agreement shall be *[his/her]* sole liabilities and obligations to be paid solely from *[his/her]* separate funds.

8.4 *[Name of party 2]* shall forever hold harmless, indemnify and defend *[name of party 1]* from any claims, liability, and any and all tax liens that might hereafter arise through the filing of a joint tax return or the failure to file proper returns or to pay the required taxes with respect to *[his/her]* separate taxable income and/or gains as defined in this Agreement.

8.5 The parties agree that if any tax liability arises from income or gains attributable to jointly held assets, each party shall pay the proportion of such liability which corresponds with his or her ownership share of said asset.

8.6 *[Name of party 2]* agrees to cooperate with *[name of party 1]*, and any tax accountants designated by *[him/her]*, in the preparation and filing of a joint tax return, in the event that *[name of party 1]* determines that such a filing method would result in a lower total tax to be paid by the parties. However, nothing contained herein shall obligate *[name of party 1]* to file a joint return if *[he/she]* prefers to file separately.

8.7 In determining the amount of tax to be paid by each party in the event that a joint return is filed, each party will pay his or her proportionate part of the joint aggregate income-tax liability of both parties based on the ratio that the net separate property taxable income of each party, computed as if he or she were a single person, bears to the aggregate net separate property income of both parties, with appropriate allowances for credits and other items (e.g. investment tax credits or recapture items) that are not reflected in the net taxable income.

8.8 *[Name of party 2]* and *[name of party 1]* each agree that upon the request of the other, he or she will consent to have gifts made by the other during his or her lifetime treated as made one-half by him or her for gift tax purposes, provided that any such gift is made during their marriage, and provided further that the total fair market value of such gifts by each completed in any calendar year qualifies under Section 2503(b) of the Internal Revenue Code (or any successor provision thereto) for the gift tax annual exclusion and is equal to or less than twice the amount of the said allowable annual exclusion. Moreover, should the Internal Revenue Code be amended to provide a limit on the dollar value of excludable annual gifts, the provisions of this Article 8 shall be void. The parties agree that they will make, execute, and file, upon the request of either of them or their respective personal representatives, whatever documents, including without limitation, gift tax returns, which are necessary in order to evidence such consent.

Article 9. WAIVER OF ESTATE RIGHTS

9.1 The parties understand that under the provisions of (state law/recite applicable estate law provisions) a surviving spouse has certain rights in and to the estate of the other, and that a surviving spouse may further be entitled to elect against the provisions of the Last Will and Testament of the other party. The parties further understand that similar rights may be conferred by the laws of the various other states in which the parties have resided in the past or may reside in the future. It is the intention of the parties that the rights of either, as a surviving spouse, shall be governed by the terms of this Agreement rather than by such statutes.

9.2 *[Name of party 2]* and *[name of party 1]* each renounces, waives, releases, and relinquishes any and all claims and rights which he or she may have or may hereafter acquire or possess to share in any capacity or to any extent in the estate of the other, whether arising by way of statutory allowance, set-off, distribution in intestacy, dower, curtesy, survivor or family allowance during administration, community property, quasi-community property, homestead interest, or election to take against any Last Will and Testament of the other; and each covenants and agrees that he or she will refrain from any action or proceeding that might change, impair, or abrogate any provision or the Last Will and Testament of the other.

9.3 The parties intend that the provisions of this Article shall constitute a waiver by each of them or the right of election granted to him or her by any statute and any rule or law of any jurisdiction, domestic or foreign, entitling a surviving spouse to all or any part of the estate or property of a deceased spouse or to any interest therein (including any income interest, dower, curtesy, community property, quasi-community property, homestead, or other marital interest of any kind whatsoever, real or personal, tangible or intangible) and of the set-off provided by law in any applicable jurisdiction, or in any other rule or law entitling a surviving spouse to all or any part of the estate or property of a deceased spouse.

9.4 Nothing contained in this Agreement shall be deemed to constitute a waiver by either of *[name of party 2]* or *[name of party 1]* of any devise or bequest to him or her actually contained in the Last Will and Testament of the other. Both *[name of party 1]* and *[name of party 2]* hereby acknowledge that no representations or promises of any kind whatsoever have been made by the other or any third person with respect to any such devise or bequest.

9.5 *[Name of party 1]* and *[name of party 2]* each hereby renounces, waives, releases, and relinquishes any and all right to act as an executor, administrator, or other fiduciary of the estate of the other unless appointed as such in the Last Will and Testament of the other.

Article 10. DISSOLUTION OF MARRIAGE

10.1 The parties are entering into this Agreement in anticipation of a long and happy marriage. Nevertheless, the parties acknowledge that differences may arise in the future and that the marriage may ultimately be terminated via an annulment, legal separation, dissolution or other judicial declaration during the lifetime of the parties. In the event of such an occurrence, it is the intention of the parties that their respective rights, duties, and entitlements be governed by the terms of this Agreement rather than by the laws of any state or nation which may have or subsequently acquire jurisdiction over the parties.

10.2 Following the marriage of *[name of party 1]* and *[name of party 2]*, if the parties should subsequently be divorced or legally separated from each other or should the marriage be annulled pursuant to a decree or order of any court or should they become separated pursuant to a separation agreement, for any reason whatsoever, including the fault of either party, *[name of party 1]* and *[name of party 2]* each hereby for himself or herself, and his or her heirs, distributees, executors, administrators, or assigns, waives, releases, relinquishes, and forever renounces any and all right in and to the income (including but not limited to the earnings from the investment thereof) or the property (including but not limited to the appreciation of such property) of the other, whether real or personal or partly real or partly personal of whatsoever nature and wheresoever located, to which he or she might be entitled by virtue of the marriage relationship under the laws of any jurisdiction.

10.3 Upon the filing by either party of a petition for divorce, dissolution of marriage, legal separation or annulment, the parties agree that it would be just, fair and equitable that the division of the property upon such termination shall restore to each party his or her separate property as defined herein along with any right to reimbursement as defined herein.

10.4 In the event of a divorce, dissolution of marriage, legal separation or annulment, the parties agree that jointly held personal property will be divided in kind, by value, in accordance with the proportionate ownership interests of the parties. In the event of any dispute over personal property, the parties will sell any commonly held personal property promptly, and the cash proceeds will be divided in accordance with the proportionate ownership interests of the parties. If there are no records reflecting such interest, the proceeds will be divided equally. Jointly held real estate will be sold and the proceeds be divided in accordance with the proportional ownership interest of the parties or the real estate will be valued at current market price and one party may buy the other party's ownership share. Gifts to both parties jointly, having a value in excess of $1,000 shall be divided equally by value.

10.5 The parties agree that prior to entry of any decree of divorce, dissolution of marriage, legal separation or annulment, they will execute a property settlement agreement setting aside to *[name of party 1]* all of the property described herein as being the separate property of *[name of party 1]*, or as belonging to the separate estate of *[name of party 1]* and setting aside to *[name of party 2]* all property described herein as being the separate property of *[name of party 2]*, or as belonging to the separate estate of *[name of party 2]*, and to divide any joint property as set forth in 10.4 above and to seek court approval of such property settlement agreement. The parties further agree that in any suit of divorce, dissolution, legal separation or annulment, neither party shall file any pleadings that request a division of property contrary to the provisions of this Agreement.

10.6 Each party hereby waives any right he or she might otherwise have or acquire to seek any alimony or spousal support from the other in any action for a divorce, dissolution of marriage, legal separation or annulment. The parties intend that this waiver shall apply to claims either might otherwise have for temporary or pendente lite alimony or spousal support during the pendency of the action as well as to claims for alimony or spousal support to be awarded in connection with any final judgment in such action. (Keep in mind that a provision of this type may not be upheld in its entirety, depending on the circumstances of the dependent spouse.)

10.7 In the event the waiver in the preceding paragraph is deemed ineffective or otherwise disregarded by a court of law for purposes of any claim for alimony or spousal support, whether during the pendency of any proceeding or in connection with any final judgment, it is the intention of the parties that the determination by the court as to the payment of alimony or spousal support be governed by the terms set forth herein.

(1) In determining the ability of *[name of party 1]* or *[name of party 2]* to pay such alimony or spousal support to the other, the court is to consider only the income from employment of *[name of party 1]* or *[name of party 2]* and the income from any joint assets to be divided between the parties pursuant to this Agreement.

(2) In making said determination as to the ability to pay, the court is not to consider the assets or net worth of the paying party, the income from any separate assets of the paying party as defined herein, any inheritance or trust interests of the paying party, any annuities to which the paying party is entitled, or any pension rights of the paying party.

(3) It is the intention of the parties that this paragraph 10.7 be given effect only if and to the extent that the waiver of alimony and spousal support set forth in paragraph 10.6 is disregarded or deemed ineffective by a court of law. The parties do not intend by this paragraph 10.7 to create or acknowledge the existence of any right or claim by either party to alimony or spousal support to be paid by the other.

10.8 In the event of any action between the parties for divorce, dissolution of marriage, legal separation or annulment, regardless of the jurisdiction in which the action is pending and regardless of the grounds upon which the action is based, neither party will request any determinations or seek any relief contrary to the terms of this Agreement.

10.9 In the event any decree of divorce, dissolution of marriage, legal separation or annulment containing an award to either party of any portion of the separate property of the other as defined herein, each party agrees to convey to the other any property which he or she may be awarded in such decree in contravention of this Agreement.

10.10 In the event of a subsequent action between the parties for divorce, dissolution of marriage, legal separation or annulment, each party shall pay his or her own accounting fees, attorney's fees, appraiser fees, and fees of expert witnesses of every kind and character and other expenses whether or not same are taxed as court costs, except that if either party unsuccessfully seeks to invalidate a portion or all of this Agreement or seeks to recover property in a manner which deviates from the terms of this Agreement, then such party shall be liable to the other party for all reasonable and necessary attorney's fees and costs incurred by the other party in successfully defending his or her rights under this Agreement.

Article 11. SEVERABILITY

If it should be determined that any provision, clause, section, or paragraph of this Agreement is invalid, is void or unenforceable for any reason, it shall be deemed severable from the remainder of the Agreement. It is the expressed intention of the parties that the remaining provisions, sections, clauses and paragraphs of this Agreement shall continue in full force and effect without being impaired or invalidated in any way and shall be considered valid and enforceable to the maximum extent possible since valid consideration exists for each and every portion of this Agreement independent from other portions of this Agreement. If a provision shall be deemed invalid due to its scope or breadth, it shall be deemed valid to the extent of the scope or breadth permitted by law. A finding by a court with jurisdiction to grant a divorce, dissolution of marriage, legal separation or annulment that any provision, clause, section or paragraph of this agreement is invalid, void or unenforceable, shall not effect an action between the parties based on the contract itself.

Article 12. AGREEMENT VOLUNTARY AND UNDERSTOOD

12.1 *[Name of party 1]* warrants and agrees that *[he/she]* executes and acknowledges this Agreement only after carefully reading same and after such reading and consultation with *[his/her]* attorney. *[He/She]* has fully considered and understands all of the terms and provisions hereof and their legal effect and ramifications. *[Name of party 1]* further acknowledges that *[he/she]* believes it is in *[his/her]* best interest to sign, execute and deliver this instrument. *[Name of party 1]* further acknowledges that this Agreement is just, fair and equitable and that this Agreement is signed willingly, freely and voluntarily as *[his/her]* act and deed without reliance upon any representation of *[name of party 2]* or any of *[his/her]* agents, other than those expressly set out in this Agreement.

12.2 *[Name of party 2]* warrants and agrees that *[he/she]* executes and acknowledges this Agreement only after carefully reading same and after such reading and consultation with *[his/her]* attorney. *[He/She]* has fully considered and understands all of the terms and provisions hereof and their legal effect and ramifications. *[Name of party 2]* further acknowledges that *[he/she]* believes it is in *[his/her]* best interest to sign, execute and deliver this instrument. *[Name of party 2]* further acknowledges that this Agreement is just, fair and equitable and that this Agreement is signed willingly, freely and voluntarily as *[his/her]* act and deed without reliance upon any representation of *[name of party 1]* or any of *[his/her]* agents, other than those expressly set out in this Agreement.

12.3 Each party acknowledges that neither party has any reason to believe that the other did not fully understand the terms and effects of the agreement or that he or she did not freely and voluntarily execute the agreement. Each party acknowledges they have signed this Agreement in full knowledge and agreement that the terms contained herein are binding on each of them.

Article 13. CHANGES IN AGREEMENT

No change shall be made in any of the provisions of this Agreement except by an instrument in writing duly executed by the parties hereto.

Article 14. MODIFICATION AND WAIVER

A modification or waiver of any of the provisions of this Agreement shall be effective only if made in writing and executed with the same formality as this Agreement. The failure of either party to insist upon strict performance of any of the provisions of this Agreement shall not be construed as a waiver of any subsequent default of the same or similar nature.

Article 15. LEGAL COUNSEL; COUNSEL FEES

15.1 The parties hereto declare and acknowledge that each has had independent legal advice of his or her own selection. *[Name of party 1]* has been represented by *[name of counsel]* of *[address of counsel]*, *[name of county]*, Connecticut; and *[name of party 2]* has been represented by *[name of counsel]* of *[address of counsel]*, *[name of county]*, Connecticut.

15.2 In the event that it shall be determined by a court of competent jurisdiction that either party shall have breached any of the provisions of this Agreement or of any court decree incorporating by reference or otherwise this Agreement or portions thereof, the offending party shall pay to the other party reasonable attorney's fees, court costs and other expenses incurred in the enforcement of the provisions of this Agreement and/or judgment or decree incorporating any or all of the provisions hereof.

15.3 Each of the parties shall be responsible for their respective counsel fees incurred in the negotiation and preparation of this Agreement and in any divorce, dissolution of marriage, legal separation or annulment action which might ever be brought by either party.

Article 16. BINDING ON PERSONAL REPRESENTATIVES

Except as otherwise provided, all of the covenants, promises, stipulations, agreements and provisions contained herein shall apply to, bind and be obligatory upon the heirs, executors, administrators, personal representatives and assigns of the parties hereto, whether so expressed or not.

Article 17. NO REPRESENTATIONS

Each party hereto agrees that no representations of any kind whatsoever have been made to him or her as an inducement to enter into this Agreement, other than the representations set forth herein, and that this Agreement contains all of the terms of the contract between the parties hereto.

Article 18. ENTIRE AGREEMENT

Both the legal and practical effect of this Agreement in each and every respect and the financial status of the parties have been fully explained to both parties by their respective counsel, and they both acknowledge that it is a fair Agreement, and is not the result of any fraud, duress or undue influence exercised by either party upon the other or by any other person or persons upon either, and they further agree that this Agreement contains the entire understanding of the parties. Each party affirms that they have had ample time to consider the terms and conditions of this Agreement and were not hurried or coerced in any manner whatsoever.

The parties agree that the preamble contained as Page 1 is an integral and essential part of this Agreement and hereby incorporated fully as part of the entire Agreement.

Article 19. AFTER-DOCUMENTS

Each of the parties hereby agrees to sign and deliver free of cost and expense, any documents which may be necessary or desirable to effectuate or implement any of the provisions of this Agreement on the request of the other party.

Article 20. ORIGINAL COPY

This Agreement may be executed in any number of counterparts, any one of which executed by both parties, shall be deemed to be the original, although the others are not produced.

Article 21. HEADINGS

The paragraph headings herein are for convenience only and shall not be construed to limit or affect any provisions of this Agreement.
IN WITNESS WHEREOF, the parties have hereunto set their hands and seals as of the day and year first above written.

Notes

The following agreement was designed to provide significant permanent separation of assets and finances. When a less restrictive or comprehensive agreement is desired, the unnecessary or inapplicable provisions should be modified or deleted. This is intended as a sample only.

Exhibit 8-C

INSTRUCTIONS FOR FLORIDA FAMILY LAW RULES OF PROCEDURE FORM 12.902(f)(3), MARITAL SETTLEMENT AGREEMENT FOR SIMPLIFIED DISSOLUTION OF MARRIAGE (11/12)

When should this form be used?

This form should be used when a **Petition for Simplified Dissolution of Marriage**, Florida Family Law Rules of Procedure Form 12.901(a), has been **filed** and the **parties** have reached an agreement on all of the issues at hand.

This form should be typed or printed in black ink. **Both** parties must sign the agreement and have their signatures witnessed by a **notary public** or **deputy clerk**. After completing this form, you should file the original with the **clerk of the circuit court** in the county where the **petition** was filed and keep a copy for your records. You should then refer to the instructions for your petition, **answer**, or answer and **counterpetition** concerning the procedures for setting a hearing or **trial** (**final hearing**).

Where can I look for more information?

Before proceeding, you should read General Information for Self-Represented Litigants found at the beginning of these forms. The words that are in **bold underline** in these instructions are defined there. For further information, see chapter 61, Florida Statutes, and the instructions for the petition which was filed in this case.

Special notes...

This form does not act to transfer title to the property. Such transfer must be done by deed or supplemental final judgment.

Remember, a person who is NOT an attorney is called a nonlawyer. If a nonlawyer helps you fill out these forms, that person must give you a copy of a **Disclosure from Nonlawyer**, Florida Family Law Rules of Procedure Form 12.900(a), before he or she helps you. A nonlawyer helping you fill out these forms also **must** put his or her name, address, and telephone number on the bottom of the last page of every form he or she helps you complete.

IN THE CIRCUIT COURT OF THE ________________________ JUDICIAL CIRCUIT,
IN AND FOR ________________________ COUNTY, FLORIDA

Case No.: ______________________________
Division: ______________________________

In re: the Marriage of:

________________________________,
Petitioner,

and

________________________________,
Respondent.

MARITAL SETTLEMENT AGREEMENT FOR SIMPLIFIED DISSOLUTION OF MARRIAGE

We, *{Husband's full legal name}*______________________________,and *{Wife's full legal name}* ____,being sworn, certify that the following statements are true:

1. We were married to each other on *{date}* ________________________.

2. Because of irreconcilable differences in our marriage (no chance of staying together), we have made this agreement to settle once and for all what we owe to each other and what we can expect to receive from each other. Each of us states that nothing has been held back, that we have honestly included everything we could think of in listing our assets (everything we own and that is owed to us) and our debts (everything we owe), and that we believe the other has been open and honest in writing this agreement.

3. We have both filed a Family Law Financial Affidavit, Florida Family Law Rules of Procedure Form 12.902(b) or (c). Because we have voluntarily made full and fair disclosure to each other of all our assets and debts, we waive any further disclosure under rule 12.285, Florida Family Law Rules of Procedure.

4. Each of us agrees to execute and exchange any papers that might be needed to complete this agreement, including deeds, title certificates, etc.

SECTION I. MARITAL ASSETS AND LIABILITIES

A. Division of Assets. We divide our assets (everything we own and that is owed to us) as follows: Any personal item(s) not listed below is the property of the party currently in possession of the item(s).

1. Wife shall receive as her own and Husband shall have no further rights or responsibilities regarding these assets:

ASSETS: DESCRIPTION OF ITEM(S) WIFE SHALL RECEIVE **(To avoid confusion at a later date, describe each item as clearly as possible. You do not need to list account numbers Where applicable, include whether the name on any title/deed/account described below is wife's, husband's, or both.)**	**Current Fair Market Value**
Cash (on hand)	$
Cash (in banks/credit unions)	
Stocks/Bonds	
Notes (money owed to you in writing)	
Money owed to you (not evidenced by a note)	
Real estate: (Home)	
(Other)	
Business interests	
Automobiles	
Boats	
Other vehicles	
Retirement plans (Profit Sharing, Pension, IRA, 401(k)s, etc.)	

Florida Family Law Rules of Procedure Form 12.902(f)(3), Marital Settlement Agreement for Simplified Dissolution of Marriage (11/12)

Furniture & furnishings in home	
Furniture & furnishings elsewhere	
Collectibles	
Jewelry	
Life insurance (cash surrender value)	
Sporting and entertainment (T.V., stereo, etc.) equipment	
Other assets	
Total Assets to Wife	$ ________

2. Husband shall receive as his own and Wife shall have no further rights or responsibilities regarding these assets:

ASSETS: DESCRIPTION OF ITEM(S) HUSBAND SHALL RECEIVE **(To avoid confusion at a later date, describe each item as clearly as possible. You do not need to list account numbers Where applicable, include whether the name on any title/deed/account described below is wife's, husband's or both.)**	**Current Fair Market Value**
Cash (on hand)	$
Cash (in banks/credit unions)	
Stocks/Bonds	
Notes (money owed to you in writing)	

Florida Family Law Rules of Procedure Form 12.902(f)(3), Marital Settlement Agreement for Simplified Dissolution of Marriage (11/12)

Money owed to you (not evidenced by a note)	
Real estate: (Home)	
(Other)	
Business interests	
Automobiles	
Boats	
Other vehicles	
Retirement plans (Profit Sharing, Pension, IRA, 401(k)s, etc.)	
Furniture & furnishings in home	
Furniture & furnishings elsewhere	
Collectibles	
Jewelry	
Life insurance (cash surrender value)	
Sporting and entertainment (T.V., stereo, etc.) equipment	
Other assets	

Florida Family Law Rules of Procedure Form 12.902(f)(3), Marital Settlement Agreement for Simplified Dissolution of Marriage (11/12)

Total Assets to Husband	$ ________

B. Division of Liabilities/Debts. We divide our liabilities (everything we owe) as follows:

1. Wife shall pay as her own the following and will not at any time ask Husband to pay these debts/bills:

LIABILITIES: DESCRIPTION OF DEBT(S) TO BE PAID BY WIFE (To avoid confusion at a later date, describe each item as clearly as possible. You do not need to list account numbers Where applicable, include whether the name on any mortgage, note, or account described below is wife's, husband's, or both.)	**Monthly Payment**	**Current Amount Owed**
Mortgages on real estate: (Home)	$	$
(Other)		
Charge/credit card accounts		
Auto loan		
Auto loan		
Bank/credit union loans		
Money you owe (not evidenced by a note)		
Judgments		
Other		
Total Debts to Be Paid by Wife	$	$

2. Husband shall pay as his own the following and will not at any time ask Wife to pay these debts/bills:

Florida Family Law Rules of Procedure Form 12.902(f)(3), Marital Settlement Agreement for Simplified Dissolution of Marriage (11/12)

LIABILITIES: DESCRIPTION OF DEBT(S) TO BE PAID BY HUSBAND (To avoid confusion at a later date, describe each item as clearly as possible. You do not need to list account numbers. Where applicable, include whether the name on any mortgage, note or account described below is wife's, husband's, or both.	**Monthly Payment**	**Current Amount Owed**
Mortgages on real estate: (Home)	$	$
(Other)		
Charge/credit card accounts		
Auto loan		
Auto loan		
Bank/credit union loans		
Money you owe (not evidenced by a note)		
Judgments		
Other		
Total Debts to Be Paid by Husband	**$**	**$**

C. Contingent Assets and Liabilities (listed in Section III of our Family Law Financial Affidavits) will be divided as follows:

____

____

____

____

____

Florida Family Law Rules of Procedure Form 12.902(f)(3), Marital Settlement Agreement for Simplified Dissolution of Marriage (11/12)

SECTION II. SPOUSAL SUPPORT (ALIMONY) Each of us forever gives up any right to spousal support (alimony) that we may have.

SECTION III. OTHER

____
____
____
____

I certify that I have been open and honest in entering into this settlement agreement. I am satisfied with this agreement and intend to be bound by it.

Dated: ______________ ______________________________

Signature of Husband
Printed Name: ______________________________
Address: ______________________________
City, State, Zip: ______________________________
Telephone Number: ______________________________
Fax Number: ______________________________
E-mail Address(es): ______________________________

STATE OF FLORIDA
COUNTY OF ___________

Sworn to or affirmed and signed before me on ___________ by ________________________.

____
NOTARY PUBLIC or DEPUTY CLERK

____
[Print, type, or stamp commissioned name of notary or clerk.]

_____ Personally known
_____ Produced identification
Type of identification produced ___________________

IF A NONLAWYER HELPED YOU FILL OUT THIS FORM, HE/SHE MUST FILL IN THE BLANKS BELOW:
[fill in **all** blanks]
This form was prepared for the Husband who is the *{choose only **one**}* (☐) Petitioner (☐) Respondent.
This form was completed with the assistance of:
{name of individual} ______________________________,
{name of business} ______________________________,
{address} ______________________________,
{city} ______________________,*{state}* ________, *{telephone number}* ______________.

Florida Family Law Rules of Procedure Form 12.902(f)(3), Marital Settlement Agreement for Simplified Dissolution of Marriage (11/12)

I certify that I have been open and honest in entering into this settlement agreement. I am satisfied with this agreement and intend to be bound by it.

Dated: ____________________ ____________________________________

Signature of Wife
Printed name:____________________________
Address:________________________________
City, State, Zip:__________________________
Telephone number:________________________
Fax number______________________________
E-mail Address(es):_______________________

STATE OF FLORIDA
COUNTY OF ____________

Sworn to or affirmed and signed before me on ____________ by ______.

____
NOTARY PUBLIC or DEPUTY CLERK

____
[Print, type, or stamp commissioned name of notary or clerk.]

☐ Personally known
☐ Produced identification
Type of identification produced ____________________

IF A NONLAWYER HELPED YOU FILL OUT THIS FORM, HE/SHE MUST FILL IN THE BLANKS BELOW:
[fill in **all** blanks]
This form was prepared for the Wife who is the *{choose only **one**}* (☐) Petitioner (☐) Respondent.
This form was completed with the assistance of:
{name of individual} ____,
{name of business} ____,
{address} ____,
*{city}*____________________,*{state}* _______, *{telephone number}* __________________.

Florida Family Law Rules of Procedure Form 12.902(f)(3), Marital Settlement Agreement for Simplified Dissolution of Marriage (11/12)

Chapter 9

Negotiating More Stressful Life Events—Dog Bites, Security Deposits, and Undue Influence

"With all this practice, I'm getting good at this negotiating thing!"

In this chapter, you will continue to practice a variety of negotiating problems using the TABLE method. As in Chapters 7 and 8, this chapter begins with an overview of legal principles, followed by three problems in which you will negotiate a dog bite lawsuit, a security deposit dispute, and a will contest involving lack of capacity and undue influence. While these topics are disparate, they can be, unfortunately, fairly common stressful life events. Regrettably, when confronted with these events, people often either ignore the problems or launch into attack mode to try to resolve them. They do not apply a cogent negotiation strategy for handling these problems. The TABLE method provides a path to resolve these matters effectively and efficiently.

Instructions

After reading the legal principles in this chapter, you will be ready to apply those principles to the practice problems below using the TABLE method The limited legal information you are given in the areas of dogs bites, security deposits, and will contests based on capacity and undue influence, should not be interpreted as a primer on these areas of the law. Rather, the information is included here solely to use as a basis for negotiating the various problems. As an alternative or in addition to negotiating these problems with the limited information about the law provided here, you may wish to research the law in your state, or another state, and negotiate the problem using that research.

The format for negotiating these problems is the same format as provided in Chapters 7 and 8. However, after introducing the problem, you are not walked through the entire TABLE method strategy, as in previous problems. Instead, because you are by now experienced with the TABLE method, you should feel comfortable applying the method on your own to the problems in this chapter.

As in Chapters 7 and 8, each problem contains general information followed by confidential information in which each negotiator will choose a bargaining position on key issues. While the general information will be known by both sides, your bargaining position is confidential, although you may disclose it, or some of it, during the negotiation session if you choose to do so. Following the confidential information, you are given guidelines and suggestions as to how to approach the negotiations using the TABLE method.

After reviewing the information, you should complete the Tactical Planning Worksheet provided in Appendix A. Each problem provides the law to use in completing your worksheet. Also, be sure to include your bargaining positions on your worksheets. After completing a Tactical Planning Worksheet for each problem, you and your counterpart are ready to conduct a negotiation in which you attempt to reach an agreement. While there is no time limit set for each problem, you should be able to complete the initial negotiations for each problem within 30 minutes.

After you complete each negotiation, you and your negotiating counterpart should exchange your Tactical Planning Worksheet so that you can analyze the bargaining positions you and your counterpart planned for the negotiation. Finally, you should complete the Post-Negotiation Self-Reflection Worksheet (found in Appendix B).

For further explanation of the methodology for negotiating the problems, please refer to the Authors' notes in Chapter 1 Introduction.

Overview of Problems 9-1, 9-2, and 9-3

Problem 9-1 is a two-person negotiation in which a woman was bitten by a dog while jogging around a park area. She has filed a lawsuit against the dog owner for her injuries resulting from the bite. In this problem, the attorneys, on behalf of their clients, are attempting to negotiate a settlement before trial. Each of you will play the role of an attorney. Since this problem involves litigation, the attorneys have taken depositions of the parties. Summaries of those depositions are included as part of the general information.

Problem 9-2 is a two-person negotiation in which a landlord is withholding a tenant's security deposit. In this problem, the landlord and tenant are attempting to negotiate a resolution before taking the matter to court. You will play the role of either the landlord or the tenant.

Problem 9-3 is a two-person negotiation involving a will contest between a decedent's son and the decedent's former nurse. In this problem, the attorneys, on behalf of their clients, are attempting to negotiate a settlement before trial. Each of you will play the role of an attorney.

Laws Relevant to Dog Bites

Dog ownership is on the rise in the United States. In 2017, there were approximately 90 million dogs living in households throughout the United States.[1] However, as dog ownership increases, so do dog bite incidents. According to the Center for Disease Control, approximately 4.5 million dog bites occur in the United States every year.[2] Given these alarming statistics, states have grappled with enacting laws that will protect and compensate people bitten by dogs, while recognizing that dogs are considered members of the family for many people, not just animals.

The majority of states have stringent laws that hold dog owners responsible for their dogs' biting with limited exceptions.[3] In fact, most states impose strict liability on owners whose dog has bitten and caused injury. This standard provides compensation for the victim and relieves the victim of the need to offer proof that the owner had knowledge of the prior viciousness of the dog, or that the owner acted negligently in handling his dog. The dog bite that results in injury to the victim is the only proof needed to state a cause of action under strict liability laws.

Florida is an example of a state that has recognized strict liability for dog bites. The statute states in part:

> **§ 767.04 Dog owner's liability for damages to persons bitten.** The owner of any dog that bites any person while such person is on or in a public place, or lawfully on or in a private place, including the property of the owner of the dog, is liable for damages suffered by persons bitten, regardless of the former viciousness of the dog or the owners' knowledge of such viciousness. However, any negligence on the part of the person bitten that is a proximate

> cause of the biting incident reduces the liability of the owner of the dog by the percentage that the bitten person's negligence contributed to the biting incident.

Note that although the Florida statute holds the dog owner strictly liable for the dog bite, the dog owner's liability may be reduced if the victim acted negligently. For example, if the victim had stepped on the dog's foot prior to the dog biting him, the jury may determine that the victim's act of stepping on the dog's foot provoked the dog and thus, the victim is partially liable for being bitten. In this case, the jury would reduce the amount of damages by the percentage of fault attributable to the victim.

A minority of states do not apply the strict liability standard, but instead rely on what is known as the "one bite rule."[4] The "one bite rule" holds a dog owner liable for a bite only if the owner had scienter, a standard which requires the dog owner to have known, or should have known, that the dog had dangerous propensities to bite prior to the dog biting the victim. The one bite rule is often referred to the one free bite rule, in that an owner can often escape liability for the first time a dog bites, since the owner can claim that he did not have knowledge of the dog's dangerous propensities prior to the bite. However, once the dog has bitten, the owner is now on notice that the dog has a propensity to bite and will be liable for any subsequent bites. The one bite rule is a bit of a misnomer. The dog owner may also be on notice of his dog's dangerous propensities even if his dog has not bitten before. If, for example, the dog was trained as an attack dog, the owner should be well aware of the dog's dangerous propensities. Further, if the dog has frequently growled or bared its teeth at people previously, this conduct may be enough to prove the required notice to the owner of the dog's dangerous propensities.

One bite rule states typically do not have statutes that address the liability of dog owners for dog bites, but instead the law is derived from common law. For example, in Kansas, a dog bite victim must prove that the dog owner either had scienter or was negligent before they can recover.[5] Therefore, if the victim is unable to prove scienter, which requires that the owner knew (or should have known) that the dog had a dangerous propensity to bite, the dog victim may be able to recover under a negligence standard.

Further, many cities and counties have leash laws, requiring that a dog owner walk his dog on a leash. For example, Palm Beach County, Florida has an ordinance that provides in part:

> It shall be unlawful for any dog to be off the owner's property (which property is exclusive to the owner) unless the dog is under the restraint or control of a person by means of a leash or other device such as a cage, crate or vehicle in accordance with section 4-24, Animal care; manner of keeping.[6]

If the owner does not leash his dog, he not only is in violation of local law, but if his dog bites, there may be a cause of action for negligence per se.[7] Negligence per se provides a cause of action when a person violates a statute that was enacted for an intended purpose.[8] One of the intended purposes of leash laws is to prevent a dog from causing harm to others. Therefore, in cities or counties with leash laws, a violation of the leash laws will likely result in a claim under negligence per se.

Due to the popularity of dogs residing in households, it is likely that you have already or will encounter a situation involving a dog bite. Many dog bites do not rise to the level of a serious injury resulting in a lawsuit, but for those that do, it is probable that the parties and their attorneys will engage in settlement negotiations. Given the adversarial nature of litigation, it may be difficult for the parties to approach negotiations in a calm and efficient manner. Nevertheless, just as in any negotiation, using the TABLE approach may help diffuse the emotion and find mutually acceptable solutions.

Problem 9-1: Dog Bite

General Information

Assume for purposes of this negotiation that the dog bite incident took place in Palm Beach County, Florida and that the Florida laws discussed above apply.

Maria Carlson is a 19-year-old single woman. She just graduated from high school and will attend college in September. Andy Tipton is a 35-year-old male, who is employed as a nurse at the local hospital. This case involves a dog bite incident, in which Tipton's dog, Mickey, bit Carlson.

As a result of this incident, Carlson hired an attorney, who filed a lawsuit on behalf of Carlson against Tipton, asking for damages in excess of $25,000. Tipton subsequently hired an attorney to defend him in the lawsuit. The parties' attorneys' have agreed to meet to negotiate and hopefully resolve this matter before going to trial.

The following information is a summary of statements from the parties and a witness.

Deposition Summary of Plaintiff Maria Carlson

I was jogging on the sidewalk that surrounds Pine Tree Park at 5:00 PM on February 23. I wear headphones and play music when I jog but keep the volume low, so I can hear my surroundings. The sidewalk is outside the park and close to the street. I jog often on the sidewalk and I'm very familiar with the area. The sidewalk is about five feet in width. I was jogging for about ten minutes when I noticed the Defendant and his dog walking about 15 feet in front of me. The Defendant's back was to me. As I approached him from about 10 feet away, I called out "excuse me," and I prepared to pass him on the left side of the sidewalk. I did not want to leave the sidewalk because even though there was a small area of grass to the left and right of the sidewalk, the grass was uneven. Of course, I didn't want to pass by Defendant on the street because of the traffic. After I said, "excuse me," the Defendant appeared to move to the right a little and his dog was on the right side on a leash. As the sidewalk is narrow, when I was about 5 feet from him, I again said, "excuse me." Defendant did not respond but as I passed him, I noticed he seemed to be talking to his watch on his left wrist.

As I jogged past him, I did not bump into Defendant and his dog, but his dog made a sudden move towards me and Defendant dropped the leash. Then the dog began to chase me, so I stopped jogging and reached down to pet the dog. I figured since this was a cute 25-pound dog, the dog was friendly, and I wanted to calm the dog down because he seemed very crazy. However, as I reached to pet him, the dog jumped at me and bit my finger before the Defendant was able to retrieve the dog. I never stepped on the dog's foot. I didn't do anything to the dog except reach out to pet him. I was in excruciating pain from the bite. The defendant called an ambulance and I was taken to the hospital. I had a bite wound on my finger that was bleeding profusely. I received five stiches at the hospital for my finger. The stiches were removed 10 days later.

Currently, my finger is still somewhat stiff and painful. I am not receiving any more medical treatment at this point. I play the trombone in my high school marching band and was planning on becoming a member of the marching band in college, but at this point, my finger is too painful for me to even practice playing the trombone. Tryouts for the marching band are in August so I may have to pass up the opportunity if my finger isn't healed by that time. My doctor has told me that my finger looks good and should not be stiff or sore by the time of the tryout, but honestly, he doesn't understand how it feels or how much you have to use your index finger to play the trombone. I will be so bummed if I can't try out for the marching band. I'm sure I would've made the marching band even though my college's marching band is one of the best in the state. But I was the third best trombone player at my high school and we came in fourth in the district marching band competition.

Deposition Summary Defendant Andy Tipton

I was walking my dog Mickey on February 23. Mickey is a 25-pound Maltese/Terrier mix that I rescued from the animal shelter. He was five years old at the time of the incident. I often walked Mickey on the sidewalk surrounding the park, but usually around 4:00 PM. However, on this date, I returned late from the dentist, so it was around 5:00 PM. I was always very careful about staying clear of other individuals on the sidewalk, and always kept Mickey on a leash. On that day, I was talking on the phone, using my watch phone on my left wrist to talk. I was not wearing headphones, so I could hear my surroundings.

On the day of the incident, I did hear Ms. Carlson's footsteps behind me, but I assumed Ms. Carlson would simply pass me by leaving the sidewalk and passing by me on the grassy part of the embankment on the left. However, Ms. Carlson decided to remain on the sidewalk and pass me. The sidewalk is so narrow that when she passed me, she bumped into me and Mickey. She was running fast, and she bumped into me and Mickey so forcefully that I dropped the leash. Mickey was confused and did start to run after Plaintiff, but not in a threatening way. However, once Plaintiff stopped and Mickey came to her, I saw Plaintiff step on Mickey's foot. I did not see her trying to pet him. Mickey did bite her finger but only because she stepped on his foot. Mickey had never bitten anyone before, and he was very obedient. Luckily, Plaintiff did not injure Mickey by stepping on his foot. By the way, I never heard her say "excuse me" or make any statements to me before she passed me. I have excellent hearing.

At the time of the incident, Mickey was a healthy dog and up to date on all of his shots. Unfortunately, two weeks after the incident, Mickey died in his sleep, apparently from a heart attack. I think it was due to all the stress he felt from the incident. He was never the same. Plaintiff was reckless. I'm sorry she was hurt, but she did provoke Mickey by stepping on his foot. By the way, her finger bite is very minor. She only required 5 stiches and it did not get infected. I'm a nurse and I've seen so many severe dog bites. This was very minor. Also, since Mickey had all his shots, she was in no danger of getting rabies or any other disease from him. She also doesn't appear to be such a great trombone player so it's doubtful she can even make her college marching band.

Deposition Summary of Witness—Francine Parker

I was walking about 20 feet from where the incident took place. I was directly facing Mr. Tipton and Ms. Carlson. I saw Ms. Carlson pass Mr. Tipton and his dog. I could not see if Ms. Carlson bumped into Mr. Tipton but I did see Mr. Tipton jump as if startled by her passing him, and he dropped the leash. It all happened so quickly that I couldn't tell if Ms. Tipton stepped on the dog's foot or if she was petting the dog when she was bitten. Everyone knows you shouldn't pass on the sidewalk so close to dogs or try to pet strange dogs. But Mr. Tipton should have been more careful with his dog and not dropped the leash.

Summary of Damages

Past medicals: $10,000 (unpaid)—**not in dispute as to amount**

Pain and Suffering: $20,000 (Plaintiff's demand)—**disputed as to amount**

No future anticipated medical bills—**not in dispute**

No psychological damages—**not in dispute**

Please Note. Assume also that neither party has insurance so do not discuss insurance coverage.

Confidential Information

Recall that the parties will prepare Tactical Planning Worksheets for the upcoming negotiation. Each party's Tactical Planning Worksheet is to be kept confidential. This information should not be shared with the other party prior to the negotiation. For purposes of this problem, your planning worksheet should include your confidential bargaining position on these issues:

A. For Carlson (Dog bite victim/Plaintiff): The minimum amount she will accept as settlement. Include the maximum percentage of comparative fault she would accept.

B. For Tipton (Dog Owner/Defendant): The maximum he will pay as settlement. Include the percentage of comparative fault, if any, he would accept.

Tactical Planning Worksheet Reveal

After concluding the negotiations, you and your counterpart should exchange your individual Tactical Planning Worksheets so that you both can see the bargaining positions you had planned to use during the negotiation. You should compare the two worksheets and see how far apart you were initially. Also, you should analyze whether and why you strayed from your worksheet, especially in the areas of offers and counteroffers. What positive aspects from your counterpart's worksheet do you wish you had included in yours?

Post-Negotiation Self-Reflection Worksheet

At the conclusion of the reveal session for this dog bite problem, be sure to complete the Post-Negotiation Self-Reflection Worksheet (found in Appendix B). Your Post-Negotiation Self-Reflection Worksheet should be completed individually and optimally within a short period of time after the Tactical Planning Worksheet reveal, while the negotiation session is fresh in your mind.

Laws Relevant to Security Deposit Disputes

Moving into an apartment is for many people a positive experience. Renters may have searched long and hard for their new apartments, and once they find it, they look forward to their new residences. Due to their optimism, they often give the lease a quick once over, and as is required by most leases, give the landlord the first and last month's rent and a security deposit. In an optimum setting, the renter lives quietly and comfortably in his apartment for the duration of the lease.

However, while moving into an apartment may be exciting, moving out is usually devoid of any entertainment value. Often, moving out of an apartment is a chaotic and exhausting experience. Packing up your belongings, cleaning the apartment, arranging for a moving company or a good friend to help you move, and cancelling cable service are some of the many mundane tasks associated with moving out. One task that should be mundane and standard is the landlord returning the security deposit. However, for many tenants, getting back their security deposit becomes a tug of war with the landlord which can quickly escalate to a stressful situation. By knowing how to effectively negotiate for return of a security deposit, both tenant and landlord can de-escalate the situation and amicably resolve their dispute.

Security deposits have been used by landlords for more than a century in order to monetarily compensate the landlord for damage done to his property by a tenant. In essence, the deposit secures the tenant's performance under the lease.[9] However, even though the security deposit has been used for over a century, courts have struggled to delineate the rights of the landlord and the tenant with respect to the deposited funds. In response to this struggle, most states have enacted specific statutes to provide clear guidance and authority on the issues involving security deposits.

State laws encompass a wide variety of issues that may arise concerning security deposits. While some states have unique provisions, most state laws uniformly address the following major issues:

Maximum Security Deposit Permitted by Law

Security deposit limits are generally established by state statutes.[10] Some states statutes do not set limits on the amount a landlord may charge as a security deposit. Many of the state statutes that impose limits set the security deposit at the price of one month's rent. However, even in those states in which there is no maximum security deposit limit, city or county ordinances may impose a limitation on the amount a landlord can hold as a security deposit.

Charges Landlord May Claim against the Security Deposit

Tenants assume that the security deposit is for the purpose of repairing damage to the apartment caused by the tenant. In fact, the security deposit is often called the damage deposit. Yet the tenant is not responsible for all damage to the apartment. Conditions caused by normal wear and tear are the responsibility of the landlord, not the tenant. For example, faded paint and frayed carpet are examples of conditions caused by normal wear and tear. However, broken windows, holes in the wall, even an excessively dirty bathroom is likely to be classified as damage and the responsibility of the tenant. The key distinction between normal wear and tear and damage is the reasonable use of the apartment. Tenants are expected to maintain their unit, but not expected, for example, to pay to replace a rug that has faded due to normal use. In contrast, broken tiles or gaping holes in the walls go beyond normal wear and tear and the tenant's security deposit may be properly used by the landlord to pay for the repair or replacement of those items.[11]

While most people consider damage to the apartment as the only legitimate deduction from their security deposit, states permit landlords to use the security deposit for other purposes. In most states, the security deposit may be used for unpaid rent. It may also be used in some states to replace or restore personal property that has been damaged or lost, such as keys. Cleaning costs, unpaid utilities, and costs associated with an early termination of the lease are other purposes for which some states permit use of the security deposit. The purposes for which the security deposit may be used must comply with state law.

Timeframe for Landlord to Return Deposit or Provide Accounting to Tenant

State laws set forth the procedure for the landlord to return the security deposit or to give notice to the tenant that there will be no return, or a partial return, of the security deposit. States vary widely in the number of days required to return or give notice of no return. For example, Arizona allows landlords fourteen days to return the deposit, while Arkansas gives landlords sixty days to return the deposit.[12] State laws strictly hold landlords to the time requirements under the principle that security deposit funds belong to the tenant, and any further delay past the time allotment is depriving that tenant of the right to his money. Of course, proper notification of the landlord's intent to retain all or part of the security deposit will forestall the tenant from receiving his money, until there is a proper resolution of the dispute. There are time requirements for notifying the tenant that the money will not be returned, which sometimes differ from the time requirement for returning the deposit.

Requirement of a Walkthrough Inspection of Apartment prior to Tenant Vacating

The majority of states do not require the landlord to conduct a walkthrough of the apartment. However, Michigan not only requires a walkthrough, but also requires that the landlord make inventory lists both before the tenant takes occupancy and again at termination of occupancy. At the end of the lease, the landlord's inventory checklist must list all the damages the landlord claims are chargeable to the tenant against the security deposit.[13] Similarly, Kentucky also requires inventory lists at the beginning and end of the tenancy, with the landlord listing damages at the end of the tenancy chargeable against the security deposit.[14] Also, in Kentucky, both the landlord and tenant must sign off to the inventory list, and if the tenant disputes the damage assessment by the landlord, the tenant must sign a separate statement listing his objections to the landlord's assessment.[15]

Landlord Placing Security Deposit in a Separate and/or Interest-Bearing Account

When a tenant pays a security deposit, that money remains the property of the tenant unless and until the time that the landlord establishes a right to retain the deposit under applicable law. As such, the landlord has a duty to safe keep the deposit on behalf of the tenant. Most states' laws require landlords to keep tenants' security deposits in a separate account from any funds of the landlord. While the landlord may be permitted to place all tenants' security deposits in the same account, he must keep his own funds in a separate account.

State law also determines whether a landlord must pay interest on a security deposit. Most states do not require a landlord to place a tenant's security deposit in an interest-bearing account for the benefit of the tenant.[16] A handful of states, however, do have that requirement. For example, North Dakota requires the landlord to deposit a tenant's security deposit in a federally insured interest-bearing account for the benefit of the tenant. Upon termination of the lease, the security deposit and interest must be paid to the tenant unless the landlord follows the procedure to make a claim against the security deposit for the reasons set forth under the statute.[17]

States are very specific as to the methodology for retaining security deposits and include numerous penalties for failure of the landlord to comply with the procedures for taking possession and retuning the security deposit. While some tenants may feel that seeking return of the deposit is not worth their time and potential court costs, familiarizing themselves with the law can go a long way in negotiating a successful return of the deposit. For example, Illinois law provides that a landlord who acts in bad faith in failing to return the security deposit is liable to the tenant for an amount equal to twice the security deposit, along with court costs and fees.[18] Therefore, as in any negotiation, it is in the best interest of tenants to research their state law in order to prepare for negotiations with the landlord concerning return of the security deposit. Furthermore, the landlord and tenant should attempt to resolve the security deposit matter before turning to the courts to settle their dispute. In fact, Florida law provides that if the landlord requires a security deposit, the lease must contain a notice that the parties try to resolve any dispute regarding security deposits informally before filing a lawsuit.[19] Hopefully, the landlord and tenant will negotiate and come to an amical resolution.

Problem 9-2: Security Deposit

General Information

Assume for purposes of this negotiation that the security deposit dispute is governed by the laws as described in the problem below.

Riley entered into a one-year lease at the Ridge Apartments. The lease required a security deposit of $1,900, which was the equivalent of one month's rent. At the time he signed the lease, Riley gave Mertz, the landlord, a check for the first and last month's rent, and the additional $1,900 for the security deposit.

Throughout the course of the year, Riley had some parties at his apartment. One of the neighbors, Mrs. Flanders, who lived across the hall, complained to Mertz about the noise. Mertz told Riley that his parties were disturbing the neighbors, and Riley had better tone it down or he would be asked to leave the apartment. Riley told Mertz that the Mrs. Flanders, the complaining neighbor, was being unreasonable, and his parties were low key and ended by midnight, in line with the city's noise ordinance. After speaking with Mertz, Riley continued to have a several parties. In fact, Mrs. Flanders recorded the noise coming from Riley's apartment during one of the parties and turned the recording over to Mertz. Mertz sent an email to Riley, informing him that if he received any more complaints about Riley, he would be evicted, as was permitted in the lease. Riley emailed Mertz back and said he would not have future parties and there would be no more problems with the noise. He also asked Mertz if he could renew his lease, which was due to expire in two months. Mertz told him he would not renew his lease. At that point, Riley emailed Mertz and told him he believed Mertz was discriminating against him, because he is Native American. Riley, who is Native American, suspected this because the young family that lived in the apartment below him had told Riley that they had overheard Mertz saying that Riley should "go back and live on the reservation." Mertz denied any discrimination and told Riley he was unaware that Riley was Native American.

The week before Riley was to vacate the apartment, Mertz contacted Riley and told him he would like to do a walkthrough inspection with Riley to determine if there was any damage to the apartment. Riley agreed to meet with Mertz on Wednesday at 3:00 PM for the walkthrough. However, at 12:00 PM on that date, Mertz emailed Riley and told him he had an emergency and had to re-schedule the walkthrough to Friday, which was the last day of Riley's lease. Riley was annoyed at the cancellation, because he had left work early Wednesday to make the appointment. Riley told Mertz he was moving out a day early on Thursday, and Mertz could inspect the apartment whenever he wanted to on Friday without Riley, since Riley could not take another day off work. Riley also told Mertz to send his security deposit to him as soon as possible, since the apartment is in great condition, better than when he moved in.

Twenty-eight days after Riley moved out, he received a letter from Mertz stating that Mertz was keeping the security deposit due to the fact that Riley had damaged the apartment, and that it was necessary for Mertz to make repairs and cleaning beyond normal wear and tear. Mertz said it was necessary to make the repair and cleaning immediately after Riley moved out, since a new tenant moved in a few days after Riley vacated the apartment. Mertz sent an itemized list to Riley, detailing the following repair and cleaning costs:

1) $400.00 for rug cleaning.

The rugs were stained, apparently with dog stains and food stains. Riley did not disclose on the lease that he had a pet and paid no extra deposit for a pet. Mertz hired a carpet cleaner, who cleaned the rug but was unable to get all the stains out of the rug. Mertz believes he may have to replace the rug due to the stains sooner than he had planned.

2) $1,200 for wall repair.

There was a hole in the wall near the patio, and it appeared to be caused by a hammer or a portable piece of furniture, like a bartender's cart, crashing into it. The wall needed drywall and a new coat of paint to repair the damage.

3) $300.00 for bathroom cleaning.

The bathroom shower and toilet were filthy and appeared as if they had not been cleaned during the lease period. Mertz hired a cleaning crew who needed to spend several hours beyond a routine apartment cleaning to clean the bathroom.

Riley responded to Mertz that he had the apartment professionally cleaned once a month and that he also personally cleaned the bathrooms. Riley also said the stains were on the rug prior to his moving in. However, neither Riley nor Mertz took pictures of the rugs before Riley moved in. Mertz did admit that the prior owner had a dog, but that he had the rugs cleaned before Riley moved in so there were no stains. Further, Mertz told Riley that a neighbor had informed him that Riley had a frequent visitor who brought her dog with her to the apartment, and that visitor often stayed overnight. Riley told Mertz that the neighbor's account was inaccurate. While he had a friend who brought her dog over one time to visit him, he did not have a frequent overnight guest, and any overnight guests he had did not have pets. As for the hole in the wall, Riley claims the hole was a result of him trying to hang a picture when the wall collapsed, due to no fault of his. Riley also claims the bathroom was not dirty beyond normal wear and tear. There are no pictures of the wall or bathroom's condition prior to Riley moving in or when Riley moved out.

Riley told Mertz again that he felt Mertz was discriminating against him, and that Riley was probably going to go to small claims court to get his money back. Mertz told him that they should try and work this out before going to court, and Mertz suggested they meet and try and come to a solution. Riley agreed to meet and negotiate a resolution.

Assume for purposes of this negotiation that the rental apartment is located in a state with the following laws concerning security deposits.

1. A Landlord shall not demand or receive as a security deposit an amount or value in excess of two months' rent.

2. Security deposits shall not be commingled with the personal funds of the Landlord. All security deposits may, but are not required, to be held in an interest-bearing account. Any interest earned on a rental deposit during the first five years of a tenancy shall be the property of the Landlord.

3. A Landlord shall, within thirty days from the date of termination of the tenancy and receipt of the Tenant's mailing address or delivery instructions, return the security deposit to the Tenant or furnish to the tenant a written statement showing the specific reason for withholding of the rental deposit or any portion thereof.

4. A Landlord may withhold from the security deposit only such amounts as are reasonably necessary for the following reasons: (1) to remedy a Tenant's default in the payment of rent or of other funds due to the landlord pursuant to the rental agreement; (2) to remedy damage caused by Tenant, ordinary wear and tear excepted. Ordinary wear and tear is defined as the expected decline in the condition of the property due to normal everyday use. The Tenant is responsible for maintaining and cleaning the property on a regular basis during the course of the tenancy.

5. A Landlord who fails to provide a written statement within thirty days of termination of the tenancy and receipt of the Tenant's mailing address or delivery instructions shall forfeit all rights to withhold any portion of the rental deposit. If no mailing address or instructions are provided to the Land-

lord within one year from the termination of the tenancy, the rental deposit shall revert to the Landlord and the Tenant will be deemed to have forfeited all rights to the rental deposit.

6. Landlord and Tenant must meet and attempt to resolve all matters concerning return of the security deposit before seeking a remedy in court.

7. The bad-faith retention of a security deposit by a Landlord, or any portion of the rental deposit, in violation of this section shall subject the Landlord to punitive damages not to exceed twice the monthly rental payment in addition to actual damages. In an action concerning the security deposit, the burden of proving, by a preponderance of the evidence, the reason for withholding all or any portion of the rental deposit shall be on the Landlord

8. The court may, in any action on a rental agreement, award reasonable attorney fees to the prevailing party.

Confidential Information

Recall that the parties will prepare Tactical Planning Worksheets for the upcoming negotiation. Each party's Tactical Planning Worksheet is to be kept confidential. This information should not be shared with the other party prior to the negotiation.

For purposes of this problem, your planning worksheet should include your confidential bargaining position on these issues:

A. For Mertz (Landlord): The maximum amount of the security deposit he would return to Riley.

B. For Riley (Tenant): The minimum amount he would accept as a return of his security deposit.

Tactical Planning Worksheet Reveal

After concluding the negotiations, you and your counterpart should exchange your individual Tactical Planning Worksheet so that you both can see the bargaining positions you had planned to use during the negotiation. You should compare the two worksheets and see how far apart you were initially. Also, you should analyze whether and why you strayed from your worksheet, especially in the areas of offers and counteroffers. What positive aspects from your counterpart's worksheet do you wish you had included in yours?

Post-Negotiation Self-Reflection Worksheet

At the conclusion of the reveal session for this problem, be sure to complete the Post-Negotiation Self-Reflection Worksheet (found in Appendix B). Your Post-Negotiation Self-Reflection Worksheet should be completed individually and optimally within a short period of time after the Tactical Planning Worksheet reveal, while the negotiation session is fresh in your mind.

Laws Relevant to Testamentary Capacity and Undue Influence

This section discusses negotiations involving will contests based on testamentary capacity and undue influence. Challenges to the validity of a will often involve claims that the person who made the will—referred to as the testator—either lacked the capacity to make the will or was unduly influenced into making the will. Claims based on undue influence often include allegations that the testator lacked capacity. However, claims of undue influence could also be brought independently of claims of lack of capacity. A person could have testamentary capacity and yet still be susceptible to undue influence by a third party such as a family member, friend, fiduciary, neighbor, or caregiver.

Generally, both lack of capacity and undue influence challenges are case law driven. State statutes do not generally address the underlying elements of such mental status challenges. Where states do have statutes regarding capacity and undue influence, the statutes are often limited to delineating which party—the will proponent or the will contestant—has the burden of proof. In most states, the proponent of the will must prove that the will was properly executed in accordance with the state's will formalities (e.g., signature, witnesses, etc.), but the contestant of the will has the burden of establishing lack of capacity or undue influence. The states vary as to the evidentiary standard required for a successful contest with some states requiring clear and convincing evidence and others accepting the lesser preponderance of evidence standard.

Testamentary Capacity

Testamentary capacity is determined at the time when the will is executed, so subsequent incapacity is not determinative. Moreover, the standard for testamentary capacity is generally lower than that required to transact ordinary business, to make a deed, or to enter into a contract.

With some variation in phrasing, the states generally use a similar analysis for determining testamentary capacity. In many states, a testator is deemed to have testamentary capacity if the testator is able to comprehend four factors: (1) the nature and extent of his property; (2) the natural objects of his bounty (e.g., the testator knows his children); (3) the disposition he wishes to make of his estate; and (4) the act of making a will. Some states refer to this analysis as a three-factor, or five-factor, rather than four-factor test, but the analysis is basically the same. For example, Florida appears to use a three-factor test. In Florida, testamentary capacity is referred to as the ability of the testator to mentally understand in a general way (1) the nature and extent of the testator's property to be disposed of, (2) the testator's relation to those who would naturally claim a substantial benefit from the will (the natural objects of the testator's bounty), and (3) the practical effect of the will as executed. Colorado appears to divide the factors into five factors such that testamentary capacity is found when the testator: (1) understood the nature of her act; (2) knew the extent of her property; (3) understood the proposed testamentary disposition; (4) knew the natural objects of her bounty; and (5) made a will that represented her wishes.[20]

Regardless of the phrasing, the tests for capacity are very fact-intensive and there is an interplay among the factors. For example, if the testator seems to have a firm grasp of the individuals who would be the natural objects of his bounty and the testator leaves those persons the bulk of his property, evidence of the testator's failure to understand in a general way the extent of the testator's property might be given little weight. Conversely, a testator does not need to leave anything in the will to the natural objects of his bounty; he meets that particular factor of the testamentary capacity test, if he simply knows the natural objects of his bounty at the time of will execution.

Undue Influence

The theory for invalidating a will based on undue influence is that the undue influence exerted on the testator destroyed the testator's free agency and substituted another person's volition for that of the testator. If a will contestant can show that a will, or a portion of a will, was the product of undue influence, that will, or portion, would be invalid, since it would not truly reflect the testator's wishes, but rather would be the product of another person's undue influence on the testator. Influence alone is not enough to invalidate a will, however. Rather the influence exerted on the testator must be such that it replaces the testator's free agency with that of the influencer. Moreover, generalized influence is not enough; the influence must be aimed towards the creation of the will.

Because finding direct evidence of undue influence is often exceedingly difficult, most states, by case law, have developed factors that give rise to procedural presumptions of undue influence. The factors for raising a procedural presumption of undue influence, while not identical, are often similar from state to state. For example, in Arizona, a presumption of undue influence arises if the will beneficiary: (1) occupies a confidential relationship with the testator; (2) actively procures or prepares the execution of the will; and (3) is a principal beneficiary. In Kansas, the presumption arises if the will beneficiary: (1) was in a confidential relationship with the testator and (2) there is clear and convincing evidence of suspicious circumstances.[21]

The Florida law of undue influence is similar. In Florida, a presumption of undue influence arises if the will contestant establishes that the will beneficiary: (1) was a substantial beneficiary; (2) occupied a confidential relationship with the testator; and (3) was actively involved in procuring the will. Generally, a substantial beneficiary is one who receives a substantial and unnatural devise. An unnatural devise may be found when the will beneficiary receives significantly more than the beneficiary would have received under intestacy, in comparison to others in the same degree of relationship to the testator, or more than the amount the beneficiary would have received under a prior will of the testator. A confidential relationship between the beneficiary and the testator may be found from fiduciary relationships and from certain relationships of special trust and confidence, including relatives handling the testator's finances and daily needs, health professionals, and advisors. The Florida courts have provided the following nonexclusive list of criteria which are relevant to determining active procurement of the disputed will: (a) presence of the beneficiary at the execution of the will; (b) presence of the beneficiary on those occasions when the testator expressed a desire to make a will; (c) recommendation by the beneficiary of an attorney to draw the will; (d) knowledge of the contents of the will by the beneficiary prior to execution; (e) giving of instructions on preparation of the will by the beneficiary to the attorney drawing the will; (f) securing of witnesses to the will by the beneficiary; and (g) safekeeping of the will by the beneficiary subsequent to execution.[22]

A state's particular case laws would have to be analyzed very carefully to determine the applicable underlying elements for undue influence, to ascertain when a procedural presumption of undue influence arises, and to establish the effect of raising a procedural presumption. In Florida, for example, once the presumption of undue influence is raised the burden of proof shifts from the contestant of the will to the proponent of the will.[23] Thus, if the presumption of undue influence is raised, the proponent of the will would have to prove that the will was not the product of undue influence. In other states, however, even if the contestant raises the presumption of undue influence, the law might only shift the burden of production (as opposed to the burden of proof) to the will proponent.

There are significant advantages in negotiating to prevent litigating will contests based on undue influence or lack of capacity. First, such contests are often costly and very fact intensive. Second, the parties may wish to preserve privacy for the deceased and the family. A will contest could provide unwanted publicity and could portray the family in a less than favorable light. Moreover, if the contest is an intra-family matter, the parties may prefer to avoid litigation in order to enhance the possibility of returning to family harmony.

Problem 9-3: Testamentary Capacity and Undue Influence

General Information

Assume for purposes of this negotiation that the decedent resided in Florida and that the Florida laws discussed above apply.

Daniel, an industrious, 90-year-old widower, had lived alone for many years after his wife died. Daniel had properly executed a will five years ago, shortly after his wife died ("First Will"). The First Will, which had been drafted by Daniel's long-time attorney and friend, devised Daniel's entire estate to his only son, Sam. Two years ago, Daniel was diagnosed with terminal cancer. His doctors explained that Daniel would need constant monitoring and assistance to administer his medical care. Daniel was determined not to "die in a sterile hospital." Sam, who lived and worked 250 miles away from his father, asked Daniel to move in with him. Daniel did not, however, want to leave his old neighborhood. Daniel reminded Sam that it was important to Daniel that the family house stay occupied and that one day the family house would be Sam's house. Since Daniel did not want to leave his house, Daniel hired a nurse, Naomi, who moved into his house to assist him. Shortly after Naomi moved into the house, she started monitoring Daniel's visitors and screening Daniel's phone calls. When Sam tried to contact his father, Naomi would say he was too ill to talk. When Sam flew in to see his father, Naomi had given Daniel so many sedatives that Daniel was barely able to recognize his son. Daniel became quite depressed, because he felt isolated.

Last year, Naomi started pestering Daniel to revise his will, saying that she would have to leave Daniel if she was not secure in the knowledge that she would be financially set after he died. Finally, at the beginning of this year, Daniel agreed to execute a new will. When Daniel tried contacting his long-time attorney, however, Daniel found out that his long-time attorney had died. That same day, Naomi called an attorney friend of hers and asked him to rush over to the house. The attorney, who Daniel had not met before, arrived and discussed the matter of a new will with Daniel while Naomi was in the room. During the conversation with the new attorney, Daniel insisted that the house had to go to Sam. When the attorney asked about the rest of Daniel's property, Daniel did not answer but Naomi said that Daniel was only worried about the house going to Sam and the rest would go to her. Daniel at that point had his eyes closed but the attorney thought that he was still awake. The next day, the attorney and his assistant, Anne, returned with a typed will. When the attorney arrived, Naomi ran and got the gardener, George, to come into the room to witness the signing. The attorney read the new will aloud in front of Daniel, Naomi, George (the gardener), and Anne (the attorney's assistant). After reading the will, the attorney directed Daniel to sign it. In his weakened state, Daniel was only able to write his initials at the end of the will. After Daniel initialed the will, Naomi, George, and Anne signed as witnesses. The attorney then served as a notary for a self-proving affidavit. As the attorney was leaving, he handed the original of the new will ("Second Will") to Naomi. The Second Will contained a clause expressly revoking any previous wills. The Second Will left Daniel's house to Sam and the rest and residue of Daniel's probate estate to Naomi. Daniel died the following week.

Assume that Daniel had no debts and that Daniel's assets consist of his house valued at $500,000, securities in his name valued at $1,000,000; a car valued at $20,000; art work valued at $5,000; and household furnishings valued at $15,000, and a bank account in his own name with cash of $30,000.

Naomi offers Daniel's Second Will for probate. Sam (Daniel's son) wants to contest the Second Will. They both hire attorneys who agree to meet prior to filing suit to try to negotiate a resolution.

Confidential Information

Before beginning the negotiation, each negotiator should prepare a Tactical Planning Worksheet (found in Appendix A). Each party's Tactical Planning Worksheet is to be kept confidential. This information should not be shared with the other party prior to the negotiation.

For purposes of this problem, your planning worksheet should include your confidential bargaining position on these issues:

A. For Naomi (Nurse/Will Proponent): The maximum amount of the residuary estate that she would concede to Sam.

B. For Sam (Son/Will Contestant): The minimum amount of the estate he would accept.

Tactical Planning Worksheet Reveal

After concluding the negotiations, you and your counterpart should exchange your individual Tactical Planning Worksheets so that you both can see the bargaining positions you had planned to use during the negotiation. You should compare the two worksheets and see how far apart you were initially. Also, you should analyze whether and why you strayed from your worksheet, especially in the areas of offers and counteroffers. What positive aspects from your counterpart's worksheet do you wish you had included in yours?

Post-Negotiation Self-Reflection Worksheet

At the conclusion of the reveal session for this problem, be sure to complete the Post-Negotiation Self-Reflection Worksheet (found in Appendix B). Your Post-Negotiation Self-Reflection Worksheet should be completed individually and optimally within a short period of time after the Tactical Planning Worksheet reveal, while the negotiation session is fresh in your mind.

Chapter 10

Conclusion

Now that you have learned to apply the TABLE method to negotiate many of life's most stressful events, you are ready to tackle some real negotiations. Here are some of our final thoughts.

First, whether you are negotiating in the boardroom or the living room, remember always to be professional and courteous. In the heat of a negotiation, we often lose sight of niceties and resort to anger and personal attacks, especially when we feel cornered. While anger may initially work for you in some instances and get you a quick concession, this bullying tactic, in the long run, will not be effective. Those negotiating with you will soon come to know your reputation as a bully and will either respond similarly or just choose not to negotiate with you at all.

Second, be willing to make concessions. A good deal does not mean you get everything you want. In a true negotiation, you make concessions and counteroffers and arrive at a mutually beneficial resolution. If you truly are not willing to give up anything, you are not negotiating, you are demanding. You do not need to wait until sitting down to negotiate to realize you are not willing to give up anything. If you cannot list what you will concede, then you are not invested in negotiating. In that case, realize that you have, in effect, chosen your alternative instead of negotiating for something better.

Third, understand that the term "discuss" often means negotiate. We used the word discuss in many of our problems because, especially in arms-open negotiations, people often say they want to discuss something with you. For example, "I'd like to discuss our living arrangements," or "I'd like to discuss our finances," or "I'd like to discuss selling our family business." These statements are really invitations to negotiations. Therefore, you should be prepared for the opportunity to make a deal. Take the offer to "discuss" and head to the negotiating table.

Fourth, remember that planning is key. You should always plan for a negotiation. Whether you have ten minutes or ten days, have a plan before you start a negotiation. If you have time, use the Tactical Planning Worksheet and map out your negotiation strategy. However, if time is short, you should at least plan your highest realistic offer, your minimal acceptable level, and analyze your alternatives. You should also write these down, or at least text them to yourself so you can refer to them during the negotiation.

Finally, remember that if you are an ethical and egalitarian negotiator, you will be more successful and will be welcome to sit at any negotiating table.

Appendices

Appendix A

Tactical Planning Worksheet

1. Identify the Relationship

   Describe whether your relationship with the other side is, arms-open or arms-length.

2. Conducting Research

   A. List the research you plan to use as objective criteria to support your goals.

   B. List the important facts you plan to rely on to support your goals.

3. Highest Realistic Goal and Minimum Acceptable Level

   A. What is your highest realistic goal?

   B. What is your minimum acceptable level?

   C. What do you think are the other side's highest realistic goal and minimum acceptable level?

4. Alternative Options If Negotiation Fails

   A. What is your best alternative if there is no agreement?

   B. What do you think is the other side's best alternative if there is no agreement?

5. Opening Offers, Concessions, and Counteroffers

   A. What is your opening offer? Does it match your highest realistic goal?

   B. What concessions are you willing to make? In what order will you make these concessions?

   C. List a minimum of three anticipated offers you intend to make after your opening offer. Explain why you would make these offers. Your last offer should be your minimum acceptable level.

6. Questions and Anticipated Responses to Questions

   A. What information do you wish to obtain from the other side?

   B. List the questions you plan to ask the other side to obtain this information.

   C. What questions do you anticipate you may be asked by the other side?

   D. How do you plan to respond to questions you may be asked?

Appendix B

Post-Negotiation Self-Reflection Worksheet

Answer the questions below and provide brief explanations with your answers.

1. Tactical Planning:
   A. What were the strengths and weaknesses of your Tactical Planning Worksheet?
   B. When did you refer to your worksheet during the negotiation?
   C. How would you change your worksheet for future negotiations?
2. Arranging:
   A. Was the forum for your negotiation optimal?
   B. What other forums might have been conducive to this negotiation?
   C. If the negotiation were to continue, would it be beneficial to change forums?
3. Bargaining:
   A. Were your offers, counteroffers, and concessions well-timed and responsive to the other side?
   B. Did you effectively communicate objective criteria to support your offers?
   C. Did you ask the questions you had planned?
   D. Did you respond adequately to questions you were asked?
   E. Were there any tricks or tactics used by the other side? If so, how did you respond?
4. Letting Go or Resolving:
   A. If you did not reach an agreement, what were the main reasons for not resolving the matter? What might you have done differently to reach an agreement?
   B. If you did reach an agreement, do you believe the agreement was fair from everyone's perspective? Did you memorialize key provisions of the agreement before leaving the negotiating table? Did you determine if you or the other side will prepare the initial draft of the agreement? Did you and the other side agree on a time schedule for completion of the agreement?

5. Ethics and Equity:
   A. Were there any ethical issues that arose during the negotiation? If so, how did you respond to those issues?
   B. Were you treated equitably by the other side? If not, how did you handle the situation?

Notes

Chapter 2

1. Charles B. Craver, Effective Legal Negotiation and Settlement § 2.02 (8th Ed. 2016).
2. *See id.* at § 2.02(1).
3. *Id.* at § 2.02(2)(d).
4. Roger Fisher & William Ury, Getting to YES: Negotiating Agreement Without Giving In, 43 (2d Ed. 1991) *available at* http://www.fd.unl.pt/docentes_docs/ma/AGON_MA_25849.pdf.
5. *See* Redfin, *How Real Estate Commission Works*, Redfin.com (*last visited July 18, 2018*), https://www.redfin.com/resources/how-much-is-real-estate-agent-commission-buyer-seller and Dina Appleton, *What Should You Look Out for in a Talent Representation Agreement?*, Backstage.com (July 13, 2011) https://www.backstage.com/advice-for-actors/business-of-acting/what-should-you-look-out-for-in-a-talent-representation-agreement/.
6. *See* G. Richard Shell, Bargaining for Advantage: Negotiation Strategies for Reasonable People, 30 (Penguin, 2d. Ed. 2006).
7. *Id.*
8. *See e.g.*, G.P. Latham & E. Locke, *New Developments In And Directions For Goal-Setting Research*, 12 European Psychologist 290, 295 (2007), *available at* http://www-2.rotman.utoronto.ca/facbios/file/28%20-%20Latham%20&%20Locke%20Euro%20Psych%202007.pdf.
9. Michael Corkey, *Wells Fargo Fined $185 Million for Fraudulently Opening Accounts*, NY Times (Sept. 8, 2016), https://www.nytimes.com/2016/09/09/business/dealbook/wells-fargo-fined-for-years-of-harm-to-customers.html.
10. *See Generally* Fisher & Ury *supra* note 4 at 50–54.
11. Shell *supra* note 6.
12. *Id.*
13. *See generally, Ask Clever Questions in Your Negotiation*, Negotiation.com (July 19, 2017), https://www.negotiations.com/articles/negotiation-questions/.
14. *See* Model Rules Prof'l Conduct R. 1.6
15. *See* Model Rules Prof'l Conduct (scope).
16. *See* Karen Wells Roby, *Ethics in Settlement: The Effect of Material Misrepresentation*, The Federal Lawyer 42 (August 2012), *available at* http://www.fedbar.org/Resources_1/Federal-Lawyer-Magazine/2012/August/Features/Ethics-in-Settlement-The-Effects-of-Material-Misrepresentation.aspx?FT=.pdf.
17. *See generally* Douglas Richmond, *Lawyer's Professional Responsibilities and Liabilities in Negotiations*, 22 Geo. J. Legal Ethics 249 (2009).

Chapter 3

1. *See* Pon Staff, *Why First Impressions Matter in Negotiation*, Harvard L. School Program on Negotiation (Jan. 25, 2018), *available at* https://www.pon.harvard.edu/daily/negotiation-skills-daily/why-first-impressions-matter/.
2. *Id.*
3. *See* Lynn A. Epstein, *Cyber E-Mail Negotiation vs. Traditional Negotiation: Will Cyber Technology Supplant Traditional Means of Settling Litigation*, 36 Tulsa L.J. 839, 845 (Summer 2001).
4. Ilan Bronstein, et al., *Source Rapport in Negotiation: The Contribution of the Verbal Channel*,

56 J. of Conflict Resolution 1089, 1092 (2012).

5. Ashley Hamer, *Body Language is Overrated*, Curiosity.com (Nov. 13, 2017), https://curiosity.com/topics/body-language-is-overrated-curiosity/.

6. *See e.g.*, Samantha Whitehorne, *When Face-to-Face Falls Short*, AssociationsNow.com (April 19, 2013), https://associationsnow.com/2013/04/when-face-to-face-falls-short/.

7. *Id.*

8. Gabriella Ziccarelli & Eric Goldman, *How a Chipmunk Emoji Cost an Israeli Texter $2,200*, Tech. & Marketing L. Blog, (May 25, 2017), https://blog.ericgoldman.org/archives/2017/05/how-a-chipmunk-emoji-cost-an-israeli-texter-2200.htm.

9. The Associated Press, *Police Add Texting to Crisis Negotiation Arsenal*, MLive.com (May 11, 2014, 12:40 PM), http://www.mlive.com/news/index.ssf/2014/05/police_add_texting_to_crisis_n.html.

Chapter 4

1. *See e.g.*, Adam D. Galinsky, *When to Make the First Offer in Negotiation*, Harv. Business Sch., (Aug. 9, 2004), https://hbswk.hbs.edu/archive/when-to-make-the-first-offer-in-negotiations.

2. Katie Shonk, What is Anchoring in Negotiation? Learn how to defuse the anchoring bias and make smart first offers. Harv. Univ. Program on Negotiation (May 15, 2018), https://www.pon.harvard.edu/daily/negotiation-skills-daily/what-is-anchoring-in-negotiation/.

3. *Id.*

4. *See generally*, Greg Northcraft & Margaret Neale, *Experts, Amateurs, and Real Estate: An Anchoring-and-Adjustment Perspective on Property Pricing Decisions*, 39 Organizational Behavior and Human Decision Processes 84, 94–96 (1986).

5. *See* Shonk *supra* note 2.

6. Joyce, Bedi, *Thomas Edison's Inventive Life*, Invention.si.edu (Apr. 18, 2004), http://invention.si.edu/thomas-edisons-inventive-life

7. *See e.g.*, Roger Fisher & William Ury, Getting to YES: Negotiating Agreement Without Giving In, 42 (2d Ed. 1981), *available at* http://www.fd.unl.pt/docentes_docs/ma/AGON_MA_25849.pdf.

8. *See* Charles B. Craver, *Classic Negotiation Techniques*, 52 Idaho L. Rev. 425, 436 (2016).

9. *See* Robert S. Adlerd & Elliot M. Silverstein, *When David Meets Goliath: Dealing with Power Differentials in Negotiations*, 5 Harv. Negotiation L. Rev. 1, 76 (2000).

10. *See* Gary Miller, *In Negotiations, Making Concessions And Reciprocating Can Lead To Great Deals*, The Denver Post (July 16, 2017), https://www.denverpost.com/2017/07/16/negotiations-concessions-reciprocating-deals/.

11. *See* PON Staff, *Negotiating Tips: Listening Skills for Dealing with Difficult People*, Harvard Law School Daily Blog (July 19, 2018), https://www.pon.harvard.edu/daily/Dealing-with-Difficult-People-daily/.

12. *See e.g.*, Craver, *supra* note 8 at 440.

13. *See* Gerben A. Van Kleef, Carsten De Dreu & Anthony Manstead, *The Interpersonal Effects of Emotions in Negotiations: A Motivated Information Processing Approach*, 87 J. Personality & Soc. Psych. 510 (2004).

Chapter 5

1. Roger Fisher & William Ury, Getting to YES: Negotiating Agreement Without Giving In, 61 (2d Ed. 1981), *available at* http://www.fd.unl.pt/docentes_docs/ma/AGON_MA_25849.pdf.

2. Dean Gesme & Charles Carver, *Principles and Tactics of Negotiation*, 3 J. of Oncology Practice 102, 104 (2007), *available at* https://www.ncbi.nlm.nih.gov/pmc/articles/PMC2793751/pdf/jop102.pdf.

3. Cliff Oxford, *Use These 16 Irrefutable Negotiation Tactics to Get What You Deserve*, Forbes, (Aug. 27, 2014), https://www.forbes.com/sites/cliffoxford/2014/08/27/use-these-16-irrefutable-negotiation-tactics-to-get-what-you-deserve/#7f55ffdd6e8c.

4. *See* Roger Dawson, *Why it's a Mistake to Offer to Split the Difference*, REIClub.com (last visited

July 19, 2018), https://www.reiclub.com/articles/mistake-split-difference.

5. *See generally* Michael J. Rainey, Choosing Your Negotiation Site: Your Place or Mine?, 13 Graziadio Bus. Rev. (2010), available at https://gbr.pepperdine.edu/2010/08/choosing-your-negotiation-site-3/.

6. *See* Gary M. McLaughlin, *Oral Contracts in the Entertainment Industry*, 1 Va. Sports & Ent. L.J. 101, 104 (2001).

7. Eric G. Andersen, *A New Look at Material Breach in the Law of Contracts*, 21 U.C. Davis L. Rev. 1073, 1077 (1988).

8. *See generally* Stephen Fishman, *The Difference Between a Lawsuit, Mediation, and Arbitration*, MileIQ.com (Jun. 11, 2017), https://www.mileiq.com/blog/legal-disputes-the-difference-between-a-lawsuit-mediation-and-arbitration/.

Chapter 6

1. *See* Roy J. Lewicki & Robert J. Robinson, *Ethical and Unethical Bargaining Tactics: An Empirical Study*, 17 J. Bus. Ethics 665, 666 (1998).

2. *See* Model Rules of Prof Conduct r. 4.1. (Am. Bar. Ass'n 2009).

3. *Id.* at cmt 2.

4. *Id.*

5. *See* James K.L. Lawrence, *Lying, Misrepresentation, Puffing, and Bluffing: Legal Ethical and Professional Standards for Negotiators and Mediation Advocates*, 29 Ohio St. J. on Disp. Resol. 35, 36 (2014).

6. *See* Jenna McGregor, *When Telling the Truth is Actually Dishonest*, Wash. Post (Dec. 29, 2016), *available at* http://www.washingtonpost.com/news/on-leadership/wp/2016/12/29/when-telling-the-truth-is-actually-dishonest/?noredirect=on&utm_term=.ddf90233cb1d.

7. *See* Lawrence, *supra* note 5 at 37.

8. *See generally* Leigh Thompson, *Negotiation Tips: Lies, Damned Lies, and Negotiations*, Kellogg. Northwestern.edu (last visited Jul. 6, 2018), http://www.kellogg.northwestern.edu/news_articles/2014/05122014-negotiation_lies.aspx.

9. *See* G. Richard Shell, *When is it Legal to Lie in Negotiations?* MIT Sloan Management Rev. (April 15, 1991), https://sloanreview.mit.edu/article/when-is-it-legal-to-lie-in-negotiations/.

10. *See id.*

11. Shell *supra* note 9.

12. *See* Joe Navarro, *The Truth About Lie Detection*, Psychol Today (Mar. 15, 2012), http://www.psychologytoday.com/us/blog/spycatcher/201203/the-truth-about-lie-detection.

13. *See* Bill Murphy, *How to Tell if Someone is Lying: Ten Tells and Clues*, INC, http://www.inc.com/bill ... jr/how-to-tell-if-someone-is-lying-10-tells-and-clues.html.

14. *See* Brianna Steinhilber, *How to Tell if Someone is Lying According to Behavioral Experts* NBC News (Aug. 15 2017), https://www.nbcnews.com/better/health/how-tell-if-someone-lying-according-behavioral-experts-ncna786326.

15. *See* Cheryl Staats, et al., *Implicit Bias*, Kirwin Inst. (July 13, 2016), http://kirwaninstitute.osu.edu/wp-content/uploads/2016/07/implicit-bias-2016.pdf.

16. L. Song Richardson & Nicole Van Cleve, *Systemic Triage: Implicit Racial Bias in the Criminal Courtroom Crook County: Racism and Injustice in America's Largest Criminal Court* 126 Yale L.J. 862, 865 (2017).

17. *See e.g.*, L. Song Richardson, *Arrest Efficiency and the Fourth Amendment*, 95 Minn. L. Rev. 2035 (2011).

18. *See generally* Ian Ayres, *Fair Driving: Gender and Race Discrimination in Retail Car Negotiations*, 104 Harv. L. Rev. 817, 856 (1991), and Ian Ayres & Peter Siegelman, *Race and Gender Discrimination in Bargaining for a New Car*, 85 Economic Review 304, 312–13 (1995). Professor Ayers' studies on racial and gender bias found overwhelming evidence that in a variety of markets—retail car sales, bail bonding, and kidney transplantation—racial minorities are consistently at a disadvantage. *Id.*

19. *See generally* Michael Z. Green, *Negotiating While Black* 17 Texas A&M Univ. *Legal Studies Research Paper* available at https://papers.ssrn.com/sol3/papers.cfm?abstract_id=2694160.

20. *See generally* Hernandez, Morela & Derek R. Avery, *Getting the Short End of the Stick: Racial Bias in Salary Negotiations*, MIT Sloan Mgmt Rev., (June 15, 2016), sloanreview.mit.edu/article/getting-the-short-end-of-the-stick-racial-bias-in-salary-negotiations.

21. *See* Rodger Volkema & Denise Fleck, *Understanding Propensity To Initiate Negotiations: An Examination Of The Effects Of Culture And Personality*, 23 Int'l J. Conflict Mgmt (2012), *available at* http://www.emeraldinsight.com/doi/pdfplus/10.1108/10444061211248976.

22. *See general* Linda Babcock, Hannah Riley Bowles, & Lei Lai, *Social Incentives For Gender Differences In The Propensity To Initiate Negotiations: Sometimes It Does Hurt To Ask*, Organizational Behav. & Hum. Decision Processes 84 (Jun. 25, 2005), *available at* https://wappp.hks.harvard.edu/files/wappp/files/social_incentives_for_gender_differences_in_the_propensity_to_initiate_negotiations-_sometimes_it_does_hurt_to_ask_0.pdf.

23. *See e.g.*, Hannah Bowles, *Psychological Perspectives on Gender in Negotiation,* HKS Faculty Research Working Paper Series RWP12-046, John F. Kennedy Sch. of Government, Harv. Univ. (2012), http://dash.harvard.edu/bitstream/handle/1/9830358/RWP12-046_Bowles.pdf?sequence=1. (Referencing studies by Rubin and Brown 1975).

24. *See generally* Jens Hüffmeier, *et al. A Meta-Analysis on Gender Differences in Negotiation Outcomes and Their Moderators, 141* Guido Psych. Bulletin 86 (2014).

25. *Id.*

26. *See e.g.*, Deborah M. Kolb, *Negotiating in the Shadows of Organizations: Gender, Negotiation, and Change,* 28 Ohio St. J. on Disp. Resol. 241, 242 (2013).

27. *Id.*

28. *Id.*

29. Julia Johnson, *Gender Differences in Negotiation: Implications for Salary Negotiations,* 23 UCLA Women's L.J. 131, 137 (2016).

30. *See* Art Hinshaw & Jess K. Alberts, *Gender and Attorney Negotiation Ethics*, 39 Wash. U. J. L. & Pol'y 145 (2012), http://openscholarship.wustl.edu/law_journal_law_policy/vol39/iss1/6.

31. *Id.* at 146.

32. *Id.*

33. *See e.g.,* Mazei, J., Freund, et al. *A Meta-Analysis on Gender Differences in Negotiation Outcomes and Their Moderators* 141 Am. Psychol. Ass'n 94, 95 (2015), https://www.apa.org/pubs/journals/releases/bul-a0038184.pdf.

34. *Id.*

35. *Id.*

36. Andrea Kupfer Schneider, Sandra Cheldelin, & Deborah Kolb, *What Travels: Teaching Gender in Cross Cultural Negotiation Classrooms*, 31 Hamline J. Pub. L. & Pol'y 531, 541 (2010).

37. *See* Leslie Cooney, *Surfing to Success as a Mindful Negotiator*, 17 Pepperdine Disp. Resol. L. J. 131 (2017), available at http://nsuworks.nova.edu/law_facarticles/327; Kaitlyn M. Murphy, *Using Meditation Techniques to Succeed During Stressful Negotiations*, Am. B. Ass'n. (Sept. 8, 2016), *available at* http://apps.americanbar.org/litigation/committees/womanadvocate/articles/summer2016-0916-using-mediation-techniques-succeed-during-stressful-negotiations.html.

38. *See* Heidi Grant, *A Second Chance to Make the Right Impression*, Harv. Bus. Rev. (Jan. 2105), *available at* https://hbr.org/2015/01/a-second-chance-to-make-the-right-impression.

Chapter 7

1. 42 U.S.C. §§ 2000e-2-e (2012).

2. Lilly Ledbetter Fair Pay Act of 2009, Pub. L. No. 111-2, 123 Stat. 5 (2009).

3. 490 U.S. 228, 251–253 (1989).

4. *See Zarda v. Altitude Express, Inc.*, 883 F.3d 100, 132 (2d Cir. 2018) (holding that plaintiffs are "entitled to bring a Title VII claim for discrimination based on sexual orientation"), and *Hively v. Ivy Tech Cmty. College*, 853 F.3d 339, 351–52 (7th Cir. 2017) (holding that "a person who alleges that she experienced employment discrimination on the basis of her sexual orientation has put forth a case of sex discrimination for Title VII purposes").

5. *Laws Enforced by the EEOC,* U.S Equal Employment Opportunity Comm'n (last visited: Jun.

15, 2018), https://www.eeoc.gov/laws/statutes/index.cfm (last visited Oct. 19, 2018).

6. *Small Business Requirements*, US Equal Opportunity Comm'n., (last visited Oct. 19, 2018), https://www.eeoc.gov/employers/smallbusiness/requirements.cfm.

7. *Id.*

8. 29 U.S.C. § 206(d) (2016).

9. *Id.*

10. *Rizo v. Yovino*, 887 F. 3d 453 (9th Cir. 2018).

11. *Id.* at 460.

12. *Id.*

13. *Id.* at 461.

14. *State Laws on Employment-Related Discrimination*, Nat'l Conference of State Legis.(last visited Oct. 19, 2018), http://www.ncsl.org/research/labor-and-employment/discrimination-employment.aspx.

15. Ala. Code § 25-1-20, et seq.

16. Ga. Code Ann. § 34-6a-1, et seq.; Ga. Code Ann. § 31-4-2, et seq.; Ga. Code Ann. § 34-5-1, et seq. Ga. Code Ann. §; Ga. Code Ann. § 45-19-20, et seq.

17. Conn. Gen. Stat. Ann. § 46a-60, et seq.

18. Conn. Gen. Stat. Ann. § 46a-60, et seq. and Conn. Gen. Stat. Ann. § 21a-408p.

19. Or. Rev. Stat. § 659a.001, et seq. Or. Rev. Stat. § 174.100.

20. *State Laws on Employment-Related Discrimination supra* note 14.

21. *See The Simple Truth About the Gender Gap*, AAUW, (2018), http://www.aauw.org/aauw_check/pdf_download/show_pdf.php?file=The-Simple-Truth.

22. *See Women's Bureau, Issue Brief: Women's Earnings and the Wage Gap*, US Dept. of Lab. (last visited Oct. 19, 2018), https://www.dol.gov/wb/resources/Womens_Earnings_and_the_Wage_Gap_17.pdf.

23. *See* Julie Anderson, Jessica Milli, & Melanie Kruvelis, *Projected Year the Wage Gap Will Close by State*, Inst. for Women's Pol. Research, (Mar. 22, 2017), https://iwpr.org/publications/projected-year-wage-gap-will-close-state/.

24. *See* AAUW, *supra* note 21.

25. *Id.*

26. Mary C. Daly, Bart Hobijn, & Joseph H. Pedtke, *Economic Letter: Disappointing Facts about the Black-White Wage Gap*, Fed. Reserve Bank of San Francisco, https://www.frbsf.org/economic-research/files/el2017-26.pdf.

27. *Id.*

28. NAWL, *2017 Annual Survey Report*, LegalExecutiveInstitute.com, http://www.legalexecutiveinstitute.com/wp-content/uploads/2018/05/130-PM-2017-NAWL-Survey-Report.pdf.

29. *2016 Report on Diversity in Law Firms*, NALP.org (Jan. 2017), https://www.nalp.org/uploads/Membership/2016NALPReportonDiversityinUSLawFirms.pdf.

30. *See* Nikki Graf, Anna Brown & Eileen Patten, *The Narrowing, but Persistent, Gender Gap in Pay*, Pew Research Ctr. http://www.pewresearch.org/fact-tank/2018/04/09/gender-pay-gap-facts/.

31. *See* Stephanie Bornstein, *Equal Work*, 77 Md. L. Rev. 581, 585 (2018).

32. *Washington signs Equal Pay Act*, HouseDeomcrats.wa.gov, (May 21, 2018), https://housedemocrats.wa.gov/news/governor-signs-equal-pay-opportunity-act/.

33. Mariela Rexach & Ana Beatriz Rivera-Beltrán, *Puerto Rico Employers Prepare for New Guidelines Governing Equal Pay in the Workplace*, Littler.com (Aug. 14, 2017), https://www.littler.com/publication-press/publication/puerto-rico-employers-prepare-new-guidelines-governing-equal-pay.

34. Allan Bloom & Laura Fant, *Vermont Enacts Salary History Inquiry Law*, LawandtheWorkplace.com, (May 16, 2018), https://www.lawandtheworkplace.com/2018/05/vermont-enacts-salary-history-inquiry-law/.

35. Kathleen Pender, *New Law Bans California Employers From Asking Applicants Their Prior Salary*, SFGate.com (Oct. 17, 2017), https://www.sfgate.com/business/networth/article/New-law-bans-California-employers-from-asking-12274431.php.

36. Duane Morris, *Delaware Enacts Pay History Ban*, Soc. For Human Resource Mgmt. (Jun. 28, 2018), https://www.shrm.org/resourcesandtools/legal-and-compliance/state-and-local-updates/

pages/delaware-enacts-pay-history-ban.aspx.

37. K. Joy Chin et al., *Massachusetts Employers Now Have Guidance on Equal Pay Law*, Soc. For Human Resource Mgmt. (Mar. 8, 2018), https://www.shrm.org/resourcesandtools/legal-and-compliance/state-and-local-updates/pages/massachusetts-employers-now-have-guidance-on-equal-pay-law.aspx.

38. *Oregon Equal Pay Law*, Oregon.gov (last visited Oct. 19, 2018), https://www.oregon.gov/boli/TA/Pages/Equal%20Pay%20Law.aspx.

39. *Asking About Salary History During the Hiring Process Is Illegal in NYC*, NYC.gov (last visited Oct. 19, 2018), https://www1.nyc.gov/assets/cchr/downloads/pdf/materials/SalaryHistory_KYO.pdf.

40. Joseph N. DiStefano, *Court: Philly Salary-History Ban Violates Free Speech, But Firms Can't Use Data To Underpay*, Philly.com (May 1, 2018), available at http://www.philly.com/philly/blogs/inq-phillydeals/phillys-job-applicant-salary-history-ban-federal-judge-20180501.html.

41. *See generally Summit Details*, USDW (last visited Oct. 19, 2018), http://www.theunitedstateofwomen.org/summit-details/.

42. Glassdoor, *Top HR Statistics: The Latest Stats for HR & Recruiting Pros*, GlassDoor.com (last visited Oct. 19, 2018), http://www.glassdoor.com/employers/popular-topics/hr-stats.htm.

43. *See* Edward Daciuk, *Salary Negotiation for Employers & Candidates*, FitSmallBusiness.com (Sept. 24 2017), https://fitsmallbusiness.com/salary-negotiaiton-employers-candidates.

44. *See Career Planning*, FarwellGroup. http://www.farwellgroup.com/services-career-salary-negotiation.asp/.

45. 18 U.S.C. § 1839(3).

46. Amit Singh, *Are Non-Solicitation/No-Hire Agreements Enforceable in California?*, StartUp Blog.com (Aug 1 2017), http://www.startupblog.com/blog/are-non-solicitation-agreements-permitted-in-california-it-depends.

47. *Id.*

48. *Non-Competition Agreements and Protection Of Trade Secrets*, Oregon.gov (last visited Oct. 19, 2018), https://www.oregon.gov/boli/TA/Pages/ta_faq_noncompete.aspx.

49. Or. Rev. Stat. Ann. § 653.295.

50. *Id.*

51. Fla. Stat. § 542.335.

52. Hank Jackson, *Florida's Noncompete Statute: "Reasonable" or "Truly Obnoxious?*, 92 Fla. Bar J. 10, 11 (2018).

53. Fla. Stat. § 688.002.

54. Jackson, *supra* note 52.

55. *Id.*

56. *Id.*

57. *See All Pro Maids, Inc. v. Layton*, 2004 WL 1878784, 5 (Del. Ch. Aug. 9, 2004); See *Delaware Exp. Shuttle, Inc. v. Older*, 2002 WL 31458243, 11 (Del. Ch. Oct. 23, 2002).

58. *See Delaware Exp. Shuttle, Inc. v. Older*, 2002 WL 31458243, 14 (Del. Ch. Oct. 23, 2002).

59. *See Faw, Casson & Co. v. Cranston*, 375 A.2d 463, 466 (Del. Ch. 1977); See *Lewmor, Inc. v. Fleming*, No. CIV.A. 8355, 1986 WL 1244, 3 (Del. Ch. Jan. 29, 1986).

60. *See Norton Petroleum Corp. v. Cameron*, No. CIV.A. 15212-NC, 1998 WL 118198, 3 (Del. Ch. Mar. 5, 1998).

61. *See Gas Oil Prod., Inc. of Delaware v. Kabino*, No. C.A. 9150, 1987 WL 18432, 2 (Del. Ch. Oct. 13, 1987).

62. *See Elite Cleaning Co. v. Capel*, No. CIV.A. 690-N, 2006 WL 1565161, 4 (Del. Ch. June 2, 2006).

63. *Id.*

64. Bloomberg, *Walmart Sues its Former Chief Tax Officer for Taking Job at Amazon*, Fortune.com (June 7, 2018) http://fortune.com/2018/06/07/walmart-sues-employee-amazon-job/.

65. *Walmart v. Waldin*, Exhibit A to Verified Compl. For Injunctive Relief, Docket No. 2018-0414 (Del. Ch. June 06, 2018).

66. Fenwick & West LLP, *Summary of Covenants Not to Compete: A Global Perspective*, The TechLaw Group 283 (last visited Oct. 19, 2018), https://www.fenwick.com/FenwickDocuments/RS_Summary-

of-Covenants.pdf.

67. *Id.* at 232.

Chapter 8

1. *See generally,* Mary Cushing Doherty & Stephanie M. Shortall, Drafting Prenup Agreements, § X Negotiating Prenuptial Agreements (2d. Aspen Pub. 2017-2 Supplement).

2. *See* Margret Ryznar & Anna Stepien-Sporek, *To Have and to Hold, for Richer or Richer: Premarital Agreements in the Comparative Context,* 13 Chap. L. Rev. 27, 31 (2009).

3. Puerto Rico also uses the community property regime. Alaska has a voluntary (opt-in) system of community property allowing spouses in Alaska to create community property by entering into a community property agreement or by creating a community property trust. See Alaska Stat. §§ 34.77.020–34.77.995. Tennessee also allows the creation of a community property trust. See TN Code § 35-17-103 (2014).

4. *See* Mark Patton, *Quasi-Community Property in Arizona: Why Just at Divorce and Not Death?,* 47 Ariz. L. Rev. 167, 168 (2005).

5. *See* Kenneth W. Kingma, *Property Division at Divorce or Death for Married Couples Migrating Between Common Law and Community Property States,* 35 ACTEC J. 74 (2009).

6. *See generally* Leslie F. Burns & Gregg A. Grauer, *Human Capital As Marital Property,* 19 Hofstra L. Rev. 499 (1990).

7. Dawn D. Nichols & Sean K. Ahmed, *Nonmarital Real Estate: Is the Appreciation Marital, Nonmarital or a Combination of Both?* 81 Fla. B. J. 75 (2007).

8. *See* Jeff Landers, *Why Divorcing Women Need to Pay Careful Attention to the Date of Separation,* Forbes, (Sep. 28, 2011), *available at* http://www.forbes.com/sites/jefflanders/2011/09/28/why-divorcing-women-need-to-pay-careful-attention-to-the-date-of-separation/#5992af03b227.

9. *See e.g.,* Cathy Meyer, *What is Marital Property and How is it Divided at Divorce?,* Liveabout.com (July 14, 2017), *available at* https://www.liveabout.com/marital-or-non-marital-property-1103103.

10. *See generally,* Kingma, *supra* note 5.

11. *See* Ryznar, *supra* note 2 at 38.

12. Of course, valuing property in order to divide the community property in half may be quite complex, especially if some of the assets are not easily marketable.

13. *See* Katherine D. Black et al., *Community Property for Non-Community Property States,* 24 Quinnipiac Prob. L. J. 260, 267 (2011).

14. *See id.* at 264.

15. *See* Kingma, *supra* note 5.

16. *See* LexisNexis, *Classification of Gifts, Inheritance, and Life Insurance in the Context of Divorce,* Lexis Legal Newsroom (Feb. 5, 2009), https://www.lexisnexis.com/legalnewsroom/lexis-hub/b/commentary/archive/2009/02/05/classification-of-gifts_2c00_-inheritance_2c00_-and-life-insurance-in-the-context-of-divorce.aspx.

17. *See* Margaret Ryznar & Anna Stepien-Sporek, *To Have and to Hold, for Richer or Richer: Premarital Agreements in the Comparative Context,* 13 Chap. L. Rev. 27, 32 (2009).

18. *See generally* Thomas M. Featherston, et al., *Handbook for Texas Martial Property Law for Estate Administration and Planning,* Baylor Univ. (2016), available at https://www.baylor.edu/law/facultystaff/doc.php/268848.pdf.

19. Cynthia Lee Starnes, *One More Time: Alimony, Intuition, and the Remarriage-Termination Rule,* 81 Ind. L.J. 971, 999 (2006).

20. *See* Jeff Landers, *Five Reasons your Prenup May be Invalid,* Forbes (Apr. 2, 2013), https://www.forbes.com/sites/jefflanders/2013/04/02/five-reasons-your-prenup-might-be-invalid/#346f9da419a5.

21. In some states, an agreement to waive death-type benefits (such as spousal elective share or intestacy) would be valid even without disclosure as long as the agreement, contract, or waiver was executed before marriage. See, e.g., FL Stat. § 732.702. Even in those states, however, disclosure would be required for the agreement to serve to waive rights upon divorce.

22. *See* Christopher J. Roman, *Protecting your Clients' Assets from their Future Son-in-Law and Daughters-in-Law: The Impact of Evolving Trust Laws on Alimony Awards,* 39 ACTEC L.J. 157, 157 (2013).

23. *See Id.*

24. Trusts provide protection against creditors of trust beneficiaries only while the assets are held in the trust. Once trust assets are distributed to the beneficiary, the assets lose their protected status.

25. *See e.g., Berlinger v. Casselberry,* 113 So. 3d 961 (Fla. 2d DCA 2013).

26. Jeff Landers, *Can A Prenup Or A Postnup With An Infidelity Clause Deter A Husband From Cheating?,* Forbes.com (Mar. 13, 2014), https://www.forbes.com/sites/jefflanders/2014/03/13/can-a-prenup-or-a-postnup-with-an-infidelity-clause-deter-a-husband-from-cheating/#20f293e97328.

27. *See For Love or Money,* Chicago Trib. (Aug. 2, 2004), http:// articles.chicagotribune.com/2004-08-02/news/0408030054_1_prenuptial-agreement-eric-benet-halle-berry.

28. *See* Elisabeth R. Feeny, *Lifestyle Clauses and Prenuptial Agreements,* MavrridesLaw.com (Feb. 19, 2015), https://mavrideslaw.com/lifestyle-clauses-prenuptial-agreements/.

29. *See* Rachel Gillet, *The Surprising 'Prenups' of America's Richest Couples,* Business Insider (Nov. 30, 2017), https://www.businessinsider.com/surprising-prenups-americas-richest-couples-2017-11.

30. *See* Jill Brooke, *No-Child Clauses More Frequent in Prenuptial Pacts,* Chic. Trib. (Oct. 23, 2002), http://articles.chicagotribune.com/2002-10-23/features/0210230012_1_prenuptial-pacts-prenuptial-agreements-younger.

31. *See* Brad Reid, *Common Prenuptial Agreement Legal Issues,* Huff Post (Feb. 18, 2018), https://www.huffingtonpost.com/brad-reid/common-prenuptial-agreeme_b_6706898.html.

32. *See Zummo v. Zummo,* 574 A.2d 1130 (Pa. Super. Ct. 1990).

33. *See* Lance Soskin, *Wondering What the Difference is Between Mediation and Arbitration?,* Huff Post (May, 9, 2014, 10:34 AM), https://www.huffingtonpost.com/lance-soskin/wondering-what-the-differ_b_5291286.html.

34. *See* Julia Marsh and Priscilla DeGregory, *Chris Rock's wife seeking huge payout in divorce,* PageSix.com, (Jun. 15, 2015, 12:30 AM), https://pagesix.com/2015/06/15/chris-rocks-estranged-wife-seeking-huge-payout-in-divorce/.

35. *See* Johnathan E. Fields, *Forbidden Provisions in Prenuptial Agreements: Legal And Practical Considerations For The Matrimonial Lawyer,* 21 J. the Am. Acad. Matrimonial Law., 413, 415 (2008).

36. *See generally* Christopher J. Roman, *Protecting your Clients' Assets from their Future Son-in-Law and Daughters-in-Law: The Impact of Evolving Trust Laws on Alimony Awards,* 39 ACTEC L. J. 157, 159–60 (2013).

37. *See* Jeffrey Pennell, Third Party Trusts in Divorce, SW037 ALI-CLE 487.

Chapter 9

1. The Statistics Portal, *Number of Pets in the United States in 2017/2018 by Species (in Millions),* Statista.com (last visited Jul. 5, 2018), https://www.statista.com/statistics/198095/pets-in-the-united-states-by-type-in-2008/.

2. Center for Disease Control, *Preventing Dog Bites,* CDC.gov (last visited Jul. 5 2018), https://www.cdc.gov/features/dog-bite-prevention/index.html.

3. Lynn A. Epstein, *There Are No Bad Dogs, Only Bad Owners: Replacing Strict Liability with A Negligence Standard in Dog Bite Cases,* 13 Animal L. 129, 131 (2006)

4. *Id.* at 134.

5. *Hahn v. Kordula,* 5 Kan. App. 142, 48 P. 896, 896 (1897)

6. Palm Beach County Ordinance 98-22 § 4-4(a).

7. *See Butler v. Frieden,* 208 Va. 352, 353, 158 S.E.2d 121, 122 (1967).

8. *Id.*

9. Sheldon F. Kurtz & Alice Noble-Allgire, *The Revised Uniform Residential Landlord and Tenant Act: A Perspective from the Reporters,* 52 Real Prop. Tr. & Est. L.J. 417, 507 (2018).

10. *See* Kaycee Miller, *Security Deposit Laws, Limits & Deadlines—State Guide for Rentals,* Rentec Direct.com (Mar. 16, 2018), https://www.rentecdirect.com/blog/security-deposit-state-guide/.

11. *See* Laura Agadoni, *The Ultimate Guide to "Normal Wear and Tear*, LANDLORDOLOGY.COM (Nov. 1 2017), https://www.landlordology.com/normal-wear-and-tear/.

12. ARIZ. REV. STAT. ANN. § 33-1321; ARK. CODE § 18-16-305.

13. MICH. COMP. LAWS § 554.608.

14. KY. REV. STAT. § 383.580.

15. KY. REV. STAT. § 383.580.

16. Sheldon F. Kurtz & Alice Noble-Allgire, *The Revised Uniform Residential Landlord and Tenant Act: A Perspective from the Reporters,* 52 REAL PROP. TR. & EST. L.J. 417, 524 (2018).

17. N.D. CENT. COD. § 47-16-07.1.

18. 765 ILL. COMP. STAT. ANN. 710/1.

19. FLA. STAT. § 83.49.

20. Marty-Nelson, Gilmore, and Rodriquez-Dod, 824-3rd T.M., *Testamentary Capacity, Undue Influence, and Validity of Wills,* A-58.

21. *Id.*

22. *In re Carpenter's Estate,* 253 So. 2d 697, 702 (Fla. 1971).

23. FLA. STAT. ANN. § 733.107 (West).

Index